Altered Egos

Altered Egos

How the Brain Creates the Self

Todd E. Feinberg, M.D.

OXFORD
UNIVERSITY PRESS

2001

OXFORD
UNIVERSITY PRESS

Oxford New York

Athens Auckland Bangkok Bogotá Buenos Aires Calcutta
Cape Town Chennai Dar es Salaam Delhi Florence Hong Kong Istanbul
Karachi Kuala Lumpur Madrid Melbourne Mexico City Mumbai
Nairobi Paris São Paulo Shanghai Singapore Taipei Tokyo Toronto Warsaw
and associated companies in
Berlin Ibadan

Published by Oxford University Press, Inc.
198 Madison Avenue, New York, N. Y. 10016

Oxford is a registered trademark of Oxford University Press.

Library of Congress Cataloging-in-Publication Data
Feinburg, Todd E.
Altered Egos : how the brain creates the self / Todd E. Feinburg.
p. cm.   Includes bibliographical references and index.
ISBN 0-19-513625-x
1. Neuropsychology.   2. Brain   3. Self.   I. Title.
[DNLM: 1. Brain–physiology.   2. Ego.   WL 103.5 F299a 2001]
QP360 .F45 2000   612.8'2–dc21   99-086181

9 8 7 6 5 4 3 2 1
Printed in the United States of America
on acid-free paper

Contents

Acknowledgments

I first wish to thank my patients and their families who have agreed to be interviewed on medical rounds, videotaped for lectures, or have participated in research protocols. As a physician who is involved in research and teaching, I frequently ask patients to take part in these activities. The majority agree in the hope that their participation will help somebody else in the future.

In preparing this book, Jim Morgan helped edit early versions of parts of the manuscript. My colleague Elizabeth Ochoa reviewed the entire manuscript and made numerous and invaluable suggestions regarding the organization and presentation of the material. I am in her debt. My editor at Oxford University Press, Fiona Stevens, believed from the start that I could write this book. Always just an e-mail away, Fiona has been a friend, supporter, and master editor throughout and this book is far better thanks to her efforts. Thanks as well to the other wonderful people at Oxford who helped make this book a reality, including Edith Barry for editorial assistance, Rosemary Wellner for expert copyediting, and Helen Mules, Trade Production Editor. My appreciation also goes to Lynn Cooper for her illustrations, and Norma Kaman and Allaya Jitsomwung for help with manuscript preparation. Permission to quote from Vladimir Nabokov's *Despair* was kindly provided by Vintage Books, a Division of Random House, Inc. Thanks to Tom Roberts for his help in obtaining permissions to quote from the Talking Heads' song, *ONCE IN A LIFETIME*, by David Byrne, Chris Frantz, Jerry Harrison, Tina Weymouth and Brian Eno © 1981 Index Music, Inc. (ASCAP) Bleu Disque Music Co., Inc. (ASCAP) & E.G. Music Ltd. (PRS) All Rights o/b/o Index Music, Inc. & Bleu Disque Music Co., Inc. administered by WB Music Corp. (ASCAP) All Rights Reserved. Used by Permission WARNER BROS. PUBLICATIONS U.S. INC., Miami, FL. 33014.

I have been enriched through discussions with many colleagues and collaborators over the years. First thanks are owed to the late Dr. Edwin Weinstein. I corresponded with Dr. Weinstein over many years about interesting neurological patients whom I had examined, and his insights never failed to illuminate the underlying dynamic of these cases. Dr. Weinstein was a great man and the influence of his ideas can be seen throughout. I also wish to thank David Roane, my collaborater on some of the research discussed in this book; Joe Giacino, for lively debates on the nature of anosognosia and for sharing important clinical material with me; and Richard Rosenthal for insightful discussions. Martha Farah, a dear friend and colleague, is a constant source of support and inspiration, and Larry Miller encouraged and advised.

I wish to express my gratitude to my many friends and colleagues at Beth Israel Medical Center, including Arnold Winston, Chairman of Psychiatry; Susan Bressman, Chairman of Neurology; and Mathew Fink, President of Beth Israel Medical Center. Special thanks to Betty and Morton Yarmon after whom our center is named. Their generosity of spirit and philanthropy make projects like this book possible.

Finally, I thank my parents Gloria and Mort, my wife Marlene, and my kids Joshua and Rachel. I love you all.

Altered Egos

1

Introduction: Soul Searching

Dissecting the Self

Early in my career as a medical student I was required to perform a dissection of the brain using an old atlas as a step-by-step guide. The brain was bathed in a jar of preservative and wrapped in white cheesecloth. I took it out carefully and placed it on an orange cafeteria tray. The first procedure called for the removal of the gray matter in order to see the underlying brain structures. Beginning in a section that the atlas identified as the temporal lobe, I slowly and gently scraped away its cortical surface using a beveled wooden probe. Having barely exposed a centimeter of brain matter, I was struck by the realization of what I was actually doing. Had this person's memory of his childhood just been scraped away? Perhaps his recall of his whole family now was gone, or simply his recollection of a family outing on a warm summer day in July. Lying inert on this cafeteria tray was the substrate of this person's mind. I picked up the brain again, held it in my hands, and looked at it anew. This was a person's essence, humanity, and entire life experience now frozen in space and time. Who might he or she have been? It became apparent that studying the physical brain would allow me to explore some fascinating questions such as: *What is the self? Where is it located in the brain? How does the brain produce a unified self? What is the relationship between the brain and the mind?* The answers to these questions reflect the knowledge I have gained over the years as a neurologist and psychiatrist from patients with disorders of the self, and are the subject of this book.

The Patients

The first part of the book looks at patients with brain damage who have altered egos, a change in the brain that transforms the boundaries of the self, the relationship between the self and the world, the self and other people, and the self to itself.[1] I use the term "ego" not in a Freudian sense, but rather to refer to the "inner I" that we feel to be the most intimate aspect of the self. As philosopher Colin McGinn points out, there are many words that refer to the "I" including "self," "subject," "person," or "ego."[2] It is to these aspects of the self that I refer when speaking of the "ego."

Patients with altered egos as a result of brain damage experience a transformation in the *personal*, the aspects of identity that are most significant to the self. These persons might reject one of their arms, disown a spouse, or claim nonexistent relationships to strangers. They might have imaginary brothers, children, or alter egos. There is much to be learned from these cases. As slicing an apple reveals its core, the neurological lesion, or damage, in these patients opens a door into the inner self; it provides an opportunity to examine the physical structure of the self and to see how the self changes and adapts in response to the damaged brain.

Most of the patients described in this book are everyday persons—people with whom any one of us could identify—who undergo transformations of their senses of identity and worldview. Before their brain disorders disrupted their normal functioning, many led rather ordinary lives. They were adults of various ages, accountants, electricians, secretaries, homemakers, business executives, accomplished musicians, or unemployed adults whose brain disorders prevented them from functioning in their previous capacities at their jobs, within their families, or in personal relationships. In some cases, a spouse, family member, or a concerned neighbor brought them to my care. Consider the following case, one of the first patients referred to me for a remarkable neurobehavioral problem.

John

The attending physician in the ER referred a middle-aged electrician, John, and his wife, Joyce G., to my office for a consultation. The patient entered alone and told me that his wife had stopped to make a phone call and would be joining us momentarily. He was a tall, husky, neatly groomed man wearing blue jeans, which oddly enough were wet on the right hip pocket. Before he took a seat, I asked him if he had sat in something wet or perhaps spilled coffee on himself. He said no. John then offered his right hand to shake mine and I was astonished to see that he had what looked like severe chemical burns on his hands; the skin was actually seared away, exposing the muscle and bone.

I asked John if he was aware of the condition of his hands. He casually responded that he had been doing some work on the plumbing in his house and had gotten a few "little burns." It was clear that John was aware of them but entirely indifferent to their severity. He had applied no bandages and had just offered to shake my hand despite the wounds. He simply did not seem to care about the injury. The most extraordinary thing about John was how normal he appeared in other respects. He spoke clearly and intelligently, and I discerned no hint of dementia or psychosis. There was a striking contrast between his superficial mental integrity and his indifference to his medical condition.

Just then his wife entered the office. "Well, Dr. Feinberg, did you get him to talk?" I inquired how her husband got burned. She reported that she had recently observed John unclogging the kitchen sink, after which she, too, had noticed that his jeans were wet at the hip. She had assumed that he merely had splashed himself with water, but later on she noticed blood and pus in his clothing while sorting it for the laundry. When she asked John about the stains, he seemed unconcerned. It was then that she noticed the horrible condition of his hands. She determined that chemicals in the drain cleaner had apparently eaten his flesh down to the muscle and he hadn't even known it. The wound had festered for days, yet John carried on his daily routine apparently without noticing the injury.

She began to cry. "Doctor, you don't realize what's going on? He seems perfectly fine to you in here. But when we go home, he will immediately head downstairs into the basement, turn out all the lights, and sit in the dark. He won't budge. I have to bring him breakfast, lunch, dinner—he won't eat if I don't bring him food."

What was the problem with John? His wife explained that John was currently out of work, and maybe this had made him a bit down. However, his mood seemed bright, and he said he did not feel depressed. Furthermore, depressed patients often lose their appetite and John had not lost any weight. He was sleeping well at night. "No, his symptoms didn't look like those of depression," I thought to myself.

I then asked why John was out of work. It turned out that he had had an accident a couple of months back. He had fallen from a scaffold, hit his head, and been hospitalized for several weeks. His wife recalled, "Come to think of it, his doctors did mention something about his brain, but I didn't quite understand the problem."

That was interesting. John's formal mental status exam—which includes tests of orientation, language, memory, and other cognitive functions—confirmed that John was cognitively intact. Indeed, it eventually turned out that every aspect of John's neurological exam was normal. On the areas of his hands that were free of burns, he was able to distinguish sharp from dull stimuli, and hot from cold stimuli. This finding meant that John's indifference to his burns could not be due to simple numbness in his hands, which would suggest a problem with the pain nerves in his hands or with the spinal cord carrying pain information to his brain.

I needed to learn more about the condition of John's brain, so I ordered an MRI (Figure 1–1.)[3] One can see from this scan that large portions of John's right frontal and parietal lobes and a part of his left frontal lobe have been destroyed by a neurotraumatic accident. This finding accounted for John's problem. Because of the extensive damage to his brain, John suffers from a rare condition known as *pain asymbolia*. He can distinguish among different types of stimuli, but painful stimuli no longer carry any emotional impact, which causes his indifference to his wounds.[4] Once the disorder was recognized, we were able to help John avoid the sort of dangerous situations that might lead to physical harm.

The Perplexing "Inner I"

John is one example of the many ways in which a change in the brain can transform the self. But from the standpoint of neurobiology, it is not clear what the self really is or how the brain creates it. The later chapters of this book will address these questions. The nature, significance, and

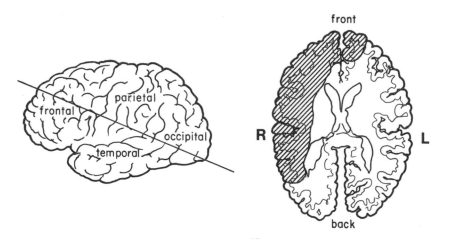

Figure 1-1.
On the left is a side view of a normal brain. The locations of the frontal, parietal, temporal, and occipital lobes are indicated. The line that runs through the brain indicates the level of the MRI slice of John's brain that appears on the right. In the scans shown in this book, cross-hatched regions represent areas of brain damage. John's scan showed regions of encephalomacia (softened, damaged, lifeless cortical tissue) that occurred as a result of John's head injury. The area of damage included large portions of the right frontal and parietal lobes. In the left hemisphere, the damage was confined to the anterior and medial portions of the frontal lobe.

even the existence of the self has been a subject of debate for centuries.[5] Philosopher Immanuel Kant (1724–1804) was a proponent of the fundamental existence and primacy of the self. He stated that even before there is thought, before we can know anything about the world or ourselves, there must be a unified "I" as the subject of experience. Kant placed the primordial, unified "I" at the center of his philosophy and argued that the inner "I" creates coherence and lends order to our experience and perception.

The psychologist and philosopher William James (1842–1910), on the other hand, was not a fan of Kant or of the notion of a primordial unified self. He devoted several pages of his monumental work *The Principles of Psychology* to criticism of Kant's theory. According to James, the "ego" was nothing but "a 'cheap and nasty' edition of the soul."[6] James held that there is something that could be appropriately referred to as the self, but he denied that there is any primordial "I" behind this self.

James maintained that there are only "passing states of consciousness," and our experience of mental unity is simply due to the fact that we as individuals experience successive mental states in our stream of consciousness that are uniquely our own. Put all these experiences together in a single mind and you get a self—without any inner "I" pulling it all together. James even made the extreme claim that if somehow one could put together several independent minds that shared the same experience and past, one could produce the same mental unity among minds that we as single minds experience:

> Successive thinkers, numerically distinct, but all aware of the same past in the same way, form an adequate vehicle for all the experience of personal unity and sameness which we actually have. And just such a train of successive thinkers is the stream of mental states . . . which psychology treated as a natural science has to assume.
>
> The logical conclusion seems then to be that *the states of consciousness are all that psychology needs to do her work with. Metaphysics or theology may prove the Soul to exist; but for psychology the hypothesis of such a substantial principle of unity is superfluous.*[7]

Unlike James, many neuroscientists since have weighed in to support the unified self, and some of their ideas will be reconsidered in this book. The neurophysiologist Charles Sherrington, for example, was a firm believer in the unified self. Sherrington beautifully summarized in his book *Man on His Nature* why he felt compelled to posit the existence of the self:

> This self is a unity. The continuity of its presence in time, some-
> times hardly broken by sleep, its inalienable "interiority" in (sensu-
> al) space, its consistency of view-point, the privacy of its experi-
> ence, combine to give it status as a unique existence. . . . It regards
> itself as one, others treat it as one. It is addressed as one, by a name
> to which it answers. The Law and the State schedule it as one. It
> and they identify it with a body which is considered by it and them
> to belong to it integrally. In short, unchallenged and unargued con-
> viction assumes it to be one. The logic of grammar endorses this by
> a pronoun in the singular. All its diversity is merged into oneness.[8]

If Kant and Sherrington are correct, as I think they are, and there is such
a thing as a self, we need to explain how the brain, which is composed
of billions of individual neurons, creates the single and unified entity we
call the self. The clinical cases will demonstrate that there are many
brain regions that play a role in creating and maintaining a self. But
modern neuroscience has now convincingly shown that there is no central place where everything in the brain "physically comes together"; no
place where the infinite diversity of the brain can physically combine to
create a centralized mind or unified self. Science writer John Horgan, in
his recent and provocative book *The Undiscovered Mind,* called this
problem the "Humpty Dumpty dilemma":

> This conundrum is sometimes called the binding problem. I would like
> to propose another term: the Humpty Dumpty dilemma. It plagues not
> only neuroscience but also evolutionary psychology, cognitive science,
> artificial intelligence—and indeed all fields that divide the mind into a
> collection of relatively discrete "modules," "intelligences," "instincts,"
> or "computational devices." Like a precocious eight-year-old tinkering
> with a radio, mind-scientists excel at taking the brain apart, but they
> have no idea how to put it back together again.[9]

The problem of mental unity poses a real challenge for any neurobiological theory of the self. If all brain regions that contribute to the self can
be enumerated and tallied as if they were computer modules, how are
they integrated so that we exist as unified, single selves? What is it about
the brain that creates the subjective sense that we possess a single and
unified point of view, an inner "I"? What keeps the neurons of our brains
from going off in their own directions?

The difficulty with previous solutions to the Humpty Dumpty dilemma
is that they tend to view the brain and mind as hierarchically organized like
a pyramid. All the brain areas that contribute to the self end up at the top

Figure 1-2.
Many models of the mind envisage the brain as a hierarchy in the shape of a pyramid. The many parts of the brain that contribute to the self and mind make up the base of the pyramid. These parts are combined and organized to create higher levels of the hierarchy. Suddenly, and somewhat mysteriously, a unified self is supposed to "emerge" at the top.

of this hierarchical system and the unified self and mind, the inner "I," mysteriously *emerge*, like the eye atop the pyramid in a dollar bill (Figure 1–2).

The problem with this account is that the brain is not organized like a pyramid, but rather operates like the living organism of which it is a part. All living things are hierarchically organized, but the hierarchy does not have a "top" or "bottom" like a pyramid. Living things represent *nested* hierarchies. In the nested hierarchy of a living thing, all parts make a contribution to the life and activity of the organism. In the nested hierarchy of the self, many parts of the living brain make a contribution to the self. I will try to show that the neurobiological self can be understood as a *nested hierarchy of meaning and purpose*.

One of the most interesting features of this view of the self is the ultimately personal nature of the nested self. Individual meaning and purpose only exist for the individual and are a part of our *being*. In our current age of miraculous computer technology, we have lost sight of the simple fact that *the mind is a living thing* that is an integral part of our existence as living beings. In the concluding chapters, I argue that when the notion of personal being is included in our theories about the brain, we can begin to comprehend the elusive neurobiological basis of the self.

Deconstructing the Self

That this is so, we have some kind of evidence in our very bodies, all whose particles, whilst vitally united to this same thinking conscious self, so that we feel when they are touched, and are affected by, and are conscious of good or harm that happens to them, are a part of our selves. Thus the limbs of his body are to everyone a part of himself; he sympathizes and is concerned for them. Cut off an hand, and thereby separate it from that consciousness we had of its heat, cold, and other affections; and it is then no longer a part of himself, any more than the remotest part of matter.

John Locke, 1690

Asomatognosia

There are many perturbations of the self in which the relatedness of the self to a part of the body, other persons, places, or experiences is severely altered. One of the most dramatic alterations of the self that the neurologist encounters in the course of clinical practice is the condition known as *asomatognosia*. Asomatognosia literally means "lack of recognition of the body." The patient with asomatognosia not only does not recognize a part of the body; he or she may totally reject it. A patient of mine serves as an example of the person with asomatognosia.[1]

Mirna

I met Mirna for the first time when she was an inpatient on the neurology service. A woman in her seventies, she was admitted to the hospital with an acute stroke. The term *stroke* refers to an injury to the brain that is caused by problems with the brain's blood vessels. All the asomatognosic patients I have examined have had strokes. As is the case in the majority of asomatognosic patients, Mirna's stroke damaged large portions of the right hemisphere of her brain (Figure 2–1).

The region of damage included the motor and sensory centers of her right hemisphere. As a result, her left arm was paralyzed and she lacked

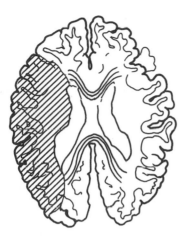

Figure 2-1.
A CAT scan of Mirna's brain demonstrated massive right frontoparietal damage, as represented by the area of infarction.
Unaware that her left arm belongs to her, Mirna ascribes it to her husband, who died of a stroke not long before Mirna's own injury.

sensation on the left side of her body. Damage to the *right* hemisphere causes problems on the *left* side of the body because the motor and sensory centers from each half of the brain have their greatest control over the opposite side of the body. Damage to the right hemisphere may also cause visual impairment on the patient's left side.

Mirna was lying quietly in her hospital bed. She was alert and responded readily to my queries, but her gaze was locked toward her extreme right, the result of a condition called hemispatial neglect. *Hemispatial neglect* (or simply *neglect*) is broadly understood to be a disorder of attention. A patient with hemispatial neglect displays a marked tendency to ignore stimuli in the area of space (referred to as the hemispace) on the side opposite a brain lesion.[2] To minimize the effects of neglect, and ensure that the patient pays attention to the left arm, one stands on the patient's right side and then gently moves the arm over to her right side, extending the left hand and forearm to the right as much as possible. After performing this maneuver, I asked Mirna to identify what I was showing her:

FEINBERG: *I want to ask you again now. What is this over here? Take a look at this over here. What is this?*
MIRNA: *Your fingers.*
FEINBERG: *My fingers?*
MIRNA: *Yes.*
FEINBERG: *Look at them again, take a good look now. OK ... tell me what they are.*
MIRNA: *Fingers ... I see two fingers and a pocket.*
FEINBERG: *Take a good look. What is it? This* [tapping the back of her hand].

MIRNA: *The back of your hand.*
FEINBERG: *The back of my hand?*
MIRNA: *Yes.*
FEINBERG: *Suppose I told you this was your hand.*
MIRNA: *I wouldn't believe you.*
FEINBERG: *You wouldn't believe me?*
MIRNA: *No, no.*
FEINBERG: *This is your hand.*
MIRNA: *No.*
FEINBERG: *Look, here's your right hand, and here's your left hand.*
MIRNA: *OK.*
FEINBERG: *Now, what's this* [holding out her left hand]*?*
MIRNA: *The back of your hand!*

How do we explain Mirna's problem? The first question to answer is how *specific* is the misidentification? For instance, could her failure of identification of her left side be due to a general problem with language? Perhaps she knew it was her left arm, but just couldn't properly communicate this idea. Alternatively, perhaps Mirna's inability to identify parts of her body was not a problem specific to her left side, and she actuality had an inability to identify parts of her body on either side. Finally, one should also consider whether her problem is limited to identification of the parts of her body or if she has difficulty identifying parts of anyone's body.

In order to evaluate these possibilities, I checked if Mirna could correctly identify her right hand. I found she could and concluded from this that her identification failure was not due to problems with language or naming body parts. Mirna also had no difficulty identifying my right or left hand, or pictures of hands, feet, eyes, or ears. Whatever the basis of Mirna's asomatognosia, her problem was specifically a difficulty with the proper identification only of the left side of *her* body.

There is another reason why general perceptual, language, or cognitive impairments do not account for Mirna's difficulties. Her asomatognosic misidentifications were refractory to correction. She could not readily be "talked out of it"; her beliefs about her hand are more delusions than simple errors. Despite my attempts to correct her, to point out that indeed it was her hand she was staring at, she never could truly be convinced of the truth of the situation. In most asomatognosic patients, with their good right hand they can trace the connection of the limp arm to the left shoulder yet remain convinced that it is not their arm. This was the case with the patient described by Dr. Clarence W.

Olsen at a meeting of the Los Angeles Neurological Society in 1937. His patient had a stroke of her right hemisphere, which paralyzed her on the left side of her body.

> She denied that the affected limbs were hers and said that "yours" or another's were in bed with her. When she was shown that they were attached to her and that the arm in question merged with her shoulder and that it must be hers, she said: "But my eyes and my feelings don't agree, and I must believe my feelings. I know they look like mine, but I can feel they are not, and I can't believe my eyes."[3]

The refractoriness to correction shown by Mirna and other asomatognosic patients is not typical of most neurobehavioral disorders. For example, the patient who gropes for words or cannot read due to aphasia generally accepts, indeed is grateful for, help when it is offered. There was something more basic going on with Mirna. Her problem was rooted in a fundamental disturbance in who and what she believed herself to be.

Mirna had all the typical features of the patient with asomatognosia. Her rejected arm is severely paralyzed and she had significant loss of sensation in the arm. Proprioception, the feeling and knowledge of the position of the limb in space, was particularly impaired in Mirna, and this is true of most asomatognosia patients. Unless she looked directly at her arm, she was unable to sense where the arm was located in space.

In Mirna's case, I was not aware that she had asomatognosia until I specifically asked her to identify her arm, but in some cases, it is obvious to the medical staff that a patient has the condition. For instance, the presence of asomatognosia was readily apparent in a patient of mine who repeatedly tried to throw his left arm out of the bed. Other patients affected with the condition complain to the hospital staff that someone is lying next to them in the bed. Nielsen described a forty-eight-year-old woman, who when asked about her left side explained, "That's an old man. Stays in bed all the time."[4] Spillane spoke of an officer-cadet in a military hospital who claimed "that there was no room for 'him'—some other person—between his own body and the wall."[5] Ullman and co-workers told of the patient who upon picking up her paralyzed left limb complained: "Nobody had any business being in my bed."[6]

Mirna had left hemispatial neglect and misidentified her left arm. The overwhelming majority of patients who display asomatognosia misidentify their left arm. A small number reject the left leg as well. I have examined over one hundred patients with asomatognosia and not a single case was caused by damage to the left hemisphere with nonrecognition of their right arm or leg. One reason the left arm is more commonly affected with the condition than the right may be due to the association between asomatognosia and hemispatial neglect.[7] Hemispatial neglect is more severe and long lasting after damage to the right hemisphere.[8] The right hemisphere has the capacity to direct attention to both sides of space. When there is damage to the left hemisphere, the right hemisphere can compensate for the loss, and the patient is still aware of both sides of the world and the self. On the other hand, the left hemisphere is much more unilateral in its attentional capabilities, and is best at directing the patient's attention to the opposite (right) side. In the presence of damage to the right hemisphere, the left hemisphere has limited capacity to adapt, and the left side of space and the body may be ignored.[9]

The clinical manifestations of neglect are among the most colorful in neurology. A patient with a right hemisphere lesion and left hemispatial neglect might not shave the left side of the face, dress the left half of the body, or eat items on the left side of the hospital tray. When attempting to walk, the patient might collide with objects on the left or ignore people who approach them from the left side. If paralyzed on the left side, which often is the case, these patients tend to ignore the immobile extremity and may carelessly (and dangerously) sit on the paralyzed extremity. When I bring a group of residents on clinical rounds to examine a patient with neglect, I often ask the patient to count the number of doctors gathered around them. The patient invariably starts counting from their right side, gets midway to the left and stops, leaving out roughly half the group.

Patients with hemispatial neglect do not simply ignore stimuli on one side; these patients act in a manner as if nothing of *personal significance* could occur on that side.[10] When asked to cross out lines distributed on a page, the so-called line cancellation task, the neglectful patient will cross out only those lines on the right. When it was pointed out that lines on the left were missed, one of my patients exclaimed, "Oh, those don't count!" and still refused to cross out the line he had missed on the left. When asked to draw a clock, neglect patients will draw only the right half; copying a flower results in a daisy with petals only on its right side. When instructed to mark a line at its center, the midline for the patient is seen to be far to the right (Figures 2–2a–c).[11]

Mirna had a powerful sense of estrangement from the hand. The patient with asomatognosia often expresses the belief that not only is it not their hand but also that it simply cannot be their hand. My patient Sonya demonstrates this estrangement from the limb.

Figure 2-2a.
In a line cancellation task, the patient is instructed to cross out all the lines on the page. The figure shows a cancellation task produced by a patient with left hemispatial neglect. This patient only marked the lines that appear on the right side of the page and she ignores all the stimuli on the left.

Figure 2-2b.
Another patient with left neglect was asked to copy the drawing of a flower shown on the left. The patient left out details from the left side of the drawing.

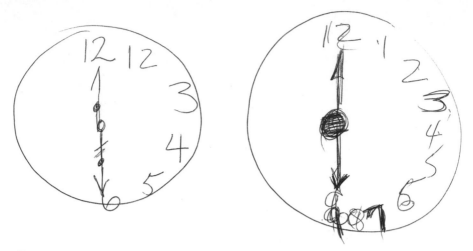

Figure 2-2c.
A third patient with left hemispatial neglect was asked to draw a clock. The patient at first drew the clock on the left, and omitted the numbers on the left. He spontaneously set the clock at 6:00. I then asked him to draw another clock and make this one 9:30. The figure he produced to these instructions is shown on the right.

Sonya

Sonya was a woman in her seventies. An accomplished musician, she was originally from Vienna and spoke with a heavy German accent. Like Mirna, Sonya was hospitalized after a stroke that damaged large portions of the parietal lobe of her right hemisphere. She was paralyzed on the left side of her body, and had considerable neglect of the left side of her body and the left side of the space about her. I moved her left arm to her right side and asked her to identify it.

FEINBERG: *What is this?*
SONYA: *A hand.*
FEINBERG: *A hand? Whose hand is it?*
SONYA: *Not mine!*
FEINBERG: *It's not yours? How do you know?*
SONYA: *Well, its just not mine.*
FEINBERG: *Are you positive?*
SONYA: *Yeah …*
FEINBERG: *Well, whose could it be? This hand here.* [Her hand is held before her eyes. No response.] *Does it have another name? What would you call it?*
SONYA: *A strange.*
FEINBERG: *A strange? You'd call it a strange?*

SONYA: *Yeah.*

FEINBERG: *But it's a hand?*

SONYA: *Yeah.*

Personification of the Limb

Some patients with asomatognosia attribute ownership of the limb to the doctor, claiming it's "your hand" or "the doctor's hand." Some patients plead ignorance and say simply, "I don't know," "I have no idea," or "How should I know? You're the doctor!" Women display a tendency to claim the arm belongs to a man, often the patient's husband. Two patients described by Ullman and coworkers also claimed that their paralyzed left arms belonged to their dead husbands.[12] Interestingly, in contrast to women, men appear more likely to claim that the misidentified arm belongs to a woman. In this case, the patient most often claims that the arm belongs to a daughter or mother-in-law.

The British neurologist Macdonald Critchley studied many patients with asomatognosia, and he highlighted the remarkable tendency of some of these patients to personify their paralyzed limbs. Critchley described the peculiar manner in which some asomatognosic patients related to the misidentified arm, as if the arm possessed a complete, independent identity. Some striking cases treated the arm as if it were a small child or a household pet. A gentleman who came under Dr. Critchley's care displayed this unique behavior. The patient spoke of his arm in the third person, referring to it as "He." This patient, when speaking of his weak left arm, reported, "He gets tired sometimes; he doesn't keep time with you; he gets out of step. He gets very lazy; he sits and hangs about and when he docs get hold of you he doesn't want to leave you. He's been doing this for a week." Critchley went on to describe the peculiar behavior that the patient directed toward the weak limb:

> Asked to open his fist, he held it up before him, still clenched, and then began to cuddle and caress it, patting it and rubbing it, talking to it and encouraging it, e.g. "Come on, you little monkey, don't let us down. Come on, "Monkey." I used to call him "Lucky." We're doing nicely now, so we'll call him "lucky." Come on, "lucky." . . . The nursing staff observed that at meal-times he would "feed" the "little monkey" with a spoon, saying, "come on, have a bit."[13]

Critchley relates the wonderful nicknames his patients gave to their limbs, such as "George," "Toby," "Silly Billy," "Floppy Joe," "Baby," "Gammy," "The Immovable One," "Curse," "Lazy Bones," and "The Nuisance." One patient designated his paretic left arm "James" and referred to his left leg as " lefty." My patient Mirna had a tendency to personify her left side. When asked to identify her left arm, she several times called it her husband's arm; she also once told me her left great toe was her husband's. Mirna's husband had been dead for years. She expressed a number of interesting beliefs regarding her husband's hands.

FEINBERG: *What is this about your husband's hands? Did you have your husband's hands?*

MIRNA: *I did.*

FEINBERG: *Tell me about that. What happened?*

MIRNA: *He left them.*

FEINBERG: *He left them to you?*

MIRNA: *He didn't want them.*

FEINBERG: *OK. Well, did he leave them to you in his will?*

MIRNA: *He just left them like he left his clothes* [tearfully].

FEINBERG: *So they were in the house? Tell me about them.*

MIRNA: *Up until the other day. They used to fall on my chest. I said " I got to get rid of them!"*

FEINBERG: *Yeah.*

MIRNA: *So I did.*

FEINBERG: *So what did you do?*

MIRNA: *Put them in the garbage.*

FEINBERG: *You put them in the garbage?*

MIRNA: *Yes … two days ago.*

FEINBERG: *Where are they now?*

MIRNA: *Still in the garbage … a black hand, with a plastic cover … you'll find them there. Be careful, though … the nails are very long … and very sharp. How come nails grew on dead hands?*

FEINBERG: *I don't know … How do you figure that?*

MIRNA: *I don't understand; if it's dead, it's dead. I don't know.*

FEINBERG: *How do you account for that?*

MIRNA: *I can't … maybe they're not completely dead.*

FEINBERG: *What would that mean?*

MIRNA: *Nothing at all.*

FEINBERG: *Why did you get rid of them?*

MIRNA: *They were bothering me. They used to fall on my chest when I slept … and they're very heavy. And the nails used to scratch me.*

FEINBERG: *Sounds like they were alive!*

MIRNA: *No … they were dead, dead, dead! I tell you, you can take my word for it.*

FEINBERG: *How many years did you have them?*

MIRNA: *Maybe two. Since I was sick.*

FEINBERG: *Since you were sick you had them? Why did you throw them out?*

MIRNA: *Because I thought they were hard luck.*

FEINBERG: *Why did you get rid of them after all those years?*

MIRNA: *Because I got the stroke ... and I thought maybe I'd die here like he did!* [At this point she began to cry.]

Mirna struggled with the reality of her new and tragic circumstances. She felt her left hand was lifeless and she expressed this feeling in her story about her dead husband's hands. Mirna's identification with the husband went beyond her left hand; she seemed to believe her entire illness was connected with her husband's death and that she might suffer the same fate he did. What is the connection between Mirna's statements about her hands and her feelings about herself?

The neurologist and psychoanalyst Edwin Weinstein, with whom I had the opportunity to study while I was a medical student and later as a resident in the Department of Neurology at the Mount Sinai School of Medicine, was, along with Critchley, among the great observers of neurological phenomena. Weinstein argued that the manner in which asomatognosic patients referred to their arms could be interpreted as *metaphorical* expressions of their feelings about themselves. It was Weinstein's position that patients with asomatognosia who misidentified parts of their body displayed a disturbance in metaphorical speech and tended to express their feelings about themselves metaphorically.[14]

Weinstein argued that the use of personification was only one example of the use of metaphorical speech in his patients. He pointed out that his patients employed a variety of tropes when speaking of the affected arm. Weinstein cited the case of the man who referred to his paralyzed arm as "a canary claw, yellow and shrivelled"; other patients of his called it "a piece of rusty machinery" or "dead wood."[15] Metaphorical misidentification was also observed by Gilliatt and Pratt in a patient who described her paralyzed arm as "poor little withered hand."[16] Critchley also noted a case that described the affected arm as "like a bird's claw."[17] Halligan, Marshall, and Wade reported a patient who felt his left arm was "like a sack of coal."[18] Another case, recounted by the same authors, described how his left foot "looked and felt like a cow's foot."[19] My patient Mirna once told me that her left arm was "nothing but a bag of bones." Another patient complained to me that his left arm was "a useless piece of machinery."

Many patients, as was the case with Mirna, describe the left arm as "dead." Sometimes the patient appears to use the word "dead" metaphorically, as in "dead tired." There are some patients, however, who seem to believe the arm is *literally dead*. The patient of Halligan and coworkers, whose left arm was "like a sack of coal," claimed he possessed a "third limb" that was "dead." Critchley observed a patient refer to his arm as "a piece of dead meat."[20]

Asomatognosic patients may express some frightening beliefs about their paralyzed arms. Although I have listened to hundreds of asomatognosic patients, I still may be surprised and taken aback by their comments about their arms. However, the use of metaphorical language in these patients actually may have an adaptive purpose. It was Weinstein's position that the use of metaphorical language demonstrated by these patients served to bring order, unity, and predictability to the frequently confusing circumstances of neurological illness. Under the conditions of brain damage, metaphorical language may seem more "real" to the patient than more conventional forms of expression and may help the patient cope with catastrophic illness. Faced with the life-threatening and chaotic circumstances posed by neurological illness, metaphor, more than everyday language, captured the way patients saw themselves and their disabilities.

Shirley

The next case beautifully illustrates the way the personification of a hemiplegic limb helps the patient adapt to illness. Shirley was a vibrant and intelligent woman in her fifties when a large stroke of her right hemisphere paralyzed her left arm and leg. Despite her recent neurological problems, Shirley remained alert and talkative. Her neurologist informed me that Shirley had some interesting things to say about her left arm:

SHIRLEY: *It took a vacation without telling me it was going. It didn't ask. It just went.*
FEINBERG: *What did?*
SHIRLEY: *My Pet Rock.* [She lifted her lifeless left arm to indicate what she was talking about.]
FEINBERG: *You call that your Pet Rock:*
SHIRLEY: *Yeah.*
FEINBERG: *Why do you call it your Pet Rock?*
SHIRLEY: *Because it doesn't do anything. It just sits there.*
FEINBERG: *When did you come up with that name?*
SHIRLEY: *Right after it went plop. I thought I'd give it a nice name even though it was something terrible.*

FEINBERG: *Do you have any other names for it?*

SHIRLEY: *Her. She belongs to me, so she's a her. She's mine but I don't like her very well. She let me down.*

FEINBERG: *In what way?*

SHIRLEY: *Plop, plop, rock, rock, nothing. I was on my way home, out the door, and then she went and did this* [Shirley pointed to her left arm]. *She didn't ask if she could* [she was shaking her head back and forth]. *I have to be the boss, not her.*

FEINBERG: *Is that its actual name? Would you say that is its real name?*

SHIRLEY: *For now. It doesn't deserve any better. I could paint it if I wanted to.*

FEINBERG: *Is it a real Pet Rock though?*

SHIRLEY: *No, it's my hand.*

FEINBERG: *So why do you refer to it as a Pet Rock? What do you mean by that?*

SHIRLEY: *It lays there like a lump. It doesn't do anything. It just lays there. It's like when you're Jewish and you go to a Jewish cemetery and put a rock on the tomb and it just lays there. It is supposed to say "I was here." [Pointing to her left arm] It's saying I'm here. But I'm not. I'm only sort of here. I'm not really here.*

FEINBERG: [I touched her left hand] *Is this part of you?*

SHIRLEY: *Un-huh. Not a part I like a lot.*

FEINBERG: *Do you dislike it?*

SHIRLEY: *Yeah.*

FEINBERG: *How do you feel about the real Pet Rocks?*

SHIRLEY: *Stupid.*

FEINBERG: *Is that something you'd give somebody as a present?*

SHIRLEY: *No.*

FEINBERG: *By calling it a Pet Rock*

SHIRLEY: [She interrupts me] *It gives it another life. Because without humor I'm nothing. I have to have a laugh a day, otherwise they're gonna put me away. So I give it a humorous reference.*

A week later I returned to re-examine Shirley. She was about to be discharged from the hospital and transferred to a rehabilitation facility. As I prepared to ask her some questions, she grabbed her left hand with her right, shook the limp arm, and began to sing to it:

SHIRLEY: *Wake up! Time to go home. What are we gonna tell your mama? What are we gonna tell your pa? What are we gonna tell your friends when they say ooo-la-la? Wake up little Susie. It's time to go home.*

[Then she held her left hand to her cheek and hugged it, kissed it, and petted it.] *She's a good girl.*

FEINBERG: *What was that?*

SHIRLEY: *"Wake Up Little Susie." Remember the Everly Brothers?* [Point to her left arm] *That's her. That's little Susie. She's been out all night long and she has to go home. That's it. She's done. She's gotta go home or they're gonna think she's the town whore* [laughing].

FEINBERG: *Why would you say that?*

SHIRLEY: *Because she's not behaving.* [She wiggled her arm again, pulling on her fingers as if to rouse it. Then she explained to me why she sang the song to her arm] *Wake up little Susie! It's a coping mechanism. It's like they used to say in* Reader's Digest, *"Laughter is the best medicine." It you can't laugh, what have you got? I thought I could bring her back with some loving kindness. So I sang it "Wake Up Little Susie," which is one of my favorite songs from the Everly Brothers.*

FEINBERG: *What's the theme of that song?*

SHIRLEY: *A girl and boyfriend were out too late at night. And the entire town is going to be talking about them. That she's being a slut. So it's a way of avoiding getting in trouble. And then he says "What are we gonna tell your friends when they they say ooo-la-la? Wake up little Susie. It's time to go home."* [Then she lifts up her left arm] *And I want to go home!*

The metaphorical personifications that Shirley used to describe her arm were condensed expressions of her feelings. A Pet Rock, like her paralyzed arm, "lays there like a lump" and is "stupid." The association Shirley made between the Pet Rock and the stones that, according to tradition, are left on a Jewish grave was a metaphorical expression of her feeling that her arm was lifeless. Shirley's choice of the Everly Brothers hit "Wake Up Little Susie" was also laden with metaphorical meaning. The words of this song eloquently expressed Shirley's feelings about her circumstances. Like Shirley's paralyzed arm, Little Susie was asleep and she must be awoken. Shirley was upset that her arm would not move and did not know who "the boss" was, and Little Susie will be in trouble if she does not listen to the entreaties of her boyfriend and wake up. In this way, Shirley expressed both her love of her arm, as well as her anger toward a hand that would not follow her instructions. Finally, Little Susie was about to go home and Shirley was about to be discharged from the hospital. If Shirley's "Little Susie" would just "wake up," Shirley would also be able to go home.

Anosognosia

Many patients who display asomatognosia have the related condition of anosognosia, or denial of illness.[21] Anosognosia literally means "lack of knowledge of the existence of disease." Even though the rejected arm in asomatognosic patients is severely weak or completely paralyzed, most patients with asomatognosia deny or minimize their paralysis. When asked to raise the paralyzed arm or wiggle the fingers of that hand, they may claim the requested actions are performed quite normally. Indeed, some patients deny they are ill in any way. They often claim the paralyzed arm is just "lazy" or perhaps "a little tired." Denial or unawareness of paralysis is called " anosognosia for hemiplegia." The three conditions—asomatognosia, hemispatial neglect, and anosognosia—often occur together, usually as a result of damage to the right hemisphere.

As is the case with asomatognosia, the manifestations of anosognosia vary from case to case, and no two patients are exactly alike. To make matters more complicated, patients may vary in their insight from day to day, even hour to hour. The truly anosognosic patient is not just "confused" about his or her circumstances. This would not be terribly interesting and hardly worth the time of the hundreds of investigators who have studied the syndrome. The patient with definite anosognosia for hemiplegia is not simply unaware of their weakness: they cannot be convinced of the paralysis. My patient Jack can serve as an example of a patient with anosognosia.

Jack

Jack was a sixty-four-year-old construction worker. He had a right hemisphere stroke, which completely paralyzed his left arm (Figure 2-3). Jack had all of the syndromes described in this chapter. He had severe left hemispatial neglect. His eyes, rather than sitting in the midline, were deviated strongly toward his right, as if he were observing something going on in the far corner of the room. He ignored people if they approached him from his left.

Jack had asomatognosia and misidentified his left arm. He also had dense anosognosia and insisted that he was in pretty good health. He made this claim, even though he was lying in a hospital bed in a gown, with an intravenous line in his right arm. Jack knew, all too well, that the *doctors* thought he was ill, that he had suffered a stroke; he even knew the hospital staff thought he could not move his left side. Despite this knowledge, he held to his belief that he was not ill in any way. Jack insist-

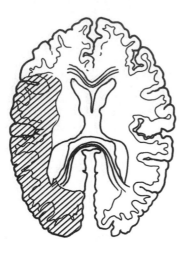

Figure 2-3.
As this CAT scan shows, Jack's infarction extended from the rear frontal portion of his brain all the way back to the occipital portion, which is responsible for visual perception.

While he cannot move his left side of his body and attend to objects in his left visual field, Jack was convinced that he is in perfectly fine shape (anosognosia).

ed that all was well, and, if the doctors would only let him, he would get right up and leave.

FEINBERG: *If everything is fine, why are you lying in the bed now?*

JACK: *I'd like to be home right now . . . I swear I'd like . . .*

FEINBERG: *I don't blame you. But why are you lying in the bed now? Is there anything wrong?*

JACK: *The doctors seem to think so*

FEINBERG: *The doctors seem to think so? What do you think they think is wrong with you?*

JACK: *They think I had a stroke or somethin.'*

FEINBERG: *Or something?*

JACK: *Yeah.*

FEINBERG: *What do you think?*

JACK: *I don't think I had a stroke.*

FEINBERG: *Why don't you think you had a stroke? Any particular reason?*

JACK: *I'm sure if I had a stroke I'd feel a lot worse than I feel.*

FEINBERG: *Than you do now? Huh! Cause you're feeling' pretty good now . . .*

JACK: *Yeah.*

FEINBERG: *OK.*

JACK: *My mother's in the hospital right now.*

FEINBERG: *Your mother is?*

JACK: *Yeah.*

FEINBERG: *What's wrong with her?*

JACK: *She had a stroke while she was in the hospital.*

FEINBERG: *She was in the hospital also?*
JACK: *Yeah.*
FEINBERG: *What's this?* [I held up Jack's hand.]
JACK: *My mother-in-law's hand. Someone's hand. I think it's my mother-in-law's hand.*

In some of the most severe cases of anosognosia, especially those in which the patient also displays asomatognosia, despite total paralysis of the left side the patient will insist that the arm is actually moving, that the fingers are wiggling, or the leg is up in the air.[22] Joseph Babinski, who introduced the term anosognosia in a 1914 paper, described how one of his patients, when she was told to raise her paralyzed arm, exclaimed "Voila, c'est fait."[23] My patient Rodney had a left hemiplegia and referred to his left arm, as a "dummy arm." He claimed the arm moved quite well:

FEINBERG: *Raise your right arm please,* [patient raises his right arm]. *Now is your right arm on the bed or in the air?*
RODNEY: *In the air.*
FEINBERG: *OK. Put your right arm down for me. Now raise your left arm.* [No movement, no response; left hand remains paralyzed on the bed, on the patient's left side.]
FEINBERG: *Where is your left arm now?*
RODNEY: *Up in the air.*
FEINBERG: *It's up in the air? How high is it now about?*
RODNEY: *Not too high.*
FEINBERG: *Not too high?* [Patient is asked to point to his left arm. With his right hand he points two and a half feet above the bed.] *Okay, good put your right arm down, now. Put your left arm down. Now, where is your left arm?* [Patient points to his left arm on the bed].

Even though Rodney's arm remained paralyzed throughout his hospital stay, his belief that he could move the arm diminished during this period. At the same time his insight into the true nature of his paralysis increased. When he started to realize the consequences of his stroke and the nature of his illness, he claimed he could lift the hand only "two inches off the bed." When he fully understood that he might never recover the use of the arm, Rodney admitted he could not lift the arm at all.

Weinstein was a strong proponent of the view that anosognosic patients were not merely unaware of their illness; they were in deep denial of their problems. For Weinstein, the presence of psychological denial was the main reason anosognosic patients could not, or would not, admit they were sick or disabled, even when the facts of their illness were obvious. Consider Patsy, who could not be convinced she wasn't well despite much evidence to the contrary.

Patsy

A woman in her sixties, Patsy was physically well and enjoyed an active career until one day when she suddenly could not move her left side. She fell to the floor, unable to get up, and wasn't discovered until hours later, when her husband returned from work. She was rushed to the hospital by ambulance, and an emergency CAT scan of her brain revealed she had a large stroke of her right hemisphere. Her doctors had told Patsy quite clearly that she had experienced a stroke. She knew what I thought was wrong with her; she just didn't agree.

FEINBERG: *OK. What are you doing here?*
PATSY: *You all tell me I have a weak left side.*
FEINBERG: *I'm sorry?*
PATSY: *You all say I have a weak left side.*
FEINBERG: *We all say you have a weak left side?*
PATSY: *And I don't agree!*
FEINBERG: *And you don't agree?*
PATSY: *No.*
FEINBERG: *Why?*
PATSY: *Because I know I don't!*
FEINBERG: *It feels fine?*
PATSY: *Yes.*
FEINBERG: *There's no weakness over there . . .*
PATSY: *No.* [She is asked to raise her right arm, which she does.]
FEINBERG: *Now raise the other arm for me. Raise your left arm for me.*
    Can't you do that for me? [Pause.] *Did you do it? Did you raise it?*
PATSY: *I did now.*
FEINBERG: *You did now? Do you have any difficulty raising it?*
PATSY: *No.*
FEINBERG: *OK then. Why don't you touch your nose?* [Touches nose
    with right hand.]
FEINBERG: *Why don't you touch it with the other hand? Can you touch it*
    with the other hand?
PATSY: *Yes.*
FEINBERG: *Could you do it for me?* [No movement.] *Are you doing it?*

[Again, no response.]

[After a pause.] *You know, it would seem to me that if you couldn't touch your nose with your left hand, that there might be some weakness over there. How does that sound to you?*

PATSY: *No.*

FEINBERG: *You adamantly disagree? You are absolutely certain there's no weakness over there? Could you tell me why you won't touch your nose with your left hand? Is there a reason for that?*

PATSY: *Because I think I'm a comedian . . . and I'd probably make an obscene gesture.*

[One week later.]

FEINBERG: *What's wrong with you?*

PATSY: *I had a slight stroke.*

FEINBERG: *Oh . . . really?* [Turning to the family who were present.] *Has she been admitting that more readily?*

PATSY: *Do they have an AA for stroke patients?*

FEINBERG: *I'm sorry.*

PATSY: *Do they have an AA for stroke patients? Yeah. Where they have to admit they had strokes.*

FEINBERG: *Would you enter that?*

PATSY: *Yes.*

In the most severe stages of anosognosia for hemiplegia that occur in the first hours or days after a stroke, the patient adamantly denies that there is a paralysis. This period of total denial generally resolves within days or weeks after the onset of the hemiplegia and gradually the patient comes to admit the true nature of their paralysis. This realization often occurs in stages. At first, the patient may admit the *doctors think* the patient is paralyzed, but the patient disagrees with their assessment. One of my patients told me "there was a rumor on the floor" that the patient was paralyzed, but "you know how unreliable rumors are." Another patient told me that it was the case that the doctors "seem to think some paralysis has set in." I asked him if he agreed with their judgment and he told me " I don't know . . . I'm not the expert!" As more time passes the patient may admit the paralysis but minimize its consequences for their lives and livelihoods. A patient in this stage of partial awareness might report that, despite the severe paralysis, he plans a swift return to physical labor or to resume jogging within a week. Ultimately, most patients understand the true nature of the paralysis and the obstacles they must face. These obstacles often include a long period of rehabilitation and the possibility of permanent disability. My patient Daryl reflected on the gradual realization that his left arm was paralyzed.

Daryl

Daryl was a very intelligent electrical engineer. He was relatively young, in his early fifties, when he sustained a massive stroke of his right hemisphere (Figure 2–4), which resulted in complete paralysis of his left side. During the initial stages of his illness, Daryl denied that there was anything wrong with him. He spoke freely about his future, and appeared ready at any moment to leave the hospital and pick up his life where he had left off. Over the next few weeks, Daryl reluctantly admitted to the painful consequences of his illness. At this point I asked him to describe what he was thinking during the period of his anosognosia.

DARYL: *That's my left hand, which I understand people who have strokes, they tend to ignore parts of their left body. They say "Go away. I don't want to know you!" It's a way of getting back. [Pointing at his left arm.] I'll hate you the rest of my life for acting this way. That's what we tend to do. I don't know the reality of it . . . the reasons for it, but apparently it's quite valid.*

FEINBERG: *That's the way you feel?*

DARYL: *This is common among stroke people. They tend to ignore . . . It could be with me too, because I was sleeping on my arm the other day. And I remember waking up and saying "Good Lord! I gotta get up and pack this before I leave or I'll leave it here" . . . we tend to admit a piece of ourselves is not a part of ourselves. We'll say it belongs to somebody else because it's sick. We'll give it away because we don't want it. That's why I slept on it. I didn't want it. I wanted*

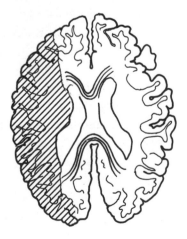

Figure 2-4.
Daryl's uncharacteristic behavior was caused by a large, right frontoparietal infarct, as seen in his remarkable CAT scan. Despite his severe paralysis, Daryl thought he was well.

to cover it up, to shield it. But when I realized it was my own arm, and I had to take it with me to be a success. I was gonna pack it, not leave it here. The only person it's going to be any good to is me. Even if it's slow to function . . .

Explaining Asomatognosia

It is amazing that people quite normal prior to a stroke could reject, misidentify, or deny a part of their body that they have known, lived with, and depended on their whole life. Asomatognosia has always struck me as one of the most bizarre, horrifying, yet fascinating manifestations of neurological disease. One perplexing thing about the syndrome is most asomatognosic patients express strange beliefs only about their arm or their illness. Furthermore, before the onset of neurological illness, they were just like everybody else and had no more psychopathology than occurs in the general population. It is clear that brain pathology can destroy the integrated self in any of us.

It would be futile to seek a single answer to the question: What causes asomatognosia? Asomatognosia does not have one cause. Rather, the syndrome occurs as the result of the many factors discussed in this chapter. Neglect surely is an important element in the production of asomatognosia. However, the presence of neglect alone is not enough to produce asomatognosia. While I have never seen a case of asomatognosia without significant neglect, there are many patients with neglect who do not misidentify their paralyzed limbs.

Most patients with asomatognosia also display anosognosia. Mirna, however, was aware she had suffered a stroke. She was even aware that her left side was paralyzed. In spite of this I could not convince her that her left arm was indeed her left arm. Furthermore, some patients with anosognosia, particularly those cases with mild forms of the condition, do not display asomatognosia.

Additionally, anosognosia occurs in many neurological illnesses besides hemiplegia. Patients may be unaware of blindness, or memory problems, or a host of other disabilities. For example, Anton's syndrome, or unawareness of blindness, is one of the classic neurobehavioral disorders. The syndrome was named after Gabriel Anton, who in 1899 described one of the earliest examples of this rather amazing condition.[24] The patient may seem alert and integrated, and often gives the appearance that nothing is amiss. On examination, however, it becomes apparent the patient is totally blind, yet oblivious to the impairment. Anton's syndrome is not a common condition, but it is not rare either. Lizzy is a typical case of Anton's syndrome.

Lizzy

Lizzy was a woman in her late sixties. A former librarian, Lizzy had a history of cardiac problems, but otherwise had no significant medical history. Unfortunately, one day she suffered acute strokes in the occipital lobes of both her left and right hemispheres. The strokes destroyed the primary visual areas of her brain, and she was rendered suddenly and totally blind.

I examined Lizzy during the initial stages of her hospitalization. She was lying comfortably in her hospital bed and appeared to be very relaxed, despite her recent neurological catastrophe. She could not have been more pleasant. Indeed, she was *too* pleasant. She seemed completely unperturbed by the dramatic shift in her fortunes. If you asked her about her vision, she would always initially deny any impairment. However, her insight fluctuated, even within the course of a single interview. She might deny her blindness, and later admit it, but never did she seem to act as if her visual impairment was of any concern. She smiled throughout the interview and acted as if she had not a care in the world.

FEINBERG: *So, how are you?*
LIZZY: *All right. Fine thanks.* [She is smiling broadly.]
FEINBERG: *Is there anything bothering you? Any problems?*
LIZZY: *No* [emphatically]. *That's the strange thing. Nothing is bothering me*
FEINBERG: *Nothing is bothering you . . . you're feeling perfectly all right?*
LIZZY: *Yeah.*
FEINBERG: *Let me ask you. Where are you right now?*
LIZZY: *I'm uh . . . well I'm near where I live. I could be at* [gives address of the hospital] *At least it looks that way.*
FEINBERG: *You could be?*
LIZZY: *Yeah . . . if I had a stroke. But the last time I looked I was home!* [After further discussion of the current location, I address her visual impairments.]
FEINBERG: *Are you having any trouble with your vision in any way?*
LIZZY: *No.* [She says this with an inflection that suggests a tone of "surprisingly enough," as if she had thought of the possibility of blindness, but is pleasantly surprised to find that she has none.]

FEINBERG: *Why don't you tell me what you see. Look around now, and just tell me what you see here.*

LIZZY: [She looks about the room, moves her head back and forth, as if she is taking a really good look.] *It's good to see friends and family, you know. It makes me feel like I'm in good hands.*

FEINBERG: *Tell me their names.*

LIZZY: [She whispers to me, as if slightly embarrassed.] *I don't know everybody. They are my brother's friends. They look friendly, but I'm not sure exactly who they are.*

FEINBERG: *How many are here?*

LIZZY: *I'd say maybe twelve.*

FEINBERG: *OK. How many are men and how many are women?*

LIZZY: *Fifty-fifty.*

FEINBERG: *Is it split right down the middle?*

LIZZY: *Yeah* [laughing]. *Pretty much.*

FEINBERG: *Look at me. What am I wearing?* [I have on a white shirt, blue tie, black pants and a white lab coat.]

LIZZY: *A casual outfit. You know, a jacket and pants.*

FEINBERG: *What color pants are they?*

LIZZY: *Mostly navy blue . . . and maroon, or something like that.*

FEINBERG: *What about my shirt? Do I have a shirt on?*

LIZZY: *You have a shirt, but it isn't dressy. Looks like navy blue and white.*

Based on the foregoing, it is fair to conclude asomatognosia and anosognosia are related conditions, but the presence of one does not explain the presence of the other. Instead, asomatognosia is multidetermined and due to the interaction of both neurological and psychiatric factors.

One of the interesting aspects of asomatognosia is that, despite the fragmentation of the self, these patients strive to maintain an integrated self and make sense of their experience. Indeed, to a large extent they succeed. The neglected left side and the misidentified left limb leave a whole, a gap, in the self, that must be filled. The patient may disavow the arm, but something is put in its place, something of personal significance. In the next chapter, we will explore another condition in which the personal world of the patient is transformed.

3

Missing Pieces;
Familiar Places

And you may ask yourself,
How do I work this?
And you may ask yourself,
Where is that large automobile?
And you may tell yourself,
This is not my beautiful house!
And you may tell yourself,
This is not my beautiful wife!

Talking Heads, "Once in a Lifetime," 1978

The Margins of the Ego

We all have a natural sense of where we as selves end and the environment begins. It is from our inside point of view, our inner personal perspective, that we experience the world. Under most conditions, the distinction between self and the world is obvious. I feel that I am not the chair on which I sit. While it may seem as if the boundaries of the self are obvious, they are in actuality more dynamic than rigid. They are not fixed; they are relative. Things or other persons can be relatively close to the inner core of the self's experience, or they can be quite removed. In this way, an object can be "ego-close" or "ego-distant."[1]

For example, your shoes on your feet are objects that are to me ego-distant. I do not feel they are a part of me, connected to me in any way, or bear any particular personal relevance to me. Now, what about the shoes on my feet? My shoes are to a certain extent felt to be part of me. They are not as close to being part of me as my feet themselves, but they are certainly closer to me personally than your shoes. I might to a certain extent *identify* with my shoes and my clothing in general. They may be incorporated into myself.

The persons, places, objects, and events that one's self experiences are imbued with feeling—the feeling of how one relates to things in a personal sense. Our identities are built around this sense of relatedness. Personal relatedness provides the structure within which the self is anchored in the world. The self is a continuum of relationships. An individual's own body, spouse, and family members are "ego-close." They bear a particular personal relationship to the self, identity with the self; we care about these items, these events, these people, in particular ways. They are significant. The objects of the world, which for us have no personal significance, could be considered "ego-distant." The impersonal world, the stranger on the street, is less likely to be imbued with any sense of personal significance.

To what extent identification with objects takes place becomes clearer whenever the degree of closeness with a particular object is *altered*. For instance, when wearing a favorite article of clothing, one to which you are particularly attached, it is commonplace not to notice the degree to which it has become worn and torn over the years. I have found that after wearing a new pair of shoes, I am startled at how worn down my old pair appear when I rediscover them a week later. As soon as one has lost the normal relatedness to the object, the degree to which one is identified with it is altered. The object is no longer apprehended as part of the self. It is no longer ego-close.

The process of going from a sense of relatedness to one of distance is commonly known as alienation. To become alienated from something, we have first to be close to it. In this way, there is a continuum of the self: from the ego-closeness of the pure "I" to the ego-distance of impersonal objects. The individual ego encompasses this continuum of personal relatedness in ways that reflect both the brain and its experience.

The conditions of jamais vu (where the familiar appears strange) and déjà vu (the opposite condition, where the unfamiliar appears familiar) are examples of alterations in relatedness. The psychologically healthy individual enjoys an integrated and comfortable relation of the self and the world. Our boundaries between the world and other people are held in delicate balance, however. This balance is maintained automatically and in large part unconsciously. We are not generally aware of these boundaries until they are violated, until someone or something gets too close or too distant, until one feels merged with or alienated from the world. This degree of relatedness also helps define what is real; it defines our reality. The peculiar, uncomfortable feeling of the loss of reality, of loss of one's psychological foothold when confronted with a déjà vu or jamais vu experience, is significant. It demonstrates how personal relatedness structures our feeling of what is real and establishes our identity in the world.

The neurological damage that we have considered perturbs ego structure in various ways, creating an alteration in the identity of the individual in the world. Remember Mirna in chapter two, the patient who misidentified her left arm as belonging to her deceased husband? The neurological lesion led to a withdrawal of personal relatedness or alienation of her limb. It no longer felt like her own arm, yet it was recognized as an element in the world that should have been her arm. No matter how connected she once was to it, no matter how impossible it might seem to us to be that her limb could be viewed as not belonging to herself, it is quite common for the arm to be disavowed under these conditions. There can also be an insertion of relatedness involved with asomatognosia. Just as this patient called it her husband's arm, many patients misidentify the paralyzed arms as belonging to a close friend, a relative, a mother-in-law, or some other part of the patient's own body, like a breast. Thus, we see an insertion of personal relatedness as well as withdrawal, and we can view the misidentification of the asomatognosic patient as both a withdrawal and an insertion of personal relatedness.

In this chapter, we will explore two more syndromes that are examples of perturbations of the self in relation to the world. The first of these, Capgras syndrome, is an example of a loss of personal relatedness; the second, Frégoli syndrome, represents an insertion of personal relatedness. By considering these disorders we may further decipher the mysteries of asomatognosia, and the relationship between the brain and self.

Capgras Syndrome

Alienation from onself or one's life is surely common. Who has not experienced the loss of the familiar at one time or other? But some patients have this experience on an enduring basis. In 1923, Joseph Capgras, a French psychiatrist, and his intern, J. Reboul-Lachaux, described the unusual case of Mme. M., a fifty-three-year-old woman who complained that imposters ("sosies") had replaced her husband, children, even herself. Her husband, according to her account, had been murdered, and the men who came to see her in his guise were his doubles. She recounted that there must have been at least eighty imposters who appeared in this fashion, and asserted: "I can assure you that the imposter husband that they are trying to insinuate is my own husband, who has not existed for ten years, is not the person who is keeping me here." Mme, M. claimed that more than two thousand doubles of her daughter had passed before her eyes: not only close family members, but eventually policemen, a concierge, doctors, nurses, and neighbors were impersonated. Eventually, she reported that there were even doubles of the doubles! Capgras and Reboul-Lachaux called her case "L'Illusion des sosies."[2]

The name they chose is derived from Greek mythology, which gives us the story of Zeus, who physically transforms himself in order to take on the appearance of Amphitryon. He performs this ruse in order to seduce Amphitryon's wife, Alcmena. Fearful that Alcmena's servant, Sosia, will alert her to the deception, he arranges for Mercury to impersonate Sosia as well. The charade is successful, and Alcmena eventually has twins: one twin is the son of Zeus and is named Hercules; the other twin is the son of Amphitryon and is named Iphicles. This myth served as the basis for the play, *Amphitrio*, by the Roman playwright Plautus, and was much later the subject of Molière's play, *Amphitryon*. The word "sosie," after Alcmena's servant, came to mean "a double" in French. It was employed to characterize someone who bears a strong twin-like resemblance to another person. The disorder subsequently became known as the Capgras syndrome.[3]

The Capgras syndrome is an example of a *delusional misidentification syndrome*. The term "delusional misidentification syndrome" applies to several clinical disorders in which a patient confuses the psychological or physical identity of a person, place, or thing.[4] The patient with Capgras syndrome knows that a certain individual *looks* like the misidentified person, but there has been a *change* in the psychological identity of the individual.

Capgras syndrome may be caused by psychiatric or neurological illness. The cause of Mme. M.'s delusional misidentification was psychiatric. Her doctor diagnosed Mme M. as suffering from "chronic psychosis"; Capgras and Reboul-Lachaux described Mme M. as a "paranoid megolamaniac." In patients with a psychiatric background, schizophrenia is a common cause of the delusion. This is especially true of patients in whom paranoia is prominent. In neurological patients, the most common causes of Capgras syndrome are head injury, stroke, or illnesses that cause dementia such as Alzheimer's disease.[5]

The person who is misidentified may be a close relative or a person significant in the patient's life. Married patients who develop Capgras syndrome often claim that an imposter has replaced their wife or husband. The patient's explanation regarding the fate of the "original" varies from case to case. When asked specifically where the original has gone, some patients simply profess that they have no idea, while other patients may hold more paranoid beliefs and claim that the original was murdered or was the object of a kidnapping plot. Some patients do not seem particularly upset about the substitution; in fact, some patients are very pleased! Others are disturbed and can become quite paranoid. I have found that women with Alzheimer's disease, especially those who have outlived their husbands, tend to misidentify a daughter. This was the case with my patient Emma.

Emma

Emma was an eighty-year-old woman who reported that there were two "versions" of her daughter: one, the actual daughter, Betty, and the other one, Betty's "assistant." Emma described at length how her daughter told me, "I'm Betty," but she reported:

EMMA: *It wasn't my daughter. Her name was Betty . . . So I said . . . her name can't be Betty because two Jewish sisters aren't called Betty.*
FEINBERG: *You thought it was her sister?*
EMMA: *No . . . I thought she worked for her. But the two girls named Betty. I mean it just . . .*
FEINBERG: *So there were two . . .*
EMMA: *Two girls both named Betty.*

The two "Bettys" were similar in most respects, except the "other" version of Betty wasn't as tall as the original, didn't wear glasses, and had shorter hair than the real Betty. The other Betty had cooked for her and took her on trips, while the real Betty wasn't around. On one of these outings, Emma reported she had bought two hats, one for the daughter Betty and one for the other Betty. There was no doubling of any of her other relatives, doctors, or friends.

EMMA: *And she had all the information about everybody in my family . . .*
FEINBERG: *The other one?*
EMMA: *The other one . . . knew everything. And she knew everyone's friend and who they were married to, and I questioned . . . because I couldn't . . .* [holding her temples as if perplexed] *. . . and then she said, "If you're my mother I'd love for you to feel the same way as maybe I felt about Betty" . . . maybe she saw how close we were . . . I came over, and then I was beginning to realize, maybe the girl, maybe I left her . . . as a . . . you know, had her adopted or something."*

She became concerned that perhaps she had done something to the other Betty as a child, maybe that she had abandoned her. She was quite upset over the substitution and asked "Why did this happen?" while crying to her daughter in perplexity. There was frequent mention of possible trickery involved. She suspected that the other Betty wanted to get rid of the original. It disturbed her to think that her daughter might also be part of this conspiracy of deception. She added that the real Betty was "nicer" than the other one. She added, "I never loved the other Betty."

As was the case with Emma, patients with Capgras often perceive differences between the original and the imposter. A well-known case reported in 1931 by Larrivé and Jasienski described a French woman who complained about her poorly endowed, inadequate, and sexually awkward lover.[6] Fortunately for her, he possessed a double, whom she described as rich, virile, handsome, and aristocratic and was a rival for her affections. Davidson also described a patient with Capgras syndrome, a thirty-year-old man with an extensive psychiatric history who reported that the woman who claimed to be his wife was an imposter:

> He had the idea that his wife was not the person he married, that she was a double, that she was not a Catholic but a Jewish woman. Also, he declared there were certain differences in temperament, and he felt even that the formations of the sexual organs of his wife and her double were different.[7]

Feelings and fears about a spouse were reflected in the Capgras delusion of my patient Louise.

Louise

I treated another eighty-year-old woman, Louise, who presented with poor memory due to the onset of Alzheimer's disease. Aside from her memory problems, however, Louise was quite intact in most respects. She was pleasant in demeanor and immaculately groomed. If you met her on the street, you would not think there was anything wrong with her. She held to no odd beliefs except one about her husband Murray, whom she claimed was not the original man she had married. Louise explained when she realized something was not right with Murray:

LOUISE: *I have found myself looking at a picture we have . . . a picture in the living room, of myself and my husband. And I made sure I picked that picture up and looked at it . . . and looked at the face, to see whether there was any form of nose or mouth or anything that was different looking and I can't see it. I can't see it on the picture.*
FEINBERG: *You can't see any difference between the picture and his face.*
LOUISE: [In agreement.] *No, no.*
FEINBERG: *They look identical?*
LOUISE: *They look identical.*

FEINBERG: *Now, when you look at the picture, you feel that that's him in the picture. But when you look at him . . .*

LOUISE: *I get the feeling . . . that he doesn't look quite the same as Murray would have looked . . . many years back.*

FEINBERG: *Doesn't look the same as Murray would have looked many years back. Now, do you ever have the feeling there's two of them?*

LOUISE: *Yes I have . . . I've had it at night, when I was alone. When I had these feelings, I did have a feeling, that there were two of them. And it's very scary so I didn't think long about it.*

FEINBERG: *Uh-huh. But you have this feeling there could be two Murrays? But when you see him and you have this feeling that that's not him, did you ever have a belief that the other Murray must be somewhere else?*

LOUISE: *I have believed that, because I've worried certain times, about that he was out in the rain . . . he's alone . . . and nobody's taking care of him . . . and he's by himself. And I was very concerned.*

Louise's comments reveal something about the basis of the Capgras delusion. When Louise stares at the picture of Murray, she realizes she is looking at a picture of a face. She doesn't mistake Murray for a hat, for example. Nor does she show evidence of any problem recognizing objects, such as keys and combs, in the world around her. We know from these observations that Louise does not suffer from *visual agnosia*. Visual agnosia is a global disorder of visual recognition in which the patient cannot recognize objects from vision alone, but may recognize the same objects through other means, such as touch.

Louise also had no difficulty with visual recognition of other members of her family, her therapists, or myself. From this we may surmise that Louise does not have the syndrome of *prosopognosia*. In prosopognosia, the patient can recognize objects in general, but has particular difficulty with assigning proper identity to faces. The patient who suffers from prosopognosia knows a face when she sees one; she just doesn't know whose face it is. Prosopognosics often compensate for their difficulty in visual face identification by using other sensory cues, such as hairstyle, voice, or clothing to improve their ability to identify people. They also do not deny a person's correct identity once it is pointed out. Moreover, prosopognosics have a problem with all faces: their problem is not selective for a particular face. Therefore, Louise knew which person was *supposed* to be Murray; it just didn't seem to her that this Murray was the *real* Murray. There was a conflict between her current perception of Murray and her *feelings* about him.

The term Capgras syndrome usually refers to the misidentification of persons, but some patients may disavow and misidentify locations, buildings, or inanimate objects. This situation was the case with my patient Oliver.

Oliver

Oliver was a distinguished gentleman in his seventies. He was a holocaust survivor who immigrated to the United States where he enjoyed great success in business. He suffered a small stroke and was admitted to the hospital. His hospitalization was uneventful, and he survived the entire episode with no obvious neurological effects.

Upon returning to his much-loved apartment, he was dismayed to find that it had been substituted for another nearly identical apartment. In other words, he was convinced that he had two apartments at the same exact address. The second apartment was "two rooms smaller than the original." When I asked him how two apartments nearly identical could be located at the same address, he calmly reported, "I have not had the opportunity to discuss it with the super(intendent) or any other official . . . about the feasibility of that apartment . . . both buildings were taken care of by the same super(intendent)."

Some patients claim that inanimate objects are substitutes, the so-called delusion of inanimate doubles. This syndrome represents a form of Capgras syndrome for objects. Anderson reported a fascinating example of this disorder.[8] He described a seventy-four-year-old man, hospitalized in Liverpool, who claimed that more than 300 items, including Wilkinson Sword razor blades, a Black & Decker electric drill, and assorted men's underwear, had been removed from his home and replaced by nearly identical doubles. The perpetrators of this heinous crime were his wife Mrs. B. and her nephew Mr. C. who were plotting to ruin him. While the substituted items bore great resemblance to the originals, the patient noted that some of the substituted items were of inferior quality to the originals. For example, there were replacement paint brushes that had "fewer bristles" than the original, a pair of replaced black Wellington boots that appeared " more worn," and a pair of replaced swimming trunks that "did not fit properly." A CAT scan of his brain revealed the patient had a large brain tumor five centimeters in diameter.

A patient of mine, Marianne, was admitted to the psychiatric ward. She reported an experience similar to Dr. Anderson's patient.

Marianne

Marianne, a woman in her seventies, had become quite agitated when she realized her apartment had been substituted for its original "just like in a mystery novel." All the furniture, posters, and even the dishware had been substituted with exact facsimiles.

MARIANNE: *And in the kitchen closet I noticed a difference.*
FEINBERG: *What was that?*
MARIANNE: *Well, first of all, the types of dishes that were there were arranged as I would never arrange it.*
FEINBERG: *In what way?*
MARIANNE: *Well, I basically size them, and then there were cups and glasses that were not quite the same.*
FEINBERG: *What were the differences? Different . . .*
MARIANNE: *Patterns.*
FEINBERG: *Different patterns that you wouldn't have picked? Or not yours?*
MARIANNE: *I'm a little fastidious. And, it's a mistake.*
FEINBERG: *What else was different about the . . . ?*
MARIANNE: *I don't use dishwash cloths that way.*
FEINBERG: *Why? What was wrong with them?*
MARIANNE: *I don't use them. I use sponges.*
FEINBERG: *Cleaner? Or different? Or . . .*
MARIANNE: *Cleaner. Different. Nothing important. But I would notice they were not the same.*

During the time Marianne was on the psychiatric service, her psychosis was treated and amazingly she began to realize that there really was only a single apartment. As she described it, "Because as the film disappears, the dreamlike experience dissolves. I know that there is one, but there must have been the illusion of two."

The Family Romance

The estrangement, disavowal, denial, or alienation from persons or objects often with their accompanying devaluation and their subsequent reduplication in fantasy is a theme that reverberates not just throughout neurology, but also throughout the study of child development, religion, literature, and, as we have just seen, mythology. In the psychology literature, the basic structure of the Capgras delusion can be found in the family romance–the fantasy of not belonging to one's family.

The term *family romance of neurotics* is derived from the writing of Freud.[9] He described how the child in his early developmental years tends to view his parents in an idealized fashion. As the child grows intellectually, the realization of the imperfections in his parents—whether imagined or real—promotes the fantasy that the child is either adopted, a stepchild, or in some fashion not actually the true biological child of his parents. When this fantasy takes on particular prominence or intensity, Freud described it as Der Familienroman der Neurotiker. The actual family is rejected as not the real family, and a "real" family is imagined to be elsewhere: the child has in essence a developmental Capgras syndrome.

The same story can be found in mythological literature. In 1909, Otto Rank, one of Freud's pupils, wrote a classic work entitled, *Der Mythus von der Geburt des Helden (The Myth of the Birth of the Hero)*, apparently at Freud's suggestion.[10] Rank's work is based on the observation that most of the great civilizations, including the Babylonians, Egyptians, Hebrews, Hindus, Persians, Greeks, and Romans, glorified their heroes, religious leaders, kings, and founders of their cities in legend and myth. These legends, despite the wide separations in space and time of the various cultures, bore a remarkable similarity regarding the circumstances of the hero's birth.

In the story, the hero is originally born of aristocratic or royal parents; he is often the son of a king. The pregnancy is preceded by extreme difficulties (i.e., a prohibition against intercourse or prolonged barrenness). During the pregnancy, a prophecy is delivered in the form of a dream or oracle that cautions against the birth and often threatens the father with misfortune should it occur. In response to the threat, the child is "surrendered to the water" in a box, but ultimately saved by either animals, lowly people, or a humble woman—in other words, the exact opposite of the child's original noble family.

As the child grows up, he experiences great adversity and many challenges; ultimately, he may take revenge upon the father for his desertion, and the hero achieves his original noble position and becomes the king himself. Freud and Rank agreed:

> The entire endeavor to replace the real father by a more distinguished one is merely the expression of the child's longing for the vanished happy time, when his father still appeared to be the strongest and greatest man, and the mother seemed the dearest and most beautiful woman.[11]

Rank lists fifteen such stories that fit the formula, including the oldest from ancient Babylon that concerns the birth of the founder of Babylon,

Sargon the First. Similar hero myths mentioned by Rank are the stories of Oedipus, Paris, Perseus, Romulus, Jesus, and none other than Hercules, where this chapter began.

It is interesting and important in the context of a discussion of the Capgras syndrome that Rank included the story of Hercules as an example of one of these hero-birth myths. Zeus is considered the royal father of Hercules, in this case the "original" father of high birth. Zeus takes on the appearance of Amphitryon, a mortal of lower birth. The two versions of Zeus—one in his original form and the other in the form of Amphitryon—correspond to the two versions of the family in the "family romance" and, by analogy, to the two versions of the person doubled in a Capgras delusion. While the French chose the word "sosies" based on the character Sosia to represent the word "double," perhaps the "Illusion des Amphitryons" would be a more accurate designation for the syndrome.

Literary references to the Capgras syndrome abound as well. One of the best known references to Capgras's syndrome is contained in *The Possessed*, by Fyodor Dostoyevsky.[12] In the book, Stravrogin, who has been secretly married to Marya Timofeyevna, fails to acknowledge her at a gathering in their hometown and, in so doing, claims he is but a stranger—not her husband, nor her betrothed. Stravrogin later visits Marya, who in turn refuses to recognize him. She tells Stravrogin, "You're like him, very like, perhaps you're a relation—only mine is a bright falcon and a prince and you're an owl and a shopman." Interestingly, not unlike the patients described in Capgras syndrome, she accuses him not only of being an imposter but of having murdered the original Stravrogin.

In the 1950s, the *Invasion of the Body Snatchers* in its many versions became a popular theme, and it too is a Capgras variant, albeit one with a paranoid flavor. Aliens from outer space take over the bodies of earthlings and possess their physical beings, masquerading as the original. As in the real Capgras syndrome, subtle personal or physical characteristics can be a tip-off to the deception. While these alien invaders have nefarious goals, another contemporary version of the Capgras delusion, the Heaven's Gate Cult, welcomed the possession. The Heaven's Gate Cult was a group led by a charismatic leader who committed mass suicide in 1997. The members believed that they were originally descended from alien beings from outer space and put on earth for a period of time, during which their bodies were merely the "vehicles" of their spirits. They had completed their time on earth, and a ritual suicide enabled them to be spiritually transported back to the "mother-ship" of their origin. This is a collective family romance in which the cult members' origins are denied and replaced by the fantasy of an alien, and, in their minds, a higher birth.

Capgras and Reboul-Lachaux proposed in their original article an explanation for the "illusion des sosies" in their patient Mme. M. These authors found that Mme M. had intact memory for faces and she showed no evidence of perceptual disturbance; however, the faces that she misidentified no longer evoked the usual emotional reaction in her. They

> . . . are nevertheless no longer accompanied by this feeling of exclusive familiarity which determines direct perception, immediate recognition.The feeling of strangeness is associated with recognition which conflicts with it. The patient, whilst picking up on a very narrow resemblance between two images, ceases to identify them because of the different emotions they elicit. Quite naturally she attributes to these similar beings, or rather to this unique, unknown personality, the name of doubles. With her, the delusion of doubles is not therefore really a sensory delusion, but rather the conclusion of an emotional judgement.[13]

For Mme. M., intact perception of certain persons bumps up against a "feeling of strangeness," and an emotional conflict is created. She then justified the lack of emotional response to the misidentified person with the confabulation that the original person has been replaced by a double, and the "illusion of sosies" is the result. What kind of brain damage could lead to the separation of intact recognition from the appropriate emotional response? I will consider this question at the end of this chapter, but first I will describe another disorder related to the Capgras syndrome.

Frégoli Syndrome

While some patients lose their sense of personal relatedness, others seem to gain the same quality. Four years after the publication of Capgras and Reboul-Lachaux's report, two other French physicians, Courbon and Fail, published a paper entitled "Syndrome d'illusion de Frégoli et schizophrénie."[14] In this report, they described a case of "delusion of doubles." But while patients with Capgras syndrome found imaginary differences between people, their patient found imaginary likenesses in the people around her—the opposite of Capgras syndrome.

Courbon and Fail described a twenty-seven-year-old woman who was diagnosed with schizophrenia. The woman developed a series of delusions in which she believed that her enemies were persecuting her. Chief among her persecutors were the famous actresses Robine and Sarah Bernhardt, both of whom she had actually once seen in the theater. She felt that these two actresses were pursuing her and were taking on the appearance or physical form of her acquaintances. Robine was able to enter the body of her neighbors or passersby, and she could force other friends and neighbors to do the same. Although the patient reported that the persons who were being impersonated, such as the nurses on her psychiatric floor, bore no physical resemblance to the actresses Robine and Bernhardt, they were still in a sense "possessed" by them or had been "psychologically occupied" by the actresses.

Courbon and Fail named the disorder after Leopoldo Frégoli, an Italian actor famous in France for his uncanny abilities of mimicry, in which he seemed to take on the physical appearance of others. Unlike the Capgras syndrome, which involves the alienation or disavowal of identity and personal relatedness, the Frégoli syndrome is actually an avowal or insertion of identity, a creation of personal relatedness. While patients with Capgras syndrome more often than not misidentify people close to them, patients with Frégoli syndrome usually misidentify people they hardly know, such as acquaintances or neighbors. The most dramatic and florid forms of Frégoli are seen in psychiatric patients with serious illness, particularly schizophrenia.

Burnham described such a patient who after a period of acute mental disorganization perceived members of the hospital staff and fellow patients as people he knew from his past, including celebrities he knew only through news and television.[15] The misidentifications were sometimes composites of more than one person. For example, the patient misidentified an aide on the floor as a combination of Art Linkletter, Lester Borden (identified as an axe murderer like his sister Lizzy Borden), and other persons from the patient's hometown, including his landlord. Another aide on the floor was misidentified as a composite of the patient's father, Abraham Lincoln, and a psychiatric aide. Other celebrity misperceptions by this patient included Walter Winchell, Dorothy Parker, Bert Lahr, Tallulah Bankhead, Gladys George, Lawrence Tibbett, Loretta Young, Alfred Gwynne Vanderbilt, William Vanderbilt, Franklin D. Roosevelt, Charlie Chaplin, and Albert Einstein. In some instances, the actual persons misidentified bore some physical similarity to their celebrity imposters: a man believed to be Roosevelt had a large head and a crippled arm, and the Vanderbilt imposters were spoken of as being aloof. My patient Fannie had Frégoli syndrome for one of her fellow patients.

Fannie

Fannie, a fifty-four-year-old executive, was admitted to the hospital for the gradual onset of a change in her personality. The CAT scan done on admission revealed bilateral brain tumors involving the frontal lobes (Figure 3–1). The lesions were diagnosed as brain metastasis from a lung cancer. She denied being ill, although she had been told many times. She claimed that her hospital roommate (whom she did not know) was familiar to her.

FEINBERG: *How are you today?*
FANNIE: *Pretty good. I've got a bit of a headache, though.*
FEINBERG: *Do you know where you are now?*
FANNIE: *In the hospital.*
FEINBERG: *You told me before you knew someone here.*
FANNIE: *Yes, the lady in the bed over there* [points to the next bed] *is the double of someone I work with! She's just like her!*
FEINBERG: *Really?*
FANNIE: *Yeah. Except this one has a different lifestyle. She's a swinger. And she has a different family. Also, this one has brain cancer!*

Fannie inserted the identity of a coworker into her hospital roommate. She denied being ill, but reported her roommate as having "brain cancer," which was the patient's own diagnosis, which Fannie had been told. Fannie actually had no knowledge of why her roommate was in the hospital. Interestingly, she later told me that even though the roommate was the double of an office coworker, she had the same initials as

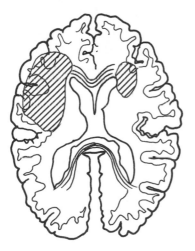

Figure 3-1.
This CAT scan shows the focal damage incurred to Fannie's brain as a result of two bilateral tumors involving her frontal lobes. Notice that the right tumor is nearly two times the size of the left.

the patient herself. This was significant in light of the fact that while the patient appeared unaware of her illness, she attributed a false diagnosis to her roommate, albeit her own diagnosis, implying some implicit awareness of her own illness. My friend and colleague neuropsychologist Joe Giacino brought to my attention the most florid case of Frégoli syndrome I have ever seen.[16]

Bart

Bart is a gentleman in his sixties. He is married and has several sons. Bart suffered a major head injury that resulted in extensive hemorrhages in his right frontal lobe, as well as smaller left temporoparietal brain contusions. He was extremely lethargic when first admitted to the hospital, but had made good improvement over the ensuing weeks.

When I spoke to Bart, he seemed fine. There was no hint of agitation or confusion. He spoke in a clear and confident voice, and his behavior gave no hint of the fact that he suffered from profound neuropsychological impairments, especially in the areas of memory and frontal lobe functions such as organization, mental flexibility, and self-monitoring.

Bart made a total of thirteen misidentifications during his hospital stay. In his mind, the hospital was populated with family, friends, and coworkers. There were five misidentifications in which Bart claimed that persons barely known to him on the hospital unit were one of his sons or daughters-in-law. Four fellow patients or visitors to the hospital were identified as coworkers or business contacts. An administrator was called the town mayor, a social worker was referred to as an old boss, and some visitors were identified as family friends. At one point, Bart even claimed that a professional ice skater on television was actually himself.

Some patients claim that their entire environment, including people, is overfamiliar. My patient JP was quite convinced that he was attending a business meeting despite substantial evidence to the contrary.

JP

JP, an insurance salesman and someone who impeccably resembled the famous financier, J. Pierpont Morgan, was hospitalized for blood clots that were compressing his frontal lobes (Figure 3–2). Despite evidence to the contrary—his supine position in a hospital bed, moaning patients in his room, the beeping of heart monitors, staff pagers, pungent antiseptic, meal trays—he insisted that we were in a conference hall. What's more, his speech was peppered with references to money.

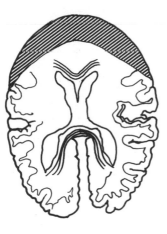

Figure 3-2.
Blood clots, known as subdural hematomas, led to the equally distributed compression of JP's frontal lobes, as depicted in this CAT scan, resulting in the bizarre belief that JP was attending a sales conference, when in fact he was lying in a hospital bed clothed only in a gown.

FEINBERG: *What are you doing here, where we are right now? Tell me what you're doing here?*

JP: *Well, this is a meeting that occurs every year set up by the sponsors. The head of that outfit this year is* [he names his boss.]

FEINBERG: *He's the head of that outfit? What's the name of the meeting?*

JP: *The name of the meeting is A Meeting for Integrated Friendship to the Poor in This Country.*

The patient reported that he was currently attending this meeting.

FEINBERG: *Are the people here . . . what are they receiving?*

JP: *They receive standard wage to my knowledge . . . very little more and I don't think much less!*

FEINBERG: *What kind of work do I do, sir?*

JP: *I take you for the vice-president for marketing for a major corporation.*

JP reported all these improbable circumstances, yet he seemed unaware of his own difficulties. He held to his misidentifications in spite of being interviewed while laying in the bed wearing a hospital gown and wrapped up in white hospital sheets.

FEINBERG: *OK, now, but one might call this a white lab coat.* [I gestured to my coat.] *And um . . . this name tag with the hospital's name on it. Do you have any other idea what I might do? Could I have another occupation? An alternative occupation? I'm asking you, Can you think of anything else I might do?*

JP: *I expect that you spend most of your time trying to sell your product.*

FEINBERG: *Trying to sell my product?*

JP: *Yes. And trying hard!*

FEINBERG: *Sir, it's not possible that you're a patient here is it? Could you be a patient?*

JP: *No, no.*

FEINBERG: *You're positive . . . There's nothing wrong with you. You feel 100%.*

JP: *Let's put it this way. I'm an "ad patient."*

The character Dorothy, as portrayed by Judy Garland in the movie *The Wizard of Oz*, is perhaps the best-known fictional case of the Frégoli syndrome. When we first meet Dorothy, she is at home in Kansas with her family and friends and her beloved dog, Toto. Almost immediately Dorothy faces psychological disaster. The nasty and merciless Miss Gulch, armed with a sheriff's order appears at Uncle Henry and Aunt Em's farm and takes Toto away. Although Toto manages to escape from Miss Gulch, Dorothy decides that if she is to save Toto's life, she must run away from home.

Not far into her journey, however, Dorothy meets Professor Marvel, who encourages her to return to her family. But it is already too late. By the time she arrives at the farm, a fierce twister is brewing, and the farmhands Hunk, Hickory, and Zeke along with Henry and Em are already safe in the storm cellar. Dorothy, now alone and exposed to the terrible winds of the cyclone, suffers a severe blow to her head and lapses into a coma. She then dreams that she travels to the mysterious and alien land of Oz.

Just as Dorothy desperately attempted to reunite with her family during the cyclone in Kansas, when she is in the Land of Oz she fervently wishes to return to her loved ones at home. But when Dorothy finally does "return home" and wakes up from unconsciousness, Auntie Em informs her that she never really left Kansas. Although Dorothy cannot accept that her experience in Oz was just a dream, she senses that many of the people in Oz were "actually" people she knew from Kansas. Rubbing the bump on her head, she protests: "No . . . but it wasn't a dream. It was a place . . . and you . . . and you . . . and you . . . and you were there!" Dorothy now realizes that the Scarecrow, the Tin Woodman, and the Cowardly Lion were transformed versions of the farmhands Hunk, Hickory, and Zeke and, further, that the Wizard was an alternative version of Professor Marvel. And we know, although Dorothy does not say it, that the recently deceased Wicked Witch of the West was in reality a duplicated Miss Gulch. Therefore, just as in a Frégoli delusion, many of the individuals Dorothy encountered in Oz were transformed versions of her personal acquaintances from Kansas. It turns out that Dorothy really never left Kansas, literally or figuratively.

Environmental Reduplication

By far the most common Frégoli-like misidentification in neurology involves the insertion of a place of personal significance into relatively unfamiliar surroundings. This often occurs in the setting of patients who have sustained serious head injury as a result of traumatic accidents, or in patients who have suffered bleeding into frontal brain areas from ruptured vessels. Disoriented patients tend to mislocalize themselves to a point closer to their own home. Sometimes the patient claims that there are two versions of a particular place, one in their own neighborhood, and another in the correct location. When a patient states that there are two or more versions of a particular place, the syndrome is called *environmental reduplication*.

The first report of environmental reduplication was described in 1903 by German neurologist Arnold Pick.[17] Dr. Pick described a sixty-seven-year-old woman who was admitted to hospital suffering from what at the time were called "psychopathic symptoms," which included depression, forgetfulness, delusions, disordered memory, nightmares, and disorientation for time. The memory disturbance appeared to be particularly prominent, and the patient demonstrated lively confabulation. While actually hospitalized in Prague, she reported that the clinic was located in her hometown of "K." When asked how Professor Pick had come to "K" and how the clinic and other doctors could have come there as well, she exclaimed, "Why, good God! Everything can go round about and back again." She spoke of two clinics, the "town" clinic and the "suburb" clinic. She tended to locate herself in the suburb clinic, nearer to her home.

Patterson and Zangwill described another interesting patient in Edinburgh, Scotland.[18] A twenty-two-year-old man fell from a height of twenty feet and sustained a severe head injury that resulted in a two-day coma. He gradually regained consciousness in the Brain Injury Unit and awoke restless, confused, and disoriented. He was diagnosed with bilateral brain damage, with most of the damage involving the right hemisphere. While he would say he was in Scotland, his behavior made it clear that he felt he was at home in Grimsby, England. Shortly thereafter, he reported that he was in a hospital two miles outside of Grimsby. When the good doctors pointed out that he could not be in both Grimsby and Scotland, he explained that Grimsby and Scotland were the same place. He even suggested that Grimsby could be a part of Scotland. He reported, "If it comes to the map, this part is the north of Scotland . . . but if people say, 'Do you live here?' I say, 'Yes

Grimsby!' . . . I feel I'm right . . . I know by my own language, by my own town streets." He suggested that there was a dividing line between England and Scotland that ran through Grimsby. At another point he reported, "I call it Grimsby and you call it Scotland . . . on the map it's Scotland." He also reported that the doctors in Grimsby were also the doctors in Scotland.

Certainly one of the most ironic twists of neurological fate occurred to a physician, Dr. Max Levin, who was a clinical professor of neurology at New York Medical College with a practice in what was at the time the Flower and Fifth Avenue Hospital. Dr. Levin wrote frequently about the nature and causes of delirium and delirious thinking.[19] He was fascinated by how the brain operated under states of confusion and paid particular attention to the delirium caused by an overdose of bromide, which was apparently a fairly common occurrence when bromide was in widespread use as a medicinal. The confusion that results from bromide intoxication became known as a "bromide delirium" or "bromide psychosis."[20] It resembles the diffuse types of brain impairment that we have already seen results in disorientation and misidentification after other generalized brain insults.

Levin was an adherent of Hughling Jackson's view of hierarchical thinking.[21] According to Jackson (who is also widely considered the father of modern neurology), the most automatic kinds of actions—those that require the least amount of complex thought—would predominate in states of brain disorganization. Under these conditions, whatever is unfamiliar to the patient, such as hospital surroundings and strangers, should be mistaken for things more familiar. In other words, the brain-damaged patient resorts to primitive, reflexive, automatic modes of thought, in which the least flexible, most overlearned association would predominate. Levin called this the law of the unfamiliar mistaken for the familiar.[22] Levin became quite an authority on this subject and wrote multiple papers and chapters on the topic. The *Encyclopaedia Britannica* even asked him to write an article on delirium for its 1961 edition. And all was well and good for Dr. Levin until, as he later put it, "Fate played a trick on me." Dr. Levin himself ran into a case of delirium in which he was the patient.

On a Wednesday afternoon in May 1966, Dr. Levin felt ill, took his temperature, and found he had several degrees of fever. It turned out that his symptoms were the onset of a severe case of cerebral meningitis due to pneumococcal infection. He was admitted to Presbyterian Hospital in New York and for several days fluctuated between coma and delirium. After a period of severe confusion, Dr. Levin reported the following experience.[23]

He had been told that he was in Presbyterian Hospital, and he knew he was in Presbyterian Hospital, but he had what he called the "remarkable misconception" that the hospital was located much closer to his home than it was in reality. His home was on Central Park West at 94th Street. The hospital is located on Broadway at 168th Street. This would place the hospital several miles from his house. During this period of disorientation, Dr. Levin thought that he was in a small "branch" of Presbyterian Hospital, on Broadway at 98th Street, which would place it less than a mile from his home. In Dr. Levin's mind, there were two Columbia Presbyterians: one, a small branch located near his home on 98th Street and Broadway, where he was hospitalized; and the real Columbia Presbyterian, in its usual location on 168th Street in Upper Manhattan. Dr. Levin had known of an observation made by Drs. Weinstein and Kahn that patients in states of confusion would often reduplicate the hospitals and erroneously mislocate themselves at a location closer to their home or place of business, often referring to this other location as an "annex" or "branch." When he recovered from his illness, he was stunned at the confirmation of their findings provided by his own experience.

When a patient misidentifies a stranger as a relation, we call it Frégoli syndrome. When the patient mislocates the hospital in his or her own backyard and doubles the place, we call it environmental reduplication. However, both syndromes represent a change in the self, in the sense that one's relatedness to the world undergoes a transformation. The boundaries of the self are altered, and one's personal world draws nearer.

The Capgras-Frégoli Dichotomy

How do these disorders relate to one another, to the self and its boundaries? The clinical material suggests that the Capgras-Frégoli dichotomy can serve as a unifying principle in understanding many perturbations of the self. We first note the similarity between the Capgras syndrome and jamais vu phenomena. Everyone has had the experience of seeing a familiar place, or person, or being involved in a familiar activity, yet feeling a strange, somewhat disturbing sensation of a lack of personal relatedness. Put another way, one might say that this entails an alienation from or estrangement from something that one knows should be familiar. The emotional force of such an experience is derived from the fact that the individual knows that a personal relationship to whatever object is involved *should* exist, yet the feeling of relatedness is gone.

In this sense, the Capgras syndrome is an alteration of *relatedness*, as opposed to an alteration in familiarity per se: the entity involved looks familiar, it appears familiar, the memory necessary for familiarity is present, but the personal relatedness is lacking. The patient recognizes the spouse as the person who *should be* the spouse, but the patient disavows the spouse because he or she does not *feel like* the spouse. It is a withdrawal of personal relatedness—a disavowal or alienation—that sets the stage for the Capgras-like misidentification.

In the same way that one can lose relatedness to a spouse or family member, asomatognosia can be interpreted as a loss or withdrawal of personal relatedness to the body. This is not to say that sensory loss, weakness, paralysis, neglect, confusion, and a myriad of other factors do not contribute to the loss of relatedness or alienation. These are important ingredients, but they do not account for the psychological reaction of the patient to this loss. The neurological conditions set the stage for the perturbation of the relatedness of the self to the misidentified entity.

Frégoli syndrome, on the other hand, represents the opposite side of the continuum. Frégoli syndrome repesents overrelatedness to something. In this sense, it resembles déjà vu, where something relatively unfamiliar or unrelated to the patient is interpreted as bearing a particular personal significance. In contrast to Capgras, which represents withdrawal of personal relatedness, one can interpret a Frégoli-like disturbance as an insertion of personal relatedness. Here, items unfamiliar to the patient are interpreted as imbued with personal relatedness that in reality does not exist.

Whether it is an arm, as in asomatognosia, or a spouse, as in Capgras, the self has withdrawn its involvement. The personal relatedness to the body part, person, place, or event is lost. There is also, however, often a compensatory insertion, a simultaneous avowal, a creation of identity with the same entity. This is how many perturbations of the self in neurology are simultaneous withdrawal and insertion of personal relatedness.[24]

It is intriguing how malleable the boundaries of the self are. The self does not exist as a rigid structure, in the way our outer skin separates us from the world. Rather, like the amoeba, the self displays an uncanny ability to change its shape, alter its margins, reform and regenerate new parts as needed. The patients described in this chapter reveal the hidden potential for an altered permeability between the self and the world, a fracture in the self-boundary. There is loss of self, but due to an increased permeability of the self-boundary, the self may expand as well.

These patients produce narratives that suggest their personal relatedness to the world has gone awry. Their self, their sense of identity, has either merged or diverged from their personal world. These patients teach us that the stuff of the self is inextricably bound up with that which has personal significance. It may be true that we are what we eat, but truer, where the mind is concerned, that we are what we love.

Disorders of Personal Relatedness and the Anatomy of the Self

Because the self displays this ability to change and adapt with existing circumstances, it is sometimes difficult to be precise regarding its neurological, material basis. In spite of this, some clues regarding the neurological basis of these conditions are emerging. The overwhelming majority of patients who misname, reject, or disown a paralyzed arm have lesions of the right hemisphere. This is partly explained by the greater frequency of neglect in patients with damage to the right hemisphere. In the patient with neglect, the left arm is ignored in the manner that all stimuli on the patient's left side are ignored. But this cannot be the whole story. If it was, when the left arm is shown to the patients on their side, in their right visual field, and viewed by the patients' left hemisphere, the arm is still rejected. Something more is going on.

There are other possible reasons why asomatognosia is more common in the presence of damage to the right hemisphere. When a patient explicitly misidentifies a limb, or calls it by another name, or personifies it, or talks about taking it home in a valise, these verbal behaviors depend in part on an intact left hemisphere. Asomatognosia is not the outcome of right hemisphere damage only, but rather results from the interaction between a damaged right hemisphere and a relatively intact, but altered, left hemisphere.

Right hemisphere damage is a factor in the production of other misidentification syndromes as well. Reduplicative paramnesia, for instance, has been found to be more common after damage to the right hemisphere. In one study, Benson and his associates analyzed a small series of patients with reduplicative paramnesia and found, in all cases, damage to posterior portions of the right hemisphere.[25] The association between right hemisphere damage and reduplicative paramnesia was corroborated in a similar study done by Ruff and Volpe.[26] In order to explore this relationship further, a colleague and I reviewed a series of sixty-nine published cases of cases of reduplicative paramnesia. We also found a strong association between this syndrome and right hemisphere damage.[27]

Some well-known cases of Capgras syndrome have been linked to right hemisphere injury. Staton and colleagues described a young man who at age twenty-three sustained extensive brain damage as the result of a serious car accident.[28] A CAT scan of his brain confirmed extensive damage to his right hemisphere, including the parietal and temporal lobes. This unfortunate young man had a major change in personality, and over the months following his injury he became withdrawn, irritable, and displayed an explosive temper. Eight years after the injury, he became convinced that his friends and relatives were "look-alikes" of the originals. He even claimed his cat wasn't "real" as evidenced by a new scar on its ear. In another case, Alexander and coworkers described a forty-four-year-old man with a head injury and damage to his right hemisphere.[29] Before the injury the patient had displayed paranoid delusions about his job; after the head injury the patient became convinced that he had two nearly identical families.

What factors could produce distorted personal relatedness in these cases? Many neuroscientists who have emphasized the right hemisphere's role in these disorders have done so on the basis of its vast temporolimbic connections—that is, the pathways that connect the temporal lobe, which is important for memory, to the limbic system, the portion of the brain linked to emotion, pain, pleasure, and motivation. Alexander and coworkers suggested that both Capgras syndrome and reduplication could result from "a distorted yet irresistible sense of familiarity, but not identity, about a place or a person."[30] This could be attributed to lesions of the right temporal and frontal lobes that disrupted the normal temporolimbic connections.

Staton and his colleagues made a similar argument to explain Capgras syndrome in their patient with right hemisphere injury.[31] These authors suggested that their patient with Capgras syndrome had a *disconnection* between his past memory stores and his current experience. The *functional* disconnection of memory and current experience was the result of an *anatomical* separation between the patient's hippocampus, a structure known to be important in forming new memories, from other brain areas important for past memory stores.

Although not specifically implicating the right hemisphere, Ellis and Young offered another suggestion regarding the origin of Capgras syndrome.[32] These authors suggested that there are two anatomically distinct routes that are involved with visual facial recognition. A "ventral route" is important for explicit recognition of facial identity. This route is crucial for matching the perceptual features of a face to stored memories, and damage to this route leads to the condition of prosopognosia.

A second "dorsal route" is necessary for the recognition of the emotional significance of faces. This route connects visual areas of the brain with the limbic system, an area of the brain that is important for emotional processing. Because the patient has an intact ventral route, faces are recognized, but a disconnection of the dorsal route leaves the patient without the proper emotional response to the face. The patient develops the Capgras delusion in an effort to resolve the conflicting perceptual and emotional information.

There are other lines of evidence that support the notion that patients with right hemisphere lesions may indeed experience a distorted sense of familiarity. Landis and his colleagues reported a series of cases, all with at least a right hemisphere lesion, and all who had lost a feeling of familiarity with their environments.[33] These patients tended to get lost in familiar surroundings, and found a lack of relatedness to their world. There is also experimental evidence that provides support for the right hemisphere's greater involvement in discerning the familiar and the personally relevant. In a series of studies, Van Lancker and colleague have demonstrated a right hemisphere superiority in a range of tasks, assessing a subject's ability to discern familiar from unfamiliar voices.[34] There is a similar right hemisphere specialization for recognizing familiar names, whether spoken or written.

Analysis of these cases appears to suggest a special role for the right hemisphere in maintaining identity. But many cases of delusional misidentification do not have selective damage to the right hemisphere. For example, Dr. Levin, who displayed environmental reduplication, suffered from pneumococcal meningitis, a bacterial infection of the outer covering of the entire brain. Meningitis most often affects brain physiology in a generalized way. The patient so affected shows decreased alertness and mental confusion, symptoms that suggest that the brain is diffusely affected by the pathological process. Many patients with environmental reduplication have diffuse brain disorders. Many patients with Capgras syndrome suffer from early Alzheimer's disease; a disorder that may affect widely distributed brain areas. A large number of patients with Frégoli or Capgras syndromes have psychiatric illness whose underlying brain pathology is unknown, but probably the disease process is not confined to the right hemisphere.

Different disorders, with a variety of underlying brain pathologies, can result in alteration of the ego. However, all the theories discussed here that consider the origin of the delusional misidentification syndromes posit that accurate recognition of the personal significance of persons, places, and things must involve multiple brain regions. Furthermore, these different brain regions have to be connected through complex pathways that integrate diverse regions of the brain. How does the brain unify these different regions in a manner that enables the creation of a coherent sense of self and personal relatedness? This is one of the many questions that must be addressed if we are to understand how the brain creates a unified ego.

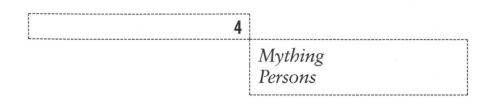

*Mything
Persons*

In Capgras syndrome, patients lose some aspect of the personal; those ego-close aspects of himself or herself are alienated from the self. In the Frégoli patient, the opposite is true: the strange and unfamiliar takes on the warmth of the personal and the related. There is another transformation of the self that I refer to as *personal confabulation.*[1] In personal confabulation, the patient misconstrues an actual event in his or her life or creates a wholly fictitious narrative about life, in which they play the starring role in another identity. The perturbation of the self here is a more subtle form than the flagrant forms of Capgras and Frégoli syndromes, but I believe that as these intricate, confabulatory narratives are appropriately analyzed, their fundamental nature can be seen as structurally similar to other varieties of misidentification.

What Is Confabulation?

The general term "confabulation" refers quite simply to an erroneous yet unintentional false statement. Confabulations occur in a wide variety of neurological and psychiatric disorders. Amnesia, when patients cannot recall some aspect of their past experience, is one of the conditions associated with profound and dramatic confabulations. Confabulation in amnesic patients traditionally has been divided into two types, although there is increasing recognition that these forms overlap. The first type is called momentary confabulation. According to Berlyne, momentary confabulations tend to be brief and are provoked in response to a question that probes the patient's defective memory.[2] He suggested that momentary confabulations are actual memories displaced in temporal context, and their content is autobiographical and refers to events in the patient's recent past. This type of confabulation is also referred to as "provoked confabulation."[3]

Patients who exhibit momentary confabulations may make frequent use of elements in their immediate environment. For example, Stuss and his colleagues described a patient who was being interviewed in an office where there was an ornamental wall map entitled "Cuttyhunk

Island, Dukes County, Massachusetts."[4] When the patient was asked the standard orientation question about where he was now located, he responded, "Massachusetts." When probed further, he responded, "Cuttyhunk Island."

I have examined many patients with this kind of "contamination" in an ongoing narrative. The following example can serve to illustrate this variety of confabulation.

Linda

Linda was a sixty-five-year-old woman who had recently undergone a surgical operation on an aneurysm in her brain. Previously, she had a successful career, but now Linda suffered from serious memory loss. Her primary problem was that she could not form any new memories, a condition called *anterograde amnesia*. Linda also had a form of memory loss known as *retrograde amnesia*, the loss of memories that had been formed in the past but that the patient can no longer recall.[5] During my clinical rounds, I videotaped an interview with Linda at her bedside in the hospital.

FEINBERG: *And why are you here?*
LINDA: [Looking around.] *We all came down here, they said it was a good idea to come down here . . . to be exposed to . . . the lights, the camera, the action. What it would be like . . .* [at this point, a nurse caring for a patient in the next bed, can be overheard to say, "The cardiac monitor stays in place while you're in this room"] *. . . what it would be like to ah . . . to get off the monitor, to get off the camera, right? So I said, "Fine with me." So that's how it started. Then I went ahead with the thing with the monitor, and they were talking to me and telling me how . . .*
FEINBERG: *So what's your point of being here?*
LINDA: *To get off the camera. I'm going to get off this . . . blah. And you know what blah, blah, blah means* [laughing]. *The camera . . . and blah, blah, blah . . .*

In this setting, confabulation seems to serve a "gap-filling" purpose, filling in the aspect of experience that the person cannot recall. The patient is simply trying to fill in lost memories in order to present a coherent sense of their world. In a face-saving effort, these patients seem to fill in their memory performance to appear as intact and socially appropriate individuals, rather than admitting that they simply cannot remember what they had for breakfast, where they are, or what they are doing there when questioned by the examiner.

Many authors have stressed the idea that confabulations are real memories displaced in time.[6] The patients who confabulate in the presence of substantial memory loss may have difficulty placing their memories in the proper sequence. Past and present memories are blurred, confused, combined, condensed, and placed out of context. These confusions bring past memories to the present and may account for the falsification of memory. For example, Victor, Adams, and Collins described a patient who was examined on a daily basis for months, but who nonetheless claimed that he had seen the examiner only "two or three times before" and "about a week ago the last time."

> According to the patient, the examiner had appeared on the last occasion together with a fat man who wore eyeglasses and they had taken him to a gymnasium, where they talked about "old times." Also on that occasion one of us allegedly upset a bottle of Coca-Cola, requiring the services of an attendant, who mopped up the mess. Actually the patient had last seen the examiner alone, on the day before. The fat man with eyeglasses was the physician in charge of the ward and the "gymnasium" was an empty, recently renovated ward. The patient had been taken there by a psychologist and an intelligence test had been performed (the patient was graded "bright–normal"). However, the patient remembered neither the prolonged testing nor the psychologist, who happened to be a thin man. The incident with the Coca-Cola bottle had indeed occurred, but several weeks before at his bedside on the ward during a visit from his wife.[7]

Momentary confabulations are often consistent with reality and plausible but false. They often involve the patient's occupation or location, which are wrong but not necessarily completely imaginary. Bonhoeffer suggested there was another variety of confabulation that appeared to go beyond the needs of memory impairment.[8] These confabulations have the names "fantastic" or "spontaneous" confabulation. Here, the emphasis is on confabulations that are elaborate, long lasting, have a delusional quality, and may be spontaneously offered by patients without the examiners attempting to probe their memories. Indeed, some patients produce narratives for anyone who will listen. Bonhoeffer compared these confabulations to dreams, daydreams, or fantasies, since they often defy reality and tolerate great inconsistency. It is possible that the patient's underlying personality plays a greater role in the production of fantastic confabulation. It may also be the case that these confabulations reflect the patient's motivation, affect, and wishes to a greater degree than the momentary variety.

Patients with both varieties of confabulation—momentary and the more fantastic or spontaneous forms—often have impairment in autobiographical memory. Autobiographical memory, according to neuropsychologist Paul Eslinger, is that aspect of memory "composed of the *personal facts, events* and *experiences* of a person's life, contributing in significant ways to a sense of identity, personal history, temporal continuity, and relationships to people and places."[9] The majority of patients who confabulate have defects in the domain of autobiographical memory known as *episodic memory.* Episodic memories are tied to particular moments of one's life, and are memories of things personally experienced. The psychologist Endel Tulving referred to this type of memory as "mental time travel, a sort of reliving of something that happened in the past."[10] Some patients confabulate exclusively to questions that test their autobiographical episodic knowledge. While we are just beginning to explore the anatomy of autobiographical memory, early indications suggest that the ability to recall specific memories from one's past requires an extensive network of neural connections involving many brain regions. Eslinger suggested that episodic autobiographical memories involve complex interactions between frontal and temporal areas bilaterally.[11]

Personal Confabulation

Memories of one's life experience are surely important for creating and maintaining the self, but the most interesting and personally meaningful confabulations are those kinds that the patient produces not just because they seem to have forgotten certain events, but because they seem to have a distorted sense of themselves. This is why I have suggested the term *personal confabulation* to describe these confabulations. The long-lasting, elaborate, and fascinating forms of confabulation are those kinds that patients produce about themselves; they are ways of expressing feelings about the self.

Patients who display personal confabulations represent themselves, their personal experiences, and their problems and preoccupations in a story. The story is a narrative of events that ostensibly but not actually have occurred to the patient in the past, or it is an account of the patient's current experiences. The narrative may involve real or fictitious places or persons; it may be rather commonplace, but it is often quite fantastic in nature. It often involves the patient's neurological problems, but it may also be about any traumatic event or circumstance of a personal nature. These confabulations can be likened to a personal myth, a story about the self in disguised form.

Weinstein and Kahn recognized these personal aspects of confabulation. I think that Weinstein's position on confabulation can best be elucidated through his analysis of one of his cases.[12]

Sick Willie

In their classic work, *Denial of Illness*, E. A. Weinstein and R. L. Kahn described a fifty-three-year-old woman who was admitted to Mount Sinai Hospital. She had lung cancer that had spread to involve the right cerebellar hemisphere. She was confused, drowsy, and incontinent of urine. The patient denied her illness and denied that she had had an operation. She was the mother of twins who at the time were twenty-six years old. One was a boy named William, whom she generally called "Bill." The other was a daughter named Hilda. During the course of her hospitalization, she confabulated that, in addition to her daughter, she had twin sons: Bill, who was her real son, and a fictitious son, "Willie." She described both Bill and Willie as sergeants in the army; but Bill had returned home on the *Queen Mary*, while Willie had returned home on the *Queen Elizabeth*. Both were commercial artists—which was Bill's real occupation—but they differed physically: Bill was taller, heavier, more athletic, and was more popular with the girls than Willie. Weinstein and Kahn emphasized that while the patient denied that she was herself ill and even seemed impervious to the thought of her own illness, she displayed great concern about the health of Willie. She reported that she had not seen him since Christmas, which was the time of the onset of her own illness; and she was concerned because she had heard that he was recuperating from an illness. She continued to express great concern about the missing Willie and insisted that he must really be very sick. She made accusations and complained that nobody would tell her the truth about him.

Weinstein and Kahn analyzed this case and suggested that the delusion of Willie was a vehicle for the expression of the patient's feelings and concerns about herself. This reduplication of her son symbolized some personal concern for the patient. Weinstein believed that the major motivating factor in the production of confabulation and reduplication was the patient's denial of their difficulties. According to Weinstein, these patients were in denial, but their personal problems and concerns would appear symbolically and metaphorically transformed in the guise of their confabulations.

In discussing the topic of delusions about children following brain injury, Weinstein, Kahn, and Morris reported that among patients with brain dysfunction the confabulation of an extra or nonexistent child was among the most common fantasies reported.[13] They found that patients with no actual children might talk about having one or more children, while a patient who had children might add an extra son or daughter to their family.

Moreover, patients often reported that the phantom child had the same illness or disability as themselves, as demonstrated in the case of the fictitious Willie. That is, in their descriptions of their phantom children, the patients were expressing feelings about themselves. Those patients who talked about children were particularly involved with their families and structured their lives around parent-child roles. Indeed, this structure was most likely the reason that the child formed an apt symbol for the patients. Weinstein and his colleagues suggested that most of the altered behavior can be interpreted as an attempt to form a relatedness and establish a self-concept or social role in terms of the significant symbols of one's experience. In other words, the child was being used as a way of representing the self. This confabulation allowed the patient to restore the self-concept, identity, and social roles in the face of significant brain dysfunction.

The following case exemplifies some of these issues.

Sam

Sam, a man in his sixties, had an aneurysm repaired after suffering severe frontal brain injury that produced anterograde and retrograde amnesia. Sam demonstrated persisting confabulation, and had been in and out of hospitals for years. His illness had created terrible marital problems and unfortunately his wife had left him after his illness. He was the biological father of three children, but he had never adopted any children. Sam denied that he had any significant cognitive or memory impairments. My colleague Dr. Giacino obtained the following interview during a session when the patient's cognitive abilities were being evaluated. Sam spoke of a fictitious adoption that he was arranging with his wife.

SAM: *I feel like I've got a little more ability than they give me credit for.*
EXAMINER: *So one last question: Has this aneurysm or the consequences of this aneurysm changed your life in any way at all?*

SAM: *No.*

EXAMINER: *So basically your life is the way it was before?*

SAM: *Yeah, like the way it was before. We have another baby . . . we've just adopted, and I have three children of my own. I've got my own house.*

EXAMINER: *When did you adopt a baby?*

SAM: *We haven't gotten the final result, but about a month ago.*

EXAMINER: *They said you could have the baby?*

SAM: *But the baby has problems now. They're trying to sort out the problems before, you know, somebody really adopts it . . . the baby. They want to make sure it's the right direction.*

EXAMINER: *Who's actually adopting the baby?*

SAM: *Me and my wife.*

EXAMINER: *Have you seen the baby at all?*

SAM: *Well, we've seen pictures. And I've seen the baby in person, too.*

EXAMINER: *And where does the baby live now?*

SAM: *The baby lives with the mother, and I think it's the mother of the boy that was dumped . . . and the mother would like to have the baby. I guess she lost her sons she might as well have the baby. That's a little problem there.*

After some discussion, the examiner asked about the child's problems.

EXAMINER: *You said before the baby has some problems.*

SAM: *That's what the psychologists are telling the guy who is in charge of the hospital. You know it's like they say certain things I go along with and certain things I don't go along with. I think there's too much pressure on the kid to really give an honest answer. I don't think a kid who is six or seven years old is capable of giving you the right answer.*

EXAMINER: *What kind of problems does this child have?*

SAM: *I don't know . . . to tell you the honest truth, I don't know. I know this kid has been in the hospital off and on for a couple of years, and they kind of rate them as far as progress goes or things like that.* [The patient was being rated during the interview.]

EXAMINER: *How do they rate them?*

SAM: *I guess they must rate them when they don't hear the things they want to hear . . . like the kid is not accomplishing anything, which I think is very unfair to basically analyze a kid that way.*

Sam's statements about the fictitious child and his planned adoption is a way of expressing concerns over his own illness, his own feeling of desertion, his current situation of being evaluated by the examiners, and other personal issues. The striking thing about personal confabulation is that the patient expresses their personal fears and desires yet they have no awareness that they are really *talking about themselves.*

Weinstein's patients confabulated not only about fictitious children but told stories in the course of their confabulation about other family members, either real or fictitious, as well. For instance, out of a group of mostly male veterans studied at Walter Reed General Hospital, all of whom had sustained head injuries in either car accidents, gunshot wounds, or ruptured aneurysms, many patients confabulated that someone in their family was ill. In most cases, it was a brother who was sick. These authors found that these stories were about an actual—not fictitious—brother, but they made up a story that one of the brothers had been ill or had a fate that corresponded closely to what in actuality had happened to the patient. The brother was said to have been in the same kind of accident and suffered similar injuries as the patient; in several instances, the brothers died.[14]

An excellent instance of this sort of self-referential confabulation was provided in a case described by Baddeley and Wilson.[15] Their patient, referred to as RJ, was a civil engineer working as a publicity manager when, at the age of forty-two, he was involved in a serious car accident. He sustained a serious head injury with intracranial hemorrhages involving both of his frontal lobes and was admitted to Rivermeed Rehabilitation Center in Oxford. Since the patient was unconscious for many days after his car accident, they concluded that he had no genuine memory of the accident. When the patient told the story of what had happened to him, he trivialized the seriousness of the accident. Although he was nearly killed in this accident, was unconscious, and was taken immediately to the hospital, he confabulated that immediately after the accident, he told the person whose car he hit, "I'm sorry, Mate," and, "Don't worry about it, it was as much my fault as yours." Despite the seriousness of his condition, his current hospitalization, and all that had transpired after this accident, RJ claimed that the hospital staff told him "there's nothing wrong with you, you'd better bugger off home." RJ had a real brother, Martin, an adult still in communication with the patient. However, RJ confabulated that he had two brothers, both named Martin, but one Martin had been killed in a car accident. He said his mother thought it was "a bit sort of morbid" that there were two Martins, but nonetheless "that's the way the situation was."

These confabulations represent an astonishing repeating pattern found all over the world. Weinstein, Kahn, and Malitz reported a twenty-year-old hospital corpsman, in Walter Reed Hospital in June 1952, who was involved in an automobile accident and sustained a severe head injury.[16] He reported that he had been killed in Korea and that his body had returned that morning, and later he stated that his brother had been killed and that his body was in a casket under his bed.

Linda, described above, also demonstrated the tendency to multiply or reduplicate other family members.

Linda

I have briefly described Linda at the beginning of this chapter. Linda is the sixty-five-year-old woman who confabulated about "the lights, the camera, the action." Linda had a ruptured anterior cerebral artery aneurysm that caused bilateral frontal lobe hemorrhages (Figure 4–1).

Linda displayed poor insight into her surgery and illnesses. Initially, she denied any surgery or illness entirely. Later, she told us that she was visiting her niece who had an "aneurysm of the brain." She also said she had an aunt who was in the hospital because "she couldn't think straight" due to an aneurysm. Although the patient did indeed have a niece and aunt, neither was in any way ill.

The following dialogue took place on a subsequent interview.

FEINBERG: *OK, anyone else here you know?*
LINDA: *Yes, a couple of more cousins.*
FEINBERG: *A couple of more cousins? They're all in this hospital?*
LINDA: *Yeah.*

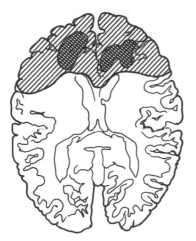

Figure 4-1.
Linda had an anterior cerebral artery aneurysm that burst. Her MRI revealed extensive damage to both frontal lobes of her brain. The dark areas on the figure represent blood from the hemorrhage, the cross-hatched areas show the regions of swelling or infarction that occurred around the hemorrhage. As a result of this extensive damage, Linda had memory impairment and personal confabulation.

FEINBERG: *Are they really?*
LINDA: *Yeah.*
FEINBERG: *Have you seen them since you've been here?*
LINDA: *Yeah.*
FEINBERG: *What are they here for?*
LINDA: *The same thing that I'm here for.*
FEINBERG: *Which is?*
LINDA: *Aneurysms, on top of their heads.*
FEINBERG: *So, you have multiple cousins here?*
LINDA: *For the same thing.*
FEINBERG: *All have . . .*
LINDA: *For the same reason . . . aneurysms on top of their heads.*
FEINBERG: *How many?*
LINDA: *Six.*
FEINBERG: *Six of them, and they all have aneurysms?*
LINDA: *Yeah.*

I told this patient a story that is usually employed to test memory but can also be used to assess a patient's degree of confabulation, denial, awareness, and tendency to project oneself into narratives. The story is adapted from an old folk legend and appears in many different cultures in various forms. We call it "The King Story."[17]

FEINBERG: *I'm going to tell you a story, and I want you to tell it back to me as best you can. Once there was a king who was very ill and his doctors couldn't cure him. But his Wisemen told him, "Oh King! You will be well, if you would wear the shirt of a happy man." So the King sent his messengers all over the kingdom, and they found a happy man, but he didn't own a shirt. Now you tell the story to me.*
LINDA: *There was a King who . . . had an aneurysm or something on his head* [at this point the patient lifted her left hand on top of her head feeling her own surgical scar]. *He could be cured forever if he found a man with a happy shirt. He went all over. The man with a happy shirt did not have a happy shirt. So, nothing was done. He never had an operation. There was no . . . nothing done for this unhappy man, and nothing was done for him! So, he was hanging around the hospital unhappy.*
FEINBERG: *So, how do you feel about what's going on?*
LINDA: *I feel that if I'm so unhappy, I should get an operation and be happy.*

Linda tended to minimize her own illness but spoke about multiple "others" with illnesses identical to her own. She did this in the context of a personal confabulation, where the boundaries of the patient are distorted and her own concerns are metaphorically represented in her narrative.

Some characters appearing in self-referential confabulations are quite fanciful and fantastic, as in the following patient.

Walter

I examined a fifty-five-year-old alcoholic man admitted to the psychiatric service for agitated behavior. He had fallen on hard times and was living in a one-flight, walk-up, single-occupancy hotel room. He apparently had been drinking quite heavily. His neighbors called 911 and had an ambulance take him to the hospital for confusion, agitation, and bizarre behavior. On admission, he was in alcohol withdrawal. Upon recovery, he recounted the reason for his admission as follows.

FEINBERG: *So, sir, tell me what brought you to the hospital? What was the problem?*

WALTER: *I thought that some creatures had invaded my apartment. I was unable to get them out, and they would have just a strange look on their face, somewhat cynical . . . not laughing, smiling. They seemed to enjoy making a fool out of me.*

FEINBERG: *Tell me more.*

WALTER: *I tried to get rid of them by changing the locks. I changed the locks twice . . . and uh . . . I tried to kick them out but invariably they seemed to get back in. They were taking little things . . . uh . . . the remote control from the television.*

FEINBERG: *They would take them?*

WALTER: *Yeah, yeah. It would disappear . . . when it first started, I thought they sort of existed because I had things taken. How could they be taken by someone who didn't exist?*

FEINBERG: *Where did you think they came from when you first saw them?*

WALTER: *I never thought of where they came from. Once I got so angry, I lifted them up . . . this was a male one, and I threw him outside . . . and this was in January when it all first started, and I put him out on a very, very cold day on the front steps of the building.*

FEINBERG: *One of these creatures?*

WALTER: *And I put a little pair of shoes beside him, and I put clothes over him. And then someone must have called in that I was being cruel to animals and swiftly the ambulance came and picked him up. I don't know what they ever did with it. Yeah, but you know if it was a live being, it was a cruel thing to do, but I did it . . . and I felt ashamed. The temperature was extremely low; but I was just trying to get him out of my apartment, and I was desperate! I had his clothes and a little pair of shoes and I had set them on the steps in the front of the building. It was the only time I tried to kill one.*

FEINBERG: *How big were the shoes?*

WALTER: *Well, I think they were my shoes. They were very old. They were discarded shoes as I remember. They never put them on . . . I set out a pair of shoes and a pair of short pants.*

Walter's story about the little creatures served many purposes. For one thing, it helped him explain his memory loss and lost items, producing an explanation for where his personal possessions were disappearing. It also served as a representation of his personal problems. When I consulted the residents caring for this man, they informed me that he had been found disheveled outside his apartment house from which he had been ejected on a cold night in the dead of the winter. He had to be taken by ambulance to the hospital. The story of his hospitalization closely parallels the story, which he doesn't consciously recall.

These confabulations, many of them in the form of reduplicated relatives, can be meaningfully interpreted as experiences of the self that are expressed in symbolic form. In other words, the experience of the patient is transformed into an experience of a real but duplicated spouse or family member or a fictitious entity on which the patient's own experiences or feelings are projected. Weinstein and his colleagues emphasized that one could view these narratives as metaphorical expressions of the patient's own feelings. They suggested that the fiction is a personification, reification, or metaphor for the patient's feeling particularly about himself, his difficulties, problems, concerns, fears, as well as motivations.[18]

Under the conditions of stress and disorganization, anomie, alienation, estrangement, and depersonalization caused by the catastrophic situation of brain dysfunction, the narrative produced by a confabulation as an explanation for the current situation takes on a greater reality than the actual circumstances in which the patients find themselves. Viewed in this way, the transformation of the self in these circumstances may be in some way an adaptation to severely disturbed brain function.

Explaining Personal Confabulation

In chapter 3, I suggested that the Capgras-Frégoli dichotomy can serve as a unifying principle that can help us understand many of the neurological perturbations of the self. According to this principle, asomatognosia and the Capgras syndrome are interpreted as the *withdrawal* of personal relatedness and environmental reduplication and Frégoli syndrome represent the *insertion* of personal relatedness. I believe this pattern of withdrawal and insertion of personal relatedness can aid our understanding of patients with personal confabulation. Consider the patient who confabulated about her missing son, Willie. This patient has lost the personal relatedness to her own experience. This may be due to many factors, including memory loss, confusion, and even the fact that some of the circumstances of the patient's illness may not have been revealed to her. This led the patient to disavow her own experience, to feel estranged from the events of her life. Through the vehicle of the fictitious Willie, as Weinstein suggested, the patient was able to reestablish relatedness to her own experience in a fashion that made sense to her. In this way, Willie represents those aspects of her experience that she had disavowed.

The same is true for the patient who confabulated that there were two Martins. This patient has lost his normal relationship to the traumatic events of his car accident, his subsequent hospitalization, his rehabilitation, and his injuries. He then confabulates a fictitious Martin to substitute for himself, in effect saying, "It doesn't feel like it happened to me, it feels like it happened to him." My patient with all the relatives who had aneurysms told me, "I don't feel like I had an operation to save my life . . . I feel like I had an operation to save someone else's life!"

This pattern of deletion and insertion of personal relatedness for events of the self is repeated over and over in the cases with disorders of the self. The patient who confabulated about the "little creatures" being taken away in an ambulance has seemingly lost the memory for his own experience. Yet, at the same time, many of the elements of his own experience appear in the confabulation about the little man being taking to the hospital. Again, the experience attributed to the fictitious entity is representative of his own experience.

Perhaps the patient who confabulated about the adopted child is the most poignant of these. This patient—after repeated hospitalizations, loss of his livelihood, destruction of his life, and estrangement of his wife—confabulates an adopted child, whom he wishes to take care of, wishes to nurture, hopes will recover, complains he must defend, whom he feels that the examiners are too hard on, too judgmental, and too critical. The patient's feelings about himself are represented in the confabulation about this child. As Weinstein argued, these confabulations provide a greater sense of identity, a greater sense of stability, and feel more real than the actual events themselves.[19] They are therapeutic, and help to restore a sense of identity and create a sense of belonging in the world that might otherwise be incomprehensible.

The elements that appear in these confabulatory narratives overwhelmingly involve things that people care about—brothers and sisters, spouses and children, jobs and homes. They reveal the structure of each individual's nexus of relationships and concerns—in short, their identities. They reveal how, in the fantasy of these patients' confabulations, the self can be represented by an elf or a soon-to-be adopted child.

There is a dream-like quality to these productions. One often gets the feeling that the disturbance in consciousness that these patients demonstrate has permitted a "waking dream," a personal myth, allowing the symbolic nature of the unconscious to speak to us directly, without the normal self-monitoring that most patients display when interviewed. It is perhaps this quality that makes these narratives in some respects so myth-like.

Personal Confabulation and the Anatomy of the Self

The area of the brain that is most often damaged in patients with fantastic and spontaneous confabulation is the frontal lobes. Stuss and co-workers described a series of cases with "extraordinary" confabulations of the fantastical variety.[20] One patient claimed he injured his head during a rescue attempt to save his child, who was drowning. Another patient, when asked about his surgical scar, told how during World War II "he surprised a teenage girl who shot him three times in the head, killing him, but that surgery had brought him back to life." The same patient "when asked about his family, he had at various times described how they had died in his arms, or been killed before his eyes, or would relate in lurid detail his sexual experiences with his daughters." The first patient had damage to both frontal and temporal lobes; the second had a large right frontal infarct.

Kapur and Coughlan described a patient with frontal lobe damage as demonstrated by CAT scan.[21] This patient initially displayed both fantastic and momentary confabulation, and on formal neuropsychological tests showed evidence for pronounced impairment of frontal lobe functioning and amnesia. Months later, the patient's confabulations decreased, and he produced only momentary confabulations comprised of memories of actual events placed in the wrong temporal order or inaccurate spatial context. Upon retesting, it was found that while the patient still had memory impairment, he no longer had the impairment in frontal lobe functioning that was present during the period of spontaneous confabulation.

Further evidence for the relationship between fantastic confabulation and frontal lobe damage came from Fischer and coworkers, who examined nine patients with ruptured anterior cerebral artery aneurysms and confabulation.[22] All five cases that displayed "spontaneous" confabulation had severe amnesia and showed evidence of frontal impairment on neuropsychological testing and brain imaging. In contrast, four cases with momentary confabulation also had severe amnesia, but did not demonstrate the degree of frontal impairment shown by the spontaneous confabulators. Finally, DeLuca and Cicerone have provided evidence in that frontal lobe impairment plays a central role in the production of confabulation.[23]

Frontal lobe dysfunction has a complex and multifactorial influence on confabulation. It is well known that the frontal lobes play an important role in self-regulation and self-monitoring. Stuss and coworkers suggested that as a result of frontal lobe impairment, these patients may not be able to inhibit their responses, which could facilitate the impulsive verbal behaviors seen in confabulation.[24] Additionally, a disturbance in self-regulation and self-awareness caused by a frontal lobe lesion could lead to a failure to monitor behavior and a lack of concern regarding incorrect performance, both of which could contribute to confabulation.[25]

Many patients with personal confabulation have damage to their frontal lobes. Both Sam, who created the story about the adopted child, and Linda who had all the fictitious cousins, had significant frontal lobe damage, particularly on the right side. RJ, the patient of Baddeley and Wilson, also had bilateral frontal lesions. Many of the "extraordinary" confabulations described by Stuss and coworkers qualify as personal confabulations. The frequent occurrence of frontal lobe damage in patients with personal confabulation suggests that the manner in which the self is perturbed in these patients, and the manner in which the ego is altered in personal confabulation, is due in part to impaired functioning of the frontal lobes. The frontal lobes must also be important in the normal functioning of the ego boundaries and the self.

Although many patients with frontal lobe damage have significant perturbations of the self, this finding does not mean that the self is "contained" in the frontal lobes or that the frontal lobes "create" the self. We could not remove the self of a person if we removed their frontal lobes. We have already seen that damage to several other brain areas can perturb the self, and to this list we will add other regions important to the creation and maintenance of the self. For example, it should be apparent from the cases we have considered that the brain-damaged person may employ language as one way to preserve the integrity of the self. Language facilitates a patient's ability to explain the catastrophic event to oneself and others. One example of this is the patient with asomatognosia. Although estranged from the limb, the patient may give the arm a name, or claim it belongs to a loved one. These verbal behaviors may help the patient sustain a relationship to the body part.

Patients with personal confabulation provide other examples of the manner in which language may sustain the self in the presence of brain damage. These patients with frontal damage create verbal narratives that provide coherence to the strange and disturbing circumstances of their present situation. In these particular conditions, we witness the role of language and dominant, usually left hemisphere functioning, in the maintenance of the self.

Michael Gazzaniga believes that language plays a key role in the creation of the self and consciousness. In his book *The Social Brain* Gazzaniga presents the view that the verbal left hemisphere is the final arbiter of individual consciousness.[26] According to Gazzaniga's account, different parts of the brain, called brain "modules," are able to perform discreet functions. For instance, some modules might be important for memory functions, other modules are involved with emotional functioning, and still others are involved with performing computations. Sometimes these modules influence our behavior in ways that are outside of our conscious awareness. When this occurs, it is the job of what Gazzaniga calls the "interpreteter" module, located in the language dominant hemisphere, to provide a rationale for the behavior.

Gazzaniga gives the example of someone who suddenly develops the urge to eat frog's legs. The impulse to consume this unusual item seems to come out of nowhere, and the "interpreter" does not actually know why this craving has occurred. Nonetheless, the interpreter module constructs a theory for the behavior. In this case, the interpreter might hypothesize the urge to consume frog's legs developed "because I want to learn about French food." According to Gazzaniga, it is the dynamics between the language-mediated interpreter module and the other modules of the brain that create our beliefs about ourselves.

Many areas of the brain make a contribution to the self. It appears that the problem is not in deciding where in the brain the self is: Rather, the question is, if the self, the ego, is widely distributed across the brain, how is it possible for a single self to exist? This problem needs to be addressed if we are to understand how the brain creates a unified person, the "I."

Auto-Bodies

"Look here, you," I blurted. "Don't you really see anything?" He rolled over and sat up. "What's the idea?" he asked, a frown of suspicion darkening his face. I said: "You must be blind." For some ten seconds we kept looking at each other's eyes. Slowly I raised my right arm, but his left arm did not rise, as I had almost expected it to do. I closed my left eye, but both his eyes remained open. I showed him my tongue. He muttered again: "What's up? What's up?" I produced a pocket mirror. Even as he took it, he pawed at his face, then glanced at his palm, but found neither blood nor bird spat. He looked at himself in the sky-blue glass. Gave it back with a shrug. "You fool." I cried. "Don't you see that we two— don't you see, you fool, that we are—Now lis-ten—take a good look at me . . . "

Vladimir Nabokov, Despair

Patients with personal confabulation confuse the margins of the self, figu-ratively speaking. By this I mean, in the context of the confabulation, that the self makes a personal appearance in the guise of a character within a story of the patient's own making. Patients with asomatognosia, on the other hand, seem to lose a part of the self in a more literal sense. The arm in the patient with severe asomatognosia may be totally rejected and per-sonified as if it belonged to someone else. I would now like to discuss another condition—mirror misidentification—in which the patient misidenti-fies not the actual body, but its mirror image.

Mirror Misidentification

It is somewhat surprising how vulnerable some aspects of self-recogni-tion actually are. In the novel *Despair*, Nabokov's protagonist, Herman, engenders a double identity in a total stranger, Felix. Faking his own death—and thinking that others will believe that he is dead—Herman kills Felix in an attempt to cash in on his insurance policy and live the good life. Like Herman, two of the more perplexing patients I have examined exhibited strange behaviors when confronted with mirrors: their reflections bore no resemblance to themselves. Both women, in their early seventies, showed signs of cognitive impairment due to either stroke or dementia. Both women demonstrated utterly fascinating misidentifications of their mirror images.

Susan

Susan, a woman in her sixties, was hearing impaired since the age of five and developed the ability to communicate by lip reading as well as sign language. She developed indications of right hemisphere dysfunction on her visual exam; this inference was confirmed by an MRI of the brain, which demonstrated atrophy of the right temporoparietal regions.

Over a period of time, Susan used sign language in front of the mirror in her bedroom. When asked what she was doing, she reported that she was communicating with the "other" Susan. She believed that there was another Susan who was identical to her in appearance, age, background, education, and so on. This other Susan was always seen in a mirror. Susan explained that the other Susan was also deaf and also used sign language to communicate. She and the other Susan had gone to the same grade school, but they "did not know each other" at that time. The other Susan had a child identical in appearance to the patient's own and she and her double were virtually identical in every respect, only the other Susan had a tendency to talk too much and did not communicate as well as the real Susan in sign language. She elaborated about the other Susan:

SUSAN: *Well, she's all right . . . sounds funny for me talking from one Susan to another, because you know she was a new person to me, and I'm surprised. She was all right, but she's very nervous, she likes to do her own ways . . . she never knew that she couldn't hear so good, and she's not a very good lip reader. I had to do mostly in sign language for her, to make her understand . . . she copies every word I say like this, like this motion . . . she doesn't even know the sign language very well, and I was confused a little bit, you know, because I wanted her. I thought she knew the sign language very well, so I won't have to repeat it twice, but then I found out that she's not that bright. I hate to say that . . . I don't want to brag, but she's a nice person; but one thing about her . . . I see her everyday through a mirror, and that's the only*

73

place I can see her. When she sees me through the mirror, she looks a little then she comes over and talks to me, and that's how we began becoming friends through our sign language. She was very nice.

Like the cases of Capgras syndrome that were described in chapter 3, Susan does not demonstrate prosopagnosia. The person with prosopagnosia has a generalized disturbance in face recognition. Patients with prosopagnosia cannot identify anyone by looking at his or her face. In other words, it is a specific visual identification disorder, not a denial of identity. Susan was able to accurately identify other family members, physicians, and neighbors. She never misidentified anyone but herself in the mirror. If either a family member or I stood behind Susan as she looked in a mirror, she always correctly identified the other person's reflection as a mirror image. Thus, we cannot say that her failure to identify her own mirror image occurred on a purely perceptual basis.

Susan's condition is a Capgras syndrome for her mirror image.[1] An early description of this condition was provided in 1968 by Gluckman.[2] In this paper, Gluckman described a sixty-one-year-old woman who suffered from cerebral atrophy and a severe psychiatric condition that Gluckman diagnosed as paranoid schizophrenia. This patient complained that a woman who was the patient's double lived in her house and imitated her in every way. The patient was afraid of the double, and she referred to her as "an old hag" or "an ugly hag." Gluckman described what happened when his patient stood in front of a full-length mirror:

> When I stood beside her she could identify my mirror image but her own mirror image was always the thing. She would on request smile, look angry, make a fist, or comb her hair in front of the mirror. She could never identify these actions in the double. They were always a take-off or a means of mocking her or insulting her. Yet she could interpret the mirror image of every gesture or facial expression or action made by me perfectly normally.

Gluckman's patient had a very negative reaction to her mirror image and she threw a bucket of water and other objects at the mirror image in an attempt to get the double to leave the house. The patient's husband had to cover all the reflecting surfaces in the house with paper, and he could not take her in a car because she saw the double reflected in the paint and windows of their car. Another patient of mine, Rosamond, displayed a striking, frightening, and sometimes dangerous, misidentification of her mirror image.

Rosamond

A semiretired gentleman from a middle-class Italian neighborhood in Queens, Richard B., brings his wife to my office. Richard and his wife, Rosamond, have been married for more than thirty years and have successfully raised two children together. Just recently she has begun to exhibit an odd behavior that worries her husband and their two grown-up children: Whenever Rosamond sees her reflection, she is convinced that a strange woman is following her. When she asks the woman to identify herself, she refuses to talk, so Rosamond—first verbally, then physically—attacks her reflection. Richard cannot let her stay alone in the bathroom because she attacks the mirror on the medicine cabinet. At night, she cannot pass the living room window without ranting and raving at the woman who is apparently outside looking in. She yells, "You tramp! Go on home! . . . Leave us alone!"

The woman appears in the windows of parked cars and in storefronts along the streets of their neighborhood. In broad daylight, Rosamond screams and wildly flails her arms at her. While Rosamond's family is quite embarrassed by her behavior, they are also afraid that she will harm herself.

Richard's account of his wife's behavior is at first quite surprising to me, since Rosamond's outward appearance is somewhat grandmotherly, prim, and proper. She adjusts the buttons on her cardigan sweater, firmly clasps her leather purse against her stomach, and brushes the lint off her pant legs while meekly answering my questions. She is obviously unaware of the wild behaviors that her husband reports to me.

During the course of my interview, Rosamond sat quietly listening while her husband described her symptoms; she didn't appear particularly agitated. I had a mirror hidden behind my back, anticipating her visit, and I presented it to her, so she could observe her own reflection. She looked at it for about ten seconds, then she stood up and down and raised her eyebrows and became quite angry and disturbed.

ROSAMOND: *Did you hear the story? Eh? Did you hear it? Now you get out . . . get home where you belong. You don't belong here . . . you don't live here! Out!* [Waving her hand.]

Her entire demeanor changed. Her face became almost contorted in agitation.

FEINBERG: *Who is that?*
ROSAMOND: [Screaming] *That's her, that's her! Yeah, that's her . . . sure*

that's her! She has no name . . . I never heard her name . . . never, never! I never! She never told me her name. No, no . . . you can't go in the house! No, you can't go in the house! She never let me know, had a lot of problems with her.

Then her eyes intensified, her face got within one foot of the mirror.

ROSAMOND: *Out!*
FEINBERG: *Does she remind you of anybody you know?*
ROSAMOND: *No . . . no, I never knew her.*

She shook her hand as if to cast the mirror image away from her. Then she pointed to it, claiming,

ROSAMOND: *Yeah, not this here one. Then she starts calling me these kind of names, street walker . . . cannot stand her.*

Her poor husband sat there worrying with his brow furrowed. She hovered over the mirror:

ROSAMOND: *You don't belong here . . . you don't belong here. Yeah, you. What are . . . you looking at? Tell them where you live . . . tell them today. Tell them where you live . . . heh? Yeah?*

As she screamed at the mirror, she started to tidy herself up, pulling her sweater together in front to produce the proper presentation.

ROSAMOND: *What do you mean we, we? Who are you? What's your name? Tell me your name? Heh? Do you know your name? Where do you live? Get the hell outta here!*

FEINBERG: *How old do you think she is?*
ROSAMOND: *I don't know, she's just an old bag . . . she's a bag. Yeah, and you, and you. Heh, I'm not afraid of you. Go ahead . . . I don't know she's just an old bag. Yeah, she's a bag . . . yeah, afraid to say it.*
FEINBERG: *You know, she looks a little like you.*
ROSAMOND: *No, she don't . . . come on, are you sure?*
FEINBERG: *Of course.*
ROSAMOND: *Look, she has no glasses.* [The patient was wearing glasses.]
FEINBERG: *Take a good look.*
ROSAMOND: *It's not . . . it's not me . . . it's not me!* [Fingering the top button of her blouse, which was closed.]
FEINBERG: *Where are your glasses? You don't have glasses?*

I turned the mirror over, so that she was now looking at the cardboard backing.

FEINBERG: *Where did she go?*
ROSAMOND: *I don't know.*
FEINBERG: *Is she gone?*
ROSAMOND: *No, not gone.*
FEINBERG: *How can I make her go away just by turning this mirror around? What is this here* [tapping the back of the mirror].
ROSAMOND: *It's a mirror . . . as if I'm some kind of idiot. Shut up.*

I turn back to the reflected side and once again she looks right at it.

ROSAMOND: *What's your name* [talking back to the mirror]*? Tell him what's your name* [shaking her finger at her reflection]*!*
FEINBERG: *Is she in the mirror?*
ROSAMOND: *Tell 'em where you live! Tell him where you live! You don't know where she lives. She's not in the mirror.*
FEINBERG: *Is she in the mirror?*
ROSAMOND: *She's not in the mirror. Heh, she's not in the mirror.*
FEINBERG: *Hold it, here, take it, look, look.* [I turned the mirror around, flipping it back and forth.]
ROSAMOND: *You want to know who she is? You want to know who she is? Because you're a . . . that's what you are. We know where you live. Where do you live? You know what? You're a good for nothin'. You know what? You're a good for nothin'. Yeah, where you walk . . . yeah, you little bitch . . . yeah. Now you know where you're gonna go? You're gonna go home . . . and when we get home, you know what? We're gonna find her right around the . . . we'll find her walkin' right around the windows. In the windows where she watches . . . listens to what we do. I can't stand her . . . she's been walking around the house, around the area for a long time . . . you know that? All the time she bothers everybody. I always wanted to hit her!*

She eventually became so agitated that I had to take the mirror away from her to calm her down. She sat hunched over, rubbing her knees back and forth.

ROSAMOND: *I'm gonna kill her . . . so mad at her.*

Her husband became concerned that Rosamond was going to stand in front of the mirror with a knife and actually stab herself, so I needed to treat her immediately before she injured herself or her husband. The hus-

band reported that the misidentification occurred in any reflective surface, from glass in store windows to car mirrors. She did not, however,
misidentify her reflection in the mirror of her cosmetic compact. It
occurred to me that perhaps its small size made it less likely for the
symptom to occur. So I first instructed her to take out the compact and
asked her to identify her image, which she did correctly. Using a series
of mirrors of increasing size, I was able to convince her as the reflection
got larger, despite her initial protestations, that they represented her own
reflection. I repeated this process over several days until her husband
reported that the behavior had vanished.

The Self as Known and Knower

Susan, my first patient with mirror misidentification, claimed that this
other version of herself in the mirror closely resembled her in all essential aspects of physical appearance, background, and education.
Although Susan reported that she was looking in the mirror when she
experienced this symptom, she did not seem aware or behave as if she
were aware of this fact when using sign language in the mirror to communicate with the other Susan. Rosamond also was able to identify the
mirror itself accurately. She could hold the mirror in her hands, examine it, identify it; yet she acted toward her image as if the reflection was
another person. Susan and Rosamond acted as if their knowledge that
they were looking in the mirror was dissociated from their behavior
vis-à-vis the mirror. There is a separation of knowledge in a psychological sense: *one domain of knowledge–perception of a person in the
mirror–is not integrated with another–a self-concept.* Susan and
Rosamond have a pathological separation of the self as *knower–the "I"*
that is the subjective aspect of the self that looks into the mirror and
the self as *known–*the "me" that is the objective aspect of the self that
is seen in the mirror.

These cases demonstrate that there may be some independence of the
"I" from "me." Psychologist William James did not believe there was an "I"
that could be separated from the "me"; rather he saw the relationship
between the self as subject and the self as object as two sides of the same
coin. This is what William James had to say about the relationship between
the subjective and objective aspects of the self:

> Whatever I may be thinking of, I am always at the same time more
> or less aware of myself, of my personal existence. At the same time
> it is I who am aware; so that the total self of me, being as it were

duplex, partly known and partly knower, partly object and partly subject, must have two aspects discriminated in it, of which for shortness we may call one the Me and the other the I. I call these "discriminated aspects" and not separate things, because the identity of I with me, even in the very act of their discrimination, is perhaps the most ineradicable dictum of common-sense.[3]

All of us must maintain a delicate balance between the subjective and objective self in order to remain integrated selves. The boundaries of the self are in flux, however, and we may be more or less self-aware depending on the circumstances. Standing in front of a mirror makes us acutely self-aware; when asleep and dreaming, self-awareness is hardly present.

The ability to focus attention to the self, as assessed by mirror recognition, appears to be a complex mental state. The evidence suggests that this highest level of the self as an object to itself does not arise until relatively late in the history of evolution. Over twenty-five years ago, Gordon G. Gallup made a rather remarkable discovery.[4] Most animals, up to the great apes, show no evidence of self-recognition when confronted with a mirror. For instance, monkeys, even after extended exposure to mirrors, react to them as if they were confronting another animal.

Gallup demonstrated how chimpanzees, when first exposed to a mirror, would initially react as if they were seeing another chimp and put on a display of social gestures directed toward her mirror image. After about two days, however, these animals began to use the mirror to groom themselves and view parts of their body they could not see using direct visual inspection. In other words, they came to act as if they were *viewing themselves.*

To be certain that these chimps had indeed developed a degree of self-awareness, Gallup marked the animals with bright red dye over an eyebrow and opposite ear and re-exposed them to the mirror. When marked in this fashion, the chimps showed clear efforts to inspect the marks on their own bodies, not on the image in the mirror. This response to mirrors has been reported to occur only in humans, chimps, and orangutans. Interestingly, gorillas show no ability to recognize themselves in the mirror.

A rhesus monkey does not recognize itself in the mirror. Yet when it sees itself "in the flesh," when it directly sees its own hands, its own feet, or tail, it doesn't react with surprise or fear. So the category of "me" must be present in many animals. It would appear that, like consciousness in general, it is just a more advanced, more complex *me* that enables self-recognition in the mirror.

Double Indemnity

Not every fictitious double is seen only in the mirror. In fact, the notion that each individual has a double that is dissociable from one's body is nearly a cultural universal. The ancient Egyptians believed in the existence of a "soul double." They held that each individual had a spirit, or Ka, which was immaterial and distinct from the body. It served as an invisible double. Created at the time of an individual's birth and persisting after an individual's death, the Ka is prototypical of the belief that each person possesses a soul that is an immaterial double of each individual. The Nagas tribe, an Indo-Mongoloid group found in Asia, believe in a ghost who is an exact image of the deceased as he was at the moment of his death. They believed that all of the alterations of the body experienced during life such as scars, marks, tattoos, and mutilations were reproduced in the ghost of the individual.[5]

Literary references to doubling also abound. The idea appears in the work of Goethe, Guy de Maupassant, Edgar Allan Poe, Oscar Wilde, and Fyodor Dostoyevsky, among numerous other authors. The corpus of the myth of the Doppelgänger is a prime example. The word "Doppelgänger" was first used by the German writer Jean Paul Richter.[6] The Doppelgänger in Richter's work appears as a pair of fellows, duplicates who together form a single individual but individually appear as half of an ego. Each half depends on the other "alter ego" for completeness. Richter writes in the novel *Siebenkes*:

> Just as women friends like to wear the same sort of dresses, so did their souls wear life's Polish coat and morning dress, I mean two bodies with the same lapels, colours, buttonholes, trimmings and cut. . . .[7]

Autoscopia

Richter's work was undoubtedly influenced by the fact that he suffered from the disorder known as autoscopia. Autoscopia (also known as heutoscopia or hallucination speculaire) is the visual hallucination of the self projected into the outside world. Richter said of his own autoscopic hallucinations, "I look at him, he looks at me, and both of us hold our ego in horror."[8] Dostoyevsky, also fascinated by idea of the double, was an epileptic, and may have suffered from autoscopic hallucinations as well, since epilepsy was one of the conditions that can cause autoscopic hallucinations.

Not surprisingly, Dostoyevsky, in his novel *The Double,* provides the most famous literary treatment of autoscopic hallucination. In this story, Petrovitch Golyadkin is an insecure bureaucrat in the midst of a period of acute anxiety and confusion. Petrovitch experiences both social and romantic rejection. On the verge of an emotional breakdown, he becomes suspicious and paranoid. During this period, Petrovitch is confronted by his double, which is presented as a palpable person, a separate visual entity. Unfortunately for poor Petrovitch, the double is a rather menacing presence. He manages to get Petrovitch in deep water with his colleagues and bosses, leaves him with bills to pay, and also gets him in trouble with women. In the end, Petrovitch has an apparition of dozens of Petrovitches and is taken off to an asylum.

Autoscopic hallucinations vary from case to case. The autoscopic vision is often semitransparent, ghost-like, or jelly-like. It has a realistic form, outline, shape, and density, but often does not approach the opacity of a real object, so that the person may be able to see through it. Some have described the autoscopic hallucination as very life-like, as if a real person were standing in front of oneself.[9] An interesting feature of the autoscopic hallucination is that the illusion or hallucination frequently mimics the patient's own actions. Drs. Todd and Dewhurst treated a young woman who suffered from severe anxiety and depression and who had autoscopic hallucinations for four years. While hospitalized in a state of anxiety, she saw a vision of herself lying in a coffin. The double faithfully copied her movements. Sitting in a chair and knitting, she saw her autoscopic double similarly engaged. "[The] chimerical double looked solid and lifelike; it was usually dressed in the clothing that she herself was wearing, but occasionally affected a dress that she had recently admired in a shop window."[10]

A central characteristic of autoscopic hallucinations is the close connection between the image and subject. There is a feeling of belonging to or of connection with the autoscopic hallucination that serves an important distinguishing feature. Unlike the Capgras patient, who denies or disavows the relationship between the image and relation, the hallucinating person feels a part of the autoscopic hallucination. There is a feeling of oneness with the hallucination. As Drs. Todd and Dewhurst put it, the hallucination is imbued with a "personal significance"; it bears a "sentiment of ownership with all the emotional and ideational accompaniments."[11]

Autoscopic hallucinations can occur in patients who suffer from psychiatric or neurological conditions. When the etiology of the autoscopy is neurological, epileptic disorders are the most common causes.[12] Some of these patients have parietal lobe damage as a cause of their seizures. A fifty-seven-year-old World War I veteran who received a shrapnel wound to his right posterior parietal lobe began to have seizures several years after the injury. On an occasion during one of these spells, he reported, "I was in the doctor's surgery staring into the garden. Then I saw the man about four feet away to my left. It suddenly dawned on me who it was. It was me." He saw a normal-sized image of himself, identical to himself, that lasted for approximately ten days. On another occasion he reported that he saw "crowds of tiny figures all the colors of the rainbow—all myself."[13]

The former soldier experienced an externalized hallucination of himself. He still maintained his usual ego-centered point of view and was aware of the position of his body in space and remain embodied within it. There are other cases, however, where the patient has what might be called an "out-of-body experience," and the person's physical self appears to be seen as if from an outside perspective.

For instance, Dr. Lippman describes a thirty-seven-year-old housewife and mother of three with autoscopic hallucinations that frequently occurred while she was serving breakfast.

> There would be my husband and children, just as usual, and in a flash they didn't seem to be quite the same. They were my husband and children all right—but they certainly weren't the same. . . . There was something queer about it all. I felt as if I were standing on an inclined plane, looking down on them from a height of a few feet, watching myself serve breakfast. It was as if I were in another dimension, looking at myself and them. I was not afraid, just amazed. I always knew that I was really with them. Yet, there was 'I', and there was 'me'—and in a moment I was one again! [14]

I am not suggesting that there is an immaterial double, astral body, or psychic self that can physically leave the material body; however, there is a very real way in which people have experiences as if this were occurring. Such experiences are far from rare and are not confined to mentally unstable persons.

The list of the medical, neurological, and psychiatric conditions that can cause autoscopy is extensive. Besides epilepsy and migraine, autoscopia has been associated with typhoid fever, influenza, various forms of brain infections, alcoholism, drug intoxications, brain tumors, and brain hemorrhages. Not every patient who suffers from autoscopy, however, has an obvious brain lesion. The symptom also has been reported in people with a variety of psychiatric conditions, including hysteria, obsessive-compulsive disorders, schizophrenia, or depression.

The Vision of the Self and the Soul

There is also a striking similarity between the autoscopic hallucination and the out-of-body experiences of the near-death survivor. And it is certainly more than coincidence that there is a common belief in folklore that the perception of a Doppelgänger is premonitory of one's death. For instance, for the natives of Alsace, the perception of one's Doppelgänger means that death is near. In Teutonic folklore, seeing one's "angel" also was a portent of impending death. This relationship occurs over and over throughout the folklore traditions in different parts of the world. Todd and Dewhurst pointed out the intriguing similarity between this folklore tradition and the fate of Narcissus, who gazed at his own reflected double in a lake and met an untimely end.[15] Consider this case described in 1890 by Barth:

> . . . a bookbinder of Strasbourgh—a young and healthy man known not to be unduly superstitious—went down to the cellar to draw a tankard of wine with which to slake his thirst; on opening the door giving access to the cellar, he saw himself crouching in front of the cask and drawing the wine. On his approach, the specter glanced round with an air of indifference before disappearing. The vision had not lasted for more than an instance. He tottered up the stairs, pale, and tremulous. The same evening he was attacked by bouts of shivering; he retired to bed and died within a few days—carried off by an acute fever.[16]

Indeed, Otto Rank believed that there were strong connections between one's own mirror reflection, with the shadow, and with the belief in the soul. In his words:

> We have seen that among primitives the designations for shadow, reflected image, and the like, also serve for the notion "soul," and that the most primitive concept of the soul of the Greeks, Egyptians, and other culturally prominent peoples coincides with a double which is essentially identical with the body.[17]

The soul, according to this belief, will leave the body and take on a material form that Rank says may become visible under favorable conditions and represent an exteriorization of the soul.[18] The double, particularly as a harbinger of death, is a form of denial of death, a tangible manifestation of the continuing life of the soul when the mortal body passes away. The appearance of the double is a moment when the soul is preparing to leave the body and take on its eternal existence beyond the material world.

The vision of the self represents a projection of the self. The remarkable feature about autoscopy is that the self, the ego, the standpoint from which the world is psychologically perceived, coheres as an entity that can be experienced outside of the body. Autoscopy teaches us that the self can be split, and one can have a dual sense of awareness or viewpoint both as experiencing and observing entities. The widespread belief in "guardian angels," the experience of the depersonalized self in out-of-body experiences in religious settings, the common occurrence of the idea of a presence under conditions of stress in normal persons, all suggest that fragmentation of the self represents a common human behavior.

Imaginary Companions and Guardian Angels

The patients with mirror misidentification demonstrate the imaginative and fantasy-like aspects of some confabulations. They bear a resemblance to another variety of doubling that occurs in the rather common childhood fantasy of the child's "imaginary companion." The imaginary companion represents the belief or fantasy of a friend, or companion, or alter ego in the developing child. Some authors have suggested that nearly all children will at one point or another have some form of imaginary companion. Certainly all psychologists who have studied the issue agree that imaginary companions occur commonly and are not necessarily abnormal. Imaginary companionship usually appears between the ages of three and six. The imaginary companion may be nice or mischievous, may be a person, another child, or an animal. It serves many purposes, including being a playmate for the child, providing companionship, or serving as a ready scapegoat. The imaginary companions are spoken to, played with, and have an almost physical space in the child's world. Interestingly, imaginary companions tend not to live in the child's own home; the exact location of the companion's home is usually significant.[19]

Some imaginary companions can rightly be considered alter egos of the child. The psychiatrist O.E. Sperling provided a particularly good description of an imaginary companion as alter ego[20] in the following case.

A boy named Rudy was brought to Sperling because his parents thought he was hallucinating. Rudy had a particularly vivid imaginary companion, whom he called "Rudyman." He demanded a chair for him to sit on and would ask permission from Rudyman to do certain things. If he was asked to eat his soup, he would report that he first had to consult Rudyman on the topic and then he would say, "Rudyman said I should eat the soup." Whenever his parents would give him an order, Rudy always reported that he needed to have a consultation with Rudyman whether to obey. Sperling observed that the child's father's name was Herman and that Rudyman was a combination of Rudy and his father's name. He also noted that many of Rudyman's characteristics, such as his height and his loud strong voice, suggested that Rudyman had features of both the child and the father.

Although it is not always the case, the imaginary companion is often a projection of the child's own ideals. Thus, the child will often endow the double with attributes that the child wishes he or she possessed, such as strength, cleanliness, cleverness, and goodness. Alternatively, the imaginary playmate will also possess characteristics that the child wishes to disavow.

Most important, the imaginary companion provides companionship for the child. Child neurologist Nagera tells the story of Tony, whose first brother was born when Tony was three years old.[21] Tony was apparently unprepared for the event and quite disturbed with the child's arrival. Right after the birth he pretended to have an imaginary friend named "Dackie." Tony would talk to Dackie for hours and hours. Dackie was his constant companion. He got up with him in the morning and went to bed with Tony every night. Dackie stayed with him until he was about five years old. A very similar story is told about Caroline, who at the age of three years and eight months invented "Dooley" shortly after the birth of her brother Barry. Caroline would spend hours talking to Dooley. Like the case of Rudy and Rudyman, she claimed that Dooley made her do many of the naughty things that she did.

Sometimes the imaginary companion can be both a playmate and an alter ego or substitute for the child. Nagera describes another fascinating case concerning a child named Miriam. Miriam was the youngest of three children. Her parents divorced and shortly thereafter Miriam's imaginary companion, Susan, appeared. Her mother suffered what was described as a "mental breakdown" and was in the hospital for several months. The father ultimately left the family. Miriam became increasingly withdrawn from both her siblings as well as her schoolmates. Interestingly, according to reports provided, she was quite reality oriented and had an excellent grasp of the difference between reality and fantasy. Despite this, she was able to maintain a fantasy life with her imaginary companion. On one hand, Miriam maintained what was described as a maternal relationship toward Susan. She reported that at night when she was cold she would put extra blankets on her. She would have to think about Susan at mealtimes because she might be hungry. It was felt that Miriam "mothered" Susan to a certain extent, and the interpretation was that the fantasy had restored to some degree Miriam's lost relationship with her then-absent mother, who was in the hospital. Interestingly, at the same time that Susan enabled Miriam to take a mothering role she simultaneously took on the identity of Susan herself. Miriam would report things like, "I think Susan is very unhappy these days" or "Susan has no family, poor Susan." At other times, she said that Susan was angry, hated her teachers, even hated Miriam herself. It was clear that Susan was expressing many of her own feelings. According to Nagera, Miriam was expressing her own difficulties by attributing them to Susan. Upon reflection four years after the disappearance of her imaginary companion, the simultaneous fantasy and reality of Susan were succinctly put by Miriam when she reported, "I invented her . . . of course, she was real."

Imaginary companions frequently occur in children who are undergoing stressful situations. L. B. Murphy provides an excellent example.[22] Three-year-old Sam had an imaginary companion named "Woody." One day, Sam had an accident in the bathroom; he had the tip of his finger cut off when the door was closed on it. He had to have stitches that were ultimately removed, but, during the procedure, the child had to be taken forcibly from his mother. Subsequent to this episode, Sam invented a little elf named Woody. Sam reported that Woody was with him during the traumatic period when others could not be present. Woody served many purposes for Sam—as a companion, sometimes as a helper, and at other times as a scapegoat. In an incredible display of insight, Sam later reported to his mother, "You know, Mommy, Woody was really you."

The point is, the existence of the imaginary child and the use of fantasy in the situations expressed can actually be a very healthy adaptation to otherwise stressful situations. According to Frailberg:

> The child who employs his imagination and the people of his imagination to solve his problems is a child who is working for his own mental health. He can maintain his human ties and his good contact with reality while he maintains his imaginary world. Moreover it can be demonstrated that the child's contact with the real world is strengthened by his periodic excursions into fantasy.

It becomes easier to tolerate the frustrations of the real world and to accede to the demands of reality if one can restore himself at intervals in a world where the deepest wishes can achieve imaginary gratification.[23]

Emotional stress therefore appears to promote the appearance of the imaginary companion. At these times, one might suppose, there is a need for one.

A related adult phenomenon is what the English neurologist McDonald Critchley called the *idea of a presence*.[24] This was described as a feeling or impression, sometimes amounting to a delusion, that one is "not alone." There is a sense of a presence of someone beyond the self. It is not a visual hallucination, nor is it a misidentification; it is rather a feeling or sense of company. Both the imaginary companion and the idea of a presence appear under conditions of stress.

While serving with the Royal Navy during World War II, Critchley had an opportunity to examine sailors who had curious experiences during the war. Once such story came from shipwreck survivors. He described two Fleet Air Arm pilots, who crashed into the sea during the Battle of the Bismarck. While adrift aboard a rubber dinghy, they had the recurring feeling that there was a third person along with them. (The Antarctic explorer Shackleton, caught in a severe blizzard, also described a similar experience.) Critchley pointed out that the common features in these stories were extreme physical and mental stress. Factors such as fatigue, exposure to the elements, starvation, dehydration, and the slim chances of survival all played a role.

Similarly, he also described the story of two sailors adrift in a raft in the Straits of Malacca. One of the sailors was attacked and eaten by sharks. The surviving sailor reported, "For the whole voyage I'd had the strange feeling that someone else was with me, watching over me, and keeping me safe from harm . . . it was as if there were sometimes three people on the raft, not two. With [his companion] dead I felt it more strongly than ever."

Critchley related the story of another patient he had seen in England, a woman with shrinkage of the parietal portion of the brain on both sides, who woke up in the night with a strong sensation that a person she was familiar with was standing near her in the room. It was someone whom she knew very well indeed: She eventually realized that this person was none other than herself. She described this person as her "alter ego"; it seemed to be located out of her sight, behind her, and to her left.

This presence, this alter ego or extension of the self, may be menacing, but it also may provide a protective function, a companion, particularly when it appears under conditions of severe stress, as in the stories of the sailor during World War II. I think it is particularly insightful that Critchley compared these autoscopic experiences to a belief in a "guardian angel."

Florence

Not every imagined presence is friendly, however. A patient of mine, Florence, is a fifty-eight-year-old woman. She suffers from mild Parkinson's disease for which she receives medication. Of late, she has been accusing her husband of infidelity. She imagines another woman in the house.[25]

FLORENCE: *Well, she wasn't heavily made-up, but she had makeup on . . .*
FEINBERG: *Who did you see with your husband?*
FLORENCE: *This particular one.*
FEINBERG: *And what happened. What did you see?*
FLORENCE: *Well I came from a store . . . and I came in a little early. You know. I had thought, well I'll go home . . . but I went home, and here they were! But he said, there's really nothing there. It's like–how would you say it?–when you see a mirage.*
FEINBERG: *A hallucination?*
FLORENCE: *Yeah, a hallucination.*
FEINBERG: *What did you see them doing?*
FLORENCE: *Kissing, their mouths pressing. You know what I mean? And he, he really didn't think nothing of it. But I, I don't know why, but I feel very bad about it.*
FEINBERG: *What did you think was happening?*
FLORENCE: *Well I thought, you know, like a . . . you know . . . he was gonna go out with her, and things like that I thought . . . which my husband never did we've been married so many years, I mean this was a shock! But he thinks nothing of it. Just one of those things.*

It came out that this symptom appeared soon after the patient's husband had a cancer operation, which made sexual relations difficult.

FEINBERG: *How has this affected your relationship [this operation]?*
FLORENCE: *Well I just feel, you know, maybe, he is not ready for it.*
FEINBERG: *Ready for what?*
FLORENCE: *For you know, an act, you know, to have intercourse. He's not ready. Or maybe I don't want it. Maybe the time hasn't come yet.*
FEINBERG: *How do you feel about that?*

FLORENCE: *It's all right. I'm not one of the sex animals. I'm not!* [laughing]

I discussed with Florence the relationship with her husband, and how to deal with the way his illness has made their more intimate moments difficult. She returned two weeks later.

FEINBERG: *Some things that came up the last time. One issue was the way your relationship has changed with your husband since his illness.*

FLORENCE: *Yeah, and it even changed a week ago.*

FEINBERG: *In what way?*

FLORENCE: *For the first time, we had intercourse in a long time . . . very long . . . Was I supposed to tell you that? I don't know. Long time.*

FEINBERG: *Really? How did that happen?*

FLORENCE: *I don't know. All of a sudden it happened.*

FEINBERG: *It was the first time since ah . . .*

FLORENCE: *Oh my God, over two or three years.*

FEINBERG: *Since he had the operation?*

FLORENCE: *Yes.*

FEINBERG: *Very interesting. Who initiated it?*

FLORENCE: *I don't know. It just came about like we were talking, and this and that, and before you know it . . .*

FEINBERG: *Hum . . . So maybe the discussion we had the last time brought you two a little closer together?*

FLORENCE: *Probably yes. Yes, it did! Because how did that come about?*

FEINBERG: *So you feel good about this?*

FLORENCE: *Oh yeah. I thought he didn't like me anymore . . .*

The imagined, the alter ego, the imaginary companion, or nemesis represent personifications, reifications of hopes or fears. The mind creates concrete representations of inner, sometimes hidden, emotions and gives them a life of their own.

6

*Keeping It
All Together*

In the foregoing chapters we have considered the various ways the unity of the self can be disturbed after damage to the brain. One of the important things we learn from these cases is the manner in which mental unity depends on the physical integrity of the brain. In this chapter we will consider a brain structure that figures prominently in the maintenance of mental unity—the *corpus callosum*.

Splitting the Brain

The upper portions of the brain, including the phylogenetically newest structure, the neocortex, are divided into left and right hemispheres. The corpus callosum, a bundle of nerves containing somewhere between 200 million and a billion fibers, is the main connecting pathway between the two hemispheres.[1] This massive fiber bundle connects anatomically symmetric regions of the hemispheres. For instance, cells of a particular region of the parietal lobe of the left hemisphere will connect with cells that mirror the same area in the right hemisphere. It enables each hemisphere of the brain to activate, communicate, and integrate its activity with the opposite side hemisphere (Figure 6–1).

As we saw in the cases of asomatognosia that were discussed in chapter 2, motor control and sensory representation on one side of the body are controlled by the opposite hemisphere. The left hemisphere controls the right side of the body, while the opposite is true of the right hemisphere. Each hemisphere can also control the ipsilateral (same side) parts of the body, but to a very limited degree; the muscles located along the body midline are one such example of parts of the body that are controlled by both hemispheres.

The two hemispheres are also specialized for certain types of activities. As is well known, the left hemisphere controls language capacities in the vast majority of right-handed people. Thus, a right-hander's ability to understand and produce speech, read, and write requires the specialized abilities of left hemisphere. The right hemisphere has a number of its own specialized abilities, including visuospatial functions, attentional

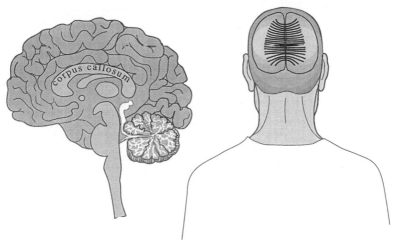

Figure 6-1.
The left side of the figure shows a sagittal section of the brain that demonstrates the topography of the corpus callosum, a bridge of axons by which the neurons of the two hemispheres of the brain communicate with one another.
Split-brain patients have this fiber "bridge" cut to control epileptic seizures from spreading from one side of the brain to the other. On the right side of the figure there is a conceptualization of the brain in a person whose corpus callosum is intact (unsplit), as seen from the rear.

control, a special role in emotional behaviors, and a whole host of other capacities to which the right hemisphere makes a greater contribution than the left. When a particular hemisphere controls the function for the entire organism, we refer to that hemisphere as being *dominant* for that capacity, although the nondominant hemisphere generally contributes as well to the overall function in question and cooperates with the other hemisphere to produce integrated behaviors.

Humans who have had their hemispheres divided by damage to the corpus callosum either surgically or as a result of stroke, tumor, or other causes demonstrate a partial lack of cross-communication between the hemispheres. These patients are referred to as "split-brain" subjects. The best known and best studied split-brain patients are people with epilepsy who have had an operation called a corpus callosotomy, in which the corpus callosum is cut to prevent the spread of a seizure from one hemisphere to the other.[2] Patients who have damage to the corpus callosum offer a unique opportunity to examine to what degree a physical separation of the brain causes a mental division as well.

Due to the manner in which the visual pathways are crossed, visual information from the left visual field goes directly to the right hemisphere, and visual information from the right visual field crosses over to the left hemisphere (Figure 6–2).

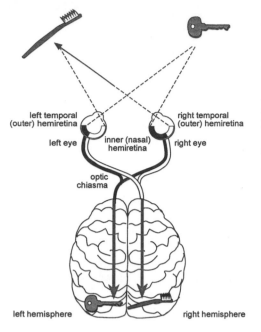

left temporal
(outer) hemiretina

right temporal
(outer) hemiretina

left eye

inner (nasal)
hemiretina

right eye

optic
chiasma

left hemisphere

right hemisphere

Figure 6-2.
The visual system.
Objects presented in the left visual field are perceived by the right hemisphere, and vice versa. Normally, information received by the left hemisphere crosses into the right hemisphere via the corpus callosum, allowing "cross-talk" between the two halves of the brain. When this fiber tract is severed, however, as in split-brain patients, visual information from one hemisphere cannot pass to the other hemisphere.

Under normal circumstances, information received by each hemisphere is shared with the opposite hemisphere via the corpus callosum and visual unity is preserved. However, if a split-brain patient fixates his gaze directly forward, and an object is briefly exposed to his right visual field, only the left hemisphere will see it (Figure 6–3). If a picture of a key is briefly flashed in the right visual field, only the speaking left hemisphere will have full knowledge of the word and will be able to say the word aloud. The right hand under the control of the left hemisphere will be able to write the word "key" and be able to pick out a key from a group of objects, but the left hand, under the predominant control of the right hemisphere, will appear completely ignorant of the stimulus.

If a toothbrush is flashed in the left visual hemifield to the right hemisphere, the now limited verbal capacities of the right hemisphere prevent the patient from reading the word aloud. The visual stimulus is received in the right hemisphere; but due to the division of the corpus callosum, the knowledge of the word cannot pass over to the speaking left hemisphere for verbalization. However, when the patient is asked to find the object corresponding to the shown word, the left hand can pick out the toothbrush from a group of tools, while the right hand cannot do this. The same principle applies when objects are placed in the patient's left hand out of sight. Objects felt in this way cannot be named aloud, but the patient may be able to draw the object with the left hand. If two visual

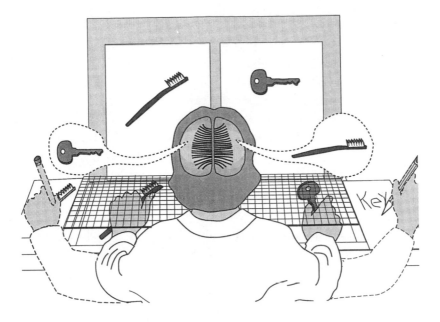

Figure 6-3.
If two objects, such as a toothbrush and a key, are simultaneously flashed in opposite visual fields, the split-brain patient can choose the object with the hand controlled by that hemisphere, but that hemisphere has no knowledge of the object that was flashed in the opposite hemisphere. (See text for full explanation.)

stimuli are simultaneously flashed, one to each hemisphere, we find that each hand can retrieve the object shown to its corresponding hemisphere; but the patient, if prohibited from naming the object seen by the right hemisphere, cannot say if the two shown stimuli were the same thing or different (Figure 6–3).[3]

The Alien Hand Syndrome

The question thus presents itself: To what extent do these patients possess two minds? The idea that two minds can exist in one head actually has a long history. Back in 1844, British physician Arthur Ladbroke Wigan contended that even when the brain was intact, the two hemispheres possessed separate consciousness—each hemisphere having a whole unto itself.[4] According to Dr. Wigan, humans possessed a "duality of mind," even when the hemispheres were in the intact, undivided condition. His belief was largely based on the observation that people who had one of their hemispheres surgically removed could still possess a normal consciousness. Wigan proposed that the two hemispheres functioned in a coordinated fashion because they had learned to do so. To Wigan, the corpus callosum was "little more than a bond of mechanical union." The experimental results in split-brain patients have led some scientists to suggest that perhaps Wigan was right, that we should view our two hemispheres as possessing independent minds.[5]

There are times when callosotomy patients do indeed seem to possess two purposeful minds. The German neurologist Kurt Goldstein described such a patient. In 1908, he reported a fifty-seven-year-old woman who claimed that her left hand acted as if it had a will of its own. The patient, not knowing what had caused this unusual symptom, concluded that her hand must be possessed.

> On one occasion the hand grabbed her own neck and tried to throttle her, and could only be pulled off by force. Similarly, it tore off the bed covers against the patient's will. . . . she soon is complaining about her hand; that it is a law unto itself, an organ without will [willenloses Werkzeug]; when once it has got hold of something, it refuses to let go: "I myself can do nothing with it; if I'm having a drink and it gets hold of the glass, it won't let go and spills [the drink] out. Then I hit it and say: 'Behave yourself, hand' [literally, mein Händchen]" (Smiling,) "I suppose there must be an evil spirit in it."[6]

At death, an autopsy of her brain revealed that she had had multiple strokes involving various regions of her brain. But in addition to her multiple strokes, Goldstein discovered an important lesion in the corpus callosum.

I have encountered several cases of this condition now known as the Alien Hand Syndrome (AHS).[7] A person with AHS has a hand that acts on its own accord, beyond the patient's conscious, voluntary control. The hand answers the phone and refuses to surrender the receiver to the other hand; it dumps a glass of water into a bowl of cereal; it tries to strangle the patient during sleep, and so on. The sine qua non of AHS is a hand that behaves in a fashion that the patient feels is beyond their control. The hand performs actions that are seemingly purposeful and voluntary, yet the patient claims that the movements are unwanted and involuntary and are not consistent with their conscious intentions.

Patients with this syndrome will differ in the hand that is alien, depending on the location of the brain lesion. When the brain lesion is confined to just the corpus callosum and involves only this structure, it is almost always the left hand that behaves in an alien manner. For instance, AHS patients who have had their corpus callosum surgically cut develop an alien left hand. Patients with damage to the frontal lobes of the brain often with callosal damage may have a left or right alien hand.[8] One of my patients, Stevie, is a good example.

Stevie

Stevie was a patient in his late sixties who had a left frontocallosal brain lesion (Figure 6–4). One day, one of the resident doctors called me to evaluate some of Stevie's unusual behaviors. After his stroke, Stevie had mild weakness of his right arm and hand, which fortunately resolved almost immediately after the stroke. However, within days, the hand that had been so affected started to display some other rather troublesome behaviors. The first thing Stevie noticed was that at times he could not *voluntarily* make the hand perform the actions he intended. For instance, if Stevie was holding a cup of juice in the right hand, he might be unable to place it back on the hospital tray, or he might involuntaily crush the cup in his hand, spilling its contents all over him in the process. On one occasion he suddenly threw a spoon across the room. All these actions were understandably of great concern to Stevie. He found these odd behaviors not only inexplicable, but also frightening.

When I first met Stevie, he was sitting in a chair near his hospital bed. He appeared composed and alert. I introduced myself and shook his hand, but he was unable to release his grasp for several seconds, although I requested several times that he do so. As I sat down on Stevie's bed and prepared to ask him about his difficulties, I suddenly noticed his right hand creeping up his leg. At first, Stevie appeared unaware that his hand was on the move,

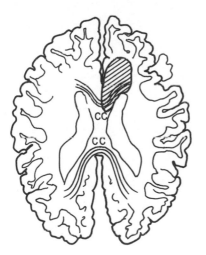

Figure 6-4.
Stevie suffered a deep, left, medial frontal infarct (loss of blood to that region of brain —what is commonly known as a "stroke"). The MRI of his brain demonstrated that the stroke resulted in damage to the corpus callosum, which led to the disinhibition of his mischievous alien right hand.

but as the alien hand inched up his leg, he noticed it. He appeared alarmed, and with his other, normal hand, he pulled the alien hand off his leg. At this point, the right hand actually seemed to resist the action of the normal hand. The right hand seemed to try to escape, but Stevie held it so tightly it couldn't get away.

When he decided the hand was quiet, he released it. Almost immediately, the right hand returned to his right knee and began to climb the leg. This time Stevie was ready, and he grabbed it before it could get very far. He held onto the hand even longer, for a good minute or two, before he released it. Nonetheless, when he let the hand go, within seconds it was pulling at his hospital gown. Now Stevie kept an eye on it, but once again it crept up his leg and he was forced to yank it off and restrain it.

FEINBERG: *What happened?*
STEVIE: *What happened . . . it got close to my genitals . . .*
FEINBERG: *Excuse me?*
STEVIE: *I got close . . .*
FEINBERG: *You got close to your genitals?*
STEVIE: *Yeah!*
FEINBERG: *Who did? What did?*
STEVIE: *This thing here* [indicating the right hand, which he was holding tightly by the left].
FEINBERG: *What is that?*
STEVIE: *My right arm. My right arm.*
FEINBERG: *What's the problem with it?*
STEVIE: *It gets out of hand!*
FEINBERG: *It gets out of hand, so to speak, huh?*
STEVIE: *Yeah.*
FEINBERG: *In what way is that, sir?*
STEVIE: *It just flies off uncontrolled.*

A few moments later I attempted to hand Stevie a spoon. He happened at this moment to be holding the left hand in his right, and with his left hand, he tried to grasp the spoon. Another fight between the hands ensued, but this time it was the left hand that struggled to get free.

FEINBERG: *What just happened there?*
STEVIE: *I was trying to take the spoon with my left hand, and there was a disagreement between my right and my left.*
FEINBERG: *What disagreed with what?*
STEVIE: *I think what happened was, I knew I wanted to take the spoon, but*

the right hand wanted to be in charge.
FEINBERG: *And your left hand didn't agree?*
STEVIE: *No sir. It never agrees . . .*
FEINBERG: *It never agrees?*
STEVIE: *That's right.*

After he was discharged from the hospital, I saw Stevie as an outpatient. Now dressed in street clothes, he appeared to be back to his former self. However, the alien hand continued to be a major problem, and Stevie complained about it bitterly. He now referred to the right hand as the "bad one" or the "naughty one," and the left hand he called "the boss." The two hands continued their fights, and the left hand, under Stevie's voluntary control, began to "beat up" the right hand. He showed me the scars on the right hand as proof of these battles.

STEVIE: *This is the bad boy* [indicating the right hand], *and this is the good boy* [pointing to the left]. *I control the good boy. I can't control the bad boy. That's been the problem. This hand over here—which is the good boy—is very dominant over the bad boy—this one here. Because he is my boy* [pointing to himself]. *You understand that? He does my wishes . . . and "bad boy" goes off on his own.*

Stevie also had a lot of difficulty with coordinating actions of the two hands. For instance, tying his shoes was difficult, and zippering up a jacket with both hands was nearly impossible. These difficulties, however, were small in comparison to the problems he experienced with the aggressive actions of the alien hand. The right hand had a mischievous, almost hostile, attitude toward Stevie. The hand was prone to tear up letters. The hand even tore up money—needless to say, a particularly troublesome symptom. He felt the hand at times seemed to try to do him harm, and he continued to retaliate against the right hand with the left.

On one visit he wore a bright blue sock, which he felt kept the hand subdued. Despite my efforts to treat the hand with a series of medications, it remained quite out of control.

STEVIE: *The fact is, I ruined about three or four pairs of pajama pants.*
FEINBERG: *Really? How?*
STEVIE: *Because I have found that I have been beating up on it and I'm beginning to feel it.*

The aggressive quality of Stevie's alien hand is not an uncommon feature of the syndrome. As was in the case in Goldstein's patient, strangling actions are a particularly frightening problem and have occurred in several cases. The case described by cognitive neuroscientist Michael Gazzaniga had a very violent left hand:

> The patient would sometimes find himself pulling his pants down with one hand and pulling them up with the other. Once, he grabbed his wife with his left hand and shook her violently, while with the right trying to come to his wife's aid in bringing the left belligerent hand under control. Once, while I was playing horse-shoes with the patient in his backyard, he happened to pick up an axe leaning against the house with his left hand. Because it was entirely likely that the more aggressive right hemisphere might be in control, I discretely left the scene—not wanting to be the victim for the test case of which half-brain does society punish or exe-cute.[9]

Another patient with an aggressive alien hand was reported by neurol-ogist D. H. Geschwind and coworkers.[10] This patient was a sixty-eight-year-old woman who had a stroke that was confined to the corpus cal-losum. Soon after the stroke, the family had noted that the patient's left hand was "performing on its own."

> She awoke several times with her left hand choking her, and while she was awake her left hand would unbutton her gown, crush cups on her tray, and fight with the right hand while she was answering the phone. To keep her left hand from doing mischief, she would subdue it with the right hand. She described this unpleasant sensa-tion as if someone "from the moon" were controlling her hand.[11]

These alien hands seem to want to do the opposite of the person's conscious intentions, a condition called *intermanual conflict.* Goldberg and Bloom described a fifty-three-year-old woman who had a stroke that damaged parts of her right frontal lobe and the corpus callosum.[12] Her left hand wandered about in what they described as the "alien mode" when it was not restrained.

> She reported an episode during a meal when the right hand was putting a spoonful of cereal in her mouth while, at the same time, the left hand brought a piece of bread to her mouth. Another incident occurred when the right hand picked up a bowl of hot soup and the left hand threw it to the ground. On another occasion, her left hand began to remove a cigarette from her mouth as she was about to light it with the right hand. She stated that the left hand "was trying to keep me from smoking."[13]

Several patients have described situations when the normal hand opens a drawer or closet and the alien limb will close it. Neurosurgeon Joseph Bogen reported that one of his callosotomy patients, RY, while buttoning up his shirt with one hand, found that the other hand was "coming along right behind it undoing the buttons."[14] Stevie's attempts to restrain the alien hand are also a characteristic feature of the disorder. It has been dubbed the "Dr. Strangelove effect."[15] This appellation derives from the character in the movie by the same name, vividly portrayed by Peter Sellers, who feels compelled to make a Nazi salute while the other limb attempts to restrain it.

The Self Finds a Way to Remain Whole

These examples do suggest that when we divide the brain physically, we also bisect the patient's mind. But to what degree is consciousness actually divided in the split-brain patient? Despite our ability to objectively demonstrate the lack of brain integration under certain circumstances, and the occasional occurrence of an alien hand syndrome, the vast majority of people with split brains do not feel different than they did prior to the division of their corpus callosums. Indeed, one of the most striking features about split-brain patients is the degree to which they act, feel, and experience themselves as completely intact.[16] I am astounded that split-brain patients never wake up after their brain surgery, shake their heads, and proclaim how peculiar they feel! These people under most circumstances have no subjective "inner sense" that their brain has been divided. How can this be?

There are a number of possibilities. First, not all the information coming into the two hemispheres is completely crossed, so each hemisphere may, independently from the other, receive a whole composite of the world. The amount of missing information is minimized, and the patient is less likely to notice anything perceptually different or wrong, even if the two hemispheres have limited "cross-talk." Incoming signals for sensations such as temperature, position of the joints in space, touch, and pain from each half of the body project for the most part to the opposite hemisphere. But sensory information passes through the spinal cord and its rostral extention, the brainstem, on its way to the cortex, and there are numerous uncrossed pathways at these lower levels. So each hemisphere receives ipsilateral (uncrossed) projections, as well as crossed contralateral projections, whether or not the callosum is intact.

The same is true for motor behavior. Each hemisphere, though predominantly controlling the opposite side of the body, also has to a certain extent control over the ipsilateral limb. Additionally, each hemisphere can control eye movements in both directions. It has also been shown that the visual fields are not entirely divided by callosotomy, and primitive visual information from right and left hemifields are partially shared; for some types of elementary visual processes, such as simple detection of light or form, cutting of the corpus callosum does not fully separate the visual fields.[17]

With the brainstem and spinal cord left intact, one does not really split the ego, or split the neurological self, by cutting the corpus callosum. Rather, one splits certain patterns of information processes and certain patterns of voluntary control that may on occasion lead to disunity of experience and action. One cannot help wondering what would happen if one actually divided the entire nervous system in half, actually split it right down the middle–through the corpus callosum, through the brainstem, all the way down through the spinal cord. While the thought of this experiment is somewhat gruesome, it is fascinating nonetheless to think about whether one would have a feeling of distinct division–a feeling of missing one's other half.

Moreover, even though the corpus callosum is sectioned, there are alternative pathways between the two hemispheres of the brain that remain intact. Some of the information that is exclusively crossed and destined for one hemisphere only may pass to the other hemisphere in the absence of a corpus callosum. One such pathway, though quite small in comparison to the corpus callosum, is called the anterior commissure. It may remain intact in some patients with callosal lesions that are either surgically or accidentally induced. An intact anterior commissure makes some degree of hemispheric "cross-communication" possible, even if the corpus callosum is divided.[18]

As we have already seen, patients who have split-brain operations do not share complex visual information such as written words across the visual fields. If a picture of a full face is flashed in the center of the visual field, only the right half of the face is seen by the left hemisphere, and only the left half of the face is seen by the right hemisphere. Under these conditions, the right hemisphere should be unaware of what the left hemisphere saw, and the left hemisphere is unaware of what the right hemisphere saw. That is, when the two halves of the stimulus don't match–if the left side is a female face and the right half is a male face, for example–the patient is unaware of the disparity. These unmatched stimuli, which neuropsychologists have used to study the divided hemispheres, are called chimerics.[19]

From the standpoint of subjective unawareness, it is a rather remarkable fact that these patients are not aware that they have seen chimeric figures. They do not comment that they have seen the halves of things, even though the hemispheres are processing simultaneously competing stimuli.

Trevarthen, a psychologist and an early investigator in this area, discovered that even though one of his patients was able to respond to *both* sides of a chimeric simultaneously, he never became aware that a stimulus was a chimeric.[20] Psychologist Jerre Levy noted that when the two hemispheres were given conflicting chimeric information,

> if the right hemisphere responded, there was no indication, by words or facial expression, that the left hemisphere had any argument with the choice made, and, similarly, if the left hemisphere responded, no behavior on the part of the patient suggested a disagreement by the right hemisphere.[21]

Levy noted that when the patient's left hemisphere responded verbally, and even confabulated a response to a stimulus that only the right hemisphere knew, the right hemisphere of this patient never indicated that it knew via a "frown or head shake" whether the response was in error. And the patient's left hemisphere did not verbally object to a right hemisphere response.[22]

Trevarthen further noted that when a verbal response was called for, split-brain patients shown only the right side of a face completed the missing left side and reported seeing a whole face.[23] Thus, each hemisphere is capable of experiencing a "whole" stimulus, though each actually saw only half. When patients fictitiously make up or fill in whatever is missing of the stimulus in the ipsilateral hemifield, we call this "confabulatory completion."[24] In this manner, each hemisphere may be capable of generating a complete and total subjective experience of the world. If this is the case, it may be that the split-brain patient has two conscious and partially independent half brains, each one aware of what it would normally be aware of in the intact brain state and making up or filling in what it is missing in the divided state (Figure 6–5).

As we have seen, some philosophers have argued that indeed this is the case, that there are two "consciousnesses" in the split-brain patient. However, if this were true, the two hands (hemispheres) would never agree on anything! So I doubt that the two hemispheres have two independent yet concurrent "consciousnesses" or volitions. Rather, I suspect that given whatever the patient's momentary intentions are, either hemisphere has the capacity to organize and control behavior. Depending on the circumstances,

Figure 6-5.
Each hemisphere of the patient with a split brain may "fill in" the missing half of a stimulus. In this case, a "chimeric" stimulus—left half a woman's face, right half a man's face—is presented to opposite visual fields. Each hemisphere of this patient's brain imagined that it saw a whole face. This is an example of confabulatory completion.

the other hemisphere will adopt a subordinate role and function in a fashion along with whichever hemisphere happens to be in control. Only momentarily does dual consciousness exist.

The separation of cognitive functions that is created when the hemispheres are divided by corpus callosotomy is one of the most striking findings in behavioral neurology. However, I am just as impressed with the split-brain patient's ability to experience a unified awareness in spite of the seemingly overwhelming obstacle of the surgical division of the hemispheres. The fact that one hemisphere may oppose the other in the split brain only highlights the extraordinary fact that under most circumstances these patients behave in a fully integrated fashion and subjectively feel unified. Moreover, despite their troublesome hands, my patients with alien hands do not experience any change in their basic personalities. In the same ways that they did before they developed neurological problems, these patients still love their wives and walk their dogs. Rather than arguing about whether the split-brain patient possesses two consciousnesses, I would contend that it is an extraordinary fact that split-brain patients largely retain their ability to function in a unified fashion despite callosal division.

I have encountered patients with other neurological conditions who demonstrate a remarkable resiliency of the self despite their neurological damage. Although the majority of patients I examine have dramatic behavioral problems that are caused by significant neurological disease, occasionally I see a patient who has relatively mild difficulties but a major neurological disorder. One case that was remarkable in this regard was Sonia.

Sonia

Sonia was a thirty-two-year-old secretary who came to me accompanied by her brother. Sonia had an unremarkable background. There was nothing unusual about her childhood and she was a good student in high school and college. She graduated from college and became an executive secretary at a large computer firm. Everything was fine with Sonia until a few months ago when her brother noticed that she had become mildly paranoid. Otherwise, Sonia had been able to function at home and on the job from day to day without any major disruptive incidents. She saw another doctor who wanted to give her antipsychotic drugs, but he first asked me to perform a neurological exam to determine whether anything else might be wrong with her.

While her neurological exam was normal, I did notice when she walked into my office that her head was unusually large. Why this characteristic did not catch anyone else's attention, I have no idea. I pulled my tape measure out of my lab coat to determine the circumference of her head. Sure enough, it was two standard deviations larger than normal, so I ordered a CAT scan (Figure 6–6). The scans shocked me. They revealed that over three-quarters of her cerebral cortex was missing: Just a ribbon of cortex around the outside of her brain remained, and her fluid-filled lateral ventricles, which are normally no

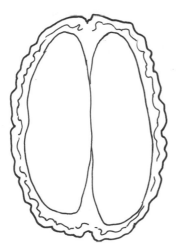

Figure 6-6.

As you can see from the figure of Stevie's brain (Figure 6-4), the lateral ventricles—the curved fluid-filled spaces inside each hemisphere of the brain—are no larger than two index fingers.

In Sonia's case, however, the ventricles have abnormally ballooned out within her hemispheres to occupy a space the size of two very large baked potatoes inside her skull.

larger than the size of two index fingers, were the size of Lake Erie. Most of her brain was composed of cerebrospinal fluid, a condition called *hydrocephalus*. It was amazing to me that Sonia had made it so far in life with so little brain. Somehow, she managed to make the most of what she did have.

Hydrocephalus as severe as Sonia's, when it develops suddenly in an adult, is fatal. If the lateral ventricles balloon out to this degree, they rapidly compress the surrounding brain, and if the condition is not immediately corrected neurosurgically, the patient goes into coma. The reason Sonia survived with this striking degree of ventricular enlargement that left her with so little brain is that her hydrocephalus was present from birth or early childhood. In her case, the ventricular enlargement developed gradually, and her nervous system was able to accommodate to the increased pressure. Also, her problem developed when Sonia was very young and, in general, the child's brain is more resilient than that of the adult.

Another patient who showed a remarkable capacity to adjust to brain damage was Seymour. The complaints that initially brought Seymour to my office were mild, so I wasn't expecting to find much wrong with him neurologically. As with Sonia, however, something had happened to Seymour's brain in the past, something that only came to light many years later.

Seymour

Seymour came to my office with the complaint that he was "a little nervous." He was an older man, well into his seventies. He was immaculate in appearance, spoke in a refined manner, and carried himself like a real gentleman. He was now retired, but had been an accountant his entire adult life. His only complaint was that he occasionally gets a little "nervous" and he would like to try some medication that might calm him down. The only unusual thing occurred when we went over his past medical history. Initially, Seymour denied any surgical procedures, but he subsequently recalled that, indeed, he did have a " bit of surgery" on his brain when he was much younger, perhaps when he was in his late teens or early twenties. He was not sure why the surgery was performed, but he thought it may have been for "nerves." In any event, that was a long time ago.

Now I was really curious. Before I treated Seymour with any medications, I suggested we get a CAT scan and see exactly what was done to his brain. When I saw the scan, once again I was amazed (Figure 6–7). Some time in his past, Seymour had had a frontal lobotomy, and substantial por-

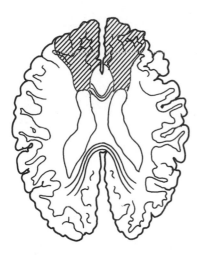

Figure 6-7.
Despite his normal appearance and neurobe-havioral exam, Seymour's CAT scan revealed that he had undergone a frontal lobotomy. The surgical procedure created symmetric areas of encepalomalacia in both of Seymour's frontal lobes. The areas of damage extended from the front of the lateral ventricles to the region where the frontal lobes should have been.

tions of his frontal lobes had been removed. I assume Seymour had the operation for a psychiatric condition, but to this day neither Seymour nor I know why the operation was performed.

Patients like Seymour do not come along every day. Indeed, I have never since seen a patient who was unaware that they had had a lobotomy.

*Journey to the
Center of the Mind*

I have shown throughout this book that many brain regions are involved in the maintenance of the self and hence it is nothing short of miraculous that the self as a coherent entity exists at all. Nonetheless, the self is highly integrated and may remain so even after serious physical disruption. Consider patients like Sonia with severe hydrocephalus and Seymour who had a frontal lobotomy. Both of these patients had preserved egos in the presence of significant alterations in their brains. Further, the patients with split brains under most circumstances have preserved mental unity despite the division of their hemispheres. This raises an important question: How does the intact brain, a brain that has no damage, maintain mental unity? How do the many regions of the brain create a coherent self? This is the question I will consider next.

How Does a Distributed Brain Create a Unified Self?

The problem of the unity of the self and individual consciousness seems remarkable when one considers the fantastic diversity and multiplicity of the brain at the microscopic level. Observation of brain matter reveals millions and millions of individual neurons that make up the structures and regions of the brain. For example, it is estimated that in the cat there are ten to fifteen different brain regions devoted to visual function alone. Add to this five areas that are involved in touch sensation and as many as eight cortical areas that are involved in audition.[1]

More evolved species have an even greater number of functionally distinct cortical regions than the cat. In the monkey, for example, there are somewhere between twenty and forty visual areas. In the human being, there is an even greater number of differentiated visual areas in the brain. Van Essen, Anderson, and Felleman suggested that there are thirty-two visual cortical areas.[2] Kaas approximates that in fact there may be over a hundred different human neocortical regions in all![3] These estimates do not include the numerous subcortical sensory processing regions in the human brain, which initially receive the incoming sensory stimuli that will be later processed in the cortex. From these investigations, it is apparent that we have numerous separate regions of the brain that need to be linked to one another in a coherent fashion for optimal functioning. Exactly how these areas of the brain are connected continues to be a vigorously investigated topic in cognitive neuroscience today.[4]

Despite the diversity of the neuroanatomical regions of the brain, the fact remains that the normally intact brain functions to produce a unified "*I.*" We experience one integrated sensory world and a single integrated self and a unified ego. But when the brain is examined neuroanatomically, we do not see a unified, homogeneous whole akin to the subjective experience that constitutes a self. We observe only a multitude of independent neurons and a host of brain structures that appear to possess a very different "grain" from the seamless self. How is it then that personal consciousness subjectively seems unified from an "inside" personal perspective for each of us when the brain is structurally diversified?[5]

Descartes' Dilemma

Obtaining the answer to this question has become a central focus in current research on the brain, but it does not represent a *new* problem. Rather, it is an old and yet-to-be-solved problem. Interest in the dilemma of mental unity goes all the way back to the seventeenth-century philosopher René Descartes (1596–1650). Descartes sometimes is considered the first "modern" psychologist, and I would concur with this judgment.[6] Descartes was also the grandfather of the mind/brain theorists, and he was among the first scholars to consider the puzzling fact of the unity of mind from both philosophical and biological perspectives.

For Descartes, the unity of the mind was a logical extension of the oneness of the soul. The soul was composed of its actions and passions, the latter encompassing its perceptions. Descartes reasoned that there were clear differences between the brain on the one hand, and the mind or soul on the other. He correctly identified the brain as a palpable organ with length, breadth and an exact spatial locus within the body. Furthermore, as is the case with all matter, he realized that the brain could be broken into parts. The soul, in contrast, is intangible and indivisible.

> and because it is of a nature which has no relation to extension, nor dimensions, nor other properties of the matter of which the body is composed, but only to the whole conglomerate of its organs, as appears from the fact that we could not in any way conceive of the half or the third of a soul, nor of the space it occupies and because

it does not become smaller owing to the cutting off of some portion of the body, but separates itself from it entirely when the union of its assembled organs is dissolved. (Descartes, 1649; I: XXX)[7]

Descartes believed that the brain was composed of parts or structures, each performing a unique function. It was also apparent to Descartes that the mind, the self, and the soul were whole entities derived from a person's internal or "inside" point of view. Put another way, the unified appearance of the self from a subjective point of view could not be reconciled with the objective divisible reality of the brain. These differences between mind and brain led Descartes to his famous theory that we now know as Cartesian Dualism, the belief that in the world there are two kinds of substances: the physical (res extensa), consisting of things that have material characteristics; and the mind or thinking substance (res cogitans), which is indivisible and hence nonmaterial.

Descartes reasoned that there must be a way for the unified mind and the immaterial "soul" to interact with the material brain. He decided that the pineal gland was a likely candidate to serve as this material liaison between brain and soul. He reasoned that the pineal gland's single midline position in the central nervous system appeared to make it ideally suited to pull together the two hemispheres of the brain to create a single and unified mind (Figure 7–1). In the following quotation, Descartes explains why he chose this relatively inconspicuous structure for such an important role:

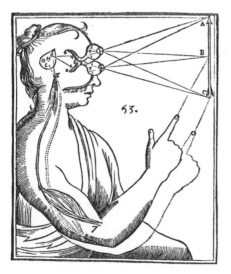

Figure 7-1.

Descartes' conception of the unity of the mind shows the converging point of the mind and the body at the only unpaired structure that Descartes could locate—the pineal gland in the center of the brain. The pineal gland is the teardrop-shaped structure in the center of the head. Descartes believed that the pineal gland was the seat of the soul.

The reason that persuades me that the soul cannot have any other place in the whole body than this gland, where it immediately exercises its functions, is that I consider that the other parts of our brain are all double so that we have two eyes, two hands, two ears, and, finally all the organs of our external senses are double; and that inasmuch as we have only one solitary and simple thought of one single thing during the same moment, it must necessarily be that there is some place where the two images which come from the two eyes, or the two other impressions which come from a single object by way of the double organs of the other senses, may unite before they reach the soul, so that they do not present to it two objects instead of one. It can easily be conceived how these images or other impressions could unite in this gland through the mediation of the spirits that fill the cavities of the brain. There is no other place in the body where they could be thus united unless it be in the gland.[8]

Sherrington Ponders the Mind's Eye

We now know that the human pineal gland is actually a neuroendocrine organ that plays no role whatsoever in neural transmission or consciousness. One might excuse Descartes' mistake as a result of the limited neurological knowledge of the time. However, hundreds of years later, at the start of the twentieth century, when a good deal more was known about the nervous system, Sir Charles Sherrington, the father of modern neurophysiology, still wondered how the brain produces a unified mind.

Sherrington asked a question similar to those posed by Descartes, but that instead involved the integration of the components of the visual system: How is it possible that there is a "singleness" of normal binocular vision when either eye alone is able to generate a separate mental image?[9] Sherrington was aware that we are capable, under certain circumstances, of being aware of *simultaneous* independent images generated by each eye. If one places, for instance, a red glass over one eye (the so-called Red Glass Test), slight deviations in the axes of the eyes can be made apparent such that the axes do not "line up" properly. The patient then experiences two independent visual images, one colored red and the other normal. In the same way, when the direction of each eye is not properly aligned, as when we are drowsy or have had one too many martinis, a person may become aware of two visual images and then we say we are "seeing double" (Figure 7–2).

Figure 7-2.
The brain under normal circumstances does an excellent job of keeping vision unified. If the axes of the eyes are not properly aligned, the retinal images from the two eyes can be disconnected, and the person "sees double."

Except for unique circumstances, like the Red Glass Test when simultaneous independent images by each eye can be generated, there typically is a remarkable unity to the visual system. Sherrington noted that under normal circumstances:

> Our binocular visual field is shown by analysis, to presuppose outlook from the body by a single eye centred at a point in the midvertical of the forehead at the level of the root of his nose. It, unconsciously, takes for granted that its seeing is done by a cyclopean eye having a center of rotation at the point of intersection just mentioned.[10]

Simply put, the mind seems to have a visual synthesis point originating somewhere smack between our eyes and behind the top of our nose, as if there were a single cyclopean eye looking out from this point on the forehead (Figure 7–3). It is from this central—and single—vantage point that we experience the world visually as a coherent entity.

The problem is, needless to say, that we do not have such an eye located in the middle of the brain; rather, the brain works in a fashion such that we *seem* to have a central, cyclopean eye. Under normal circumstances, we experience a unified visual world within a single integrated self. But where

Figure 7-3.
Although we have two eyes that possess overlapping visual fields, the brain creates a single "mind's eye" that seems to be located at a point somewhere between and behind the actual eyes.

does the unified visual field come from? How do the material parts of the brain involved with vision combine to bring this novel unified visual field into being? And where is the "mind's eye" physically located? Can it even be said to have a physical location?

One might suppose that the brain could achieve visual and by extension mental unity if every part of the brain that contributes to the self goes to a central place in the brain where it can be organized into a coherent whole. But, as Sherrington pointed out, there is no "psychic pineal gland":

> Where it is a question of "mind" the nervous system does not integrate itself by centralization upon one pontifical cell. Rather it elaborates a million fold democracy whose each unit is a cell.[11]

Sherrington was confronted with a paradox. On the one hand, he believed that the mind is able to integrate information from both eyes and create a single visual image in the mind from a particular vantage point behind and between the eyes. On the other hand, Sherrington could not find, or even imagine, a particular place, or "pontifical cell" in the brain where this integration occurs. Sherrington consequently arrived at a solution to the mind-brain problem that was similar to Descartes' solution: He asserted that the integration of the mind and the body is *mental* not *physical*.

Was Sherrington correct? Is there reason to believe, based on our current knowledge of the operations of the visual system, that the mental and physical worlds are two separate domains? The questions raised by Sherrington about the visual system parallel those asked about the neurology of the self. Just as the cyclopean eye is built up from the inputs of the two eyes, the self is created from the unification of many parts of the brain. If it can be shown, as asserted by Sherrington, that within the visual system there really is a split between the mental and physical, this finding would have profound implications for the neurology of the self. If the "mind's eye" proves to be a *mental integration but not a physical reality*, this could mean that the unified self is an immaterial entity as well. It is important therefore to understand how the brain creates visual unity in order to understand how the brain creates mental unity.

Mental Unity and the Visual System

Modern neuroscientists, unlike Descartes and Sherrington, have at their disposal an enormous amount of information about the operation of the visual system. The visual pathways can be thought of as streams of information flowing from the eye to the brain.[12] Vision begins at the eye's retina that has millions of rods and cones, the specialized cells that respond to light. These specialized cells enable the eye to transform light energy into electrical neural signals for processing later on in the visual regions of the brain. Each cell of the retina responds to a particular area of the visual world and this region of space that each cell monitors is called the cell's *receptive field*. For instance, a single retinal cell responds most strongly when a tiny circular light in a particular point in space stimulates a specific point on the retina within that cell's receptive field. The receptive field of each retinal cell is quite small, and somehow the brain must build up whole, and hence unified, mental representations of objects from these minuscule and discrete points of contact with the world.

After many complicated intermediary steps, the stream of incoming visual information eventually reaches the brain for additional processing. The brain area known as V1 is the primary cortical area to receive visual information. In the 1960s, Torsten Hubel and David Wiesel, in work that led to their receiving the Noble Prize in 1981, demonstrated that cells in V1, which they called *simple* cortical cells, responded not to points of light—as in the retina—but to a thin bar of light.[13] Hubel and Wiesel questioned how a *single* neuron in the brain could respond to a *line* in the world. They reasoned that if a line of adjacent firing cells—each responsive to an individual point of light—converged on a single simple cortical cell further along the processing stream, that single cortical cell could "add up" the points of light that each lower order cell had responded to. In this way, a *single* higher order cell could respond to a *line*.

Hubel and Wiesel further traced the visual processing stream for a line in the brain and found that multiple simple cortical cells converged on other single higher order cells to create what they called *complex* cortical cells. These complex cells displayed even more complicated properties than the simple cells: they converged on single neurons to create *hypercomplex* cells with increasingly specific and complex response properties. The model of Hubel and Wiesel is hierarchical in that simple cells lower or earlier in the neural processing chain create cells of ever-increasing complexity higher up on the neural hierarchy.

In this schema, the progression from simple to complex to hypercomplex cells is an example of what the visual neurobiologist Semir Zeki terms "topical convergence."[14] This is the process whereby many lower order, simple visual cells simultaneously *converge* on a smaller number of higher order complex cells. Topical convergence ultimately produces advanced "higher order" cells that possess amazingly specific response properties. These very complex cells, or neurons, are found in the inferior temporal cortex, way up the neural hierarchy and far "downstream" from the simple cells found early in the primary visual region. Higher order visual cells respond preferentially to highly specific and complex stimuli such as hands or faces. Some of these neurons respond best to the frontal view of a face and others to a side view. Neurons of this type led to the somewhat fanciful notion of the "grandmother" cell, a cell so specific that it fires only to the vision of one's grandmother![15] Cells of that degree of specificity do not exist, but it is true that the farther along a sensory processing stream that one looks, the more specific a cell's response characteristics become (Figure 7–4).

The creation of a hypercomplex cell like a face cell poses a problem for mental unity. In the process of creating higher order cells, like the hypothetical "grandmother cell," *the receptive fields of these cells increase in size.* Although a retinal cell early in the stream monitors a tiny specific point in the visual field, a hypercomplex cell such as a face cell will react to a face that appears almost *anywhere* in the person's entire visual field. While the cells early in the visual stream have small receptive fields and "know" where each line of the face is, these early cells do not "know" that a given line is part of a face. They do not have knowledge of the "big picture" of the face that will emerge later on in the processing stream. The face cells, on the other hand, "know" there is a face, but due to the process of topical convergence, these cells don't know where the face is located in space. Cells of the brain project higher and higher in a hierarchical fashion in order to code for increasingly specific complex and abstract properties, but information coded by cells earlier in the process

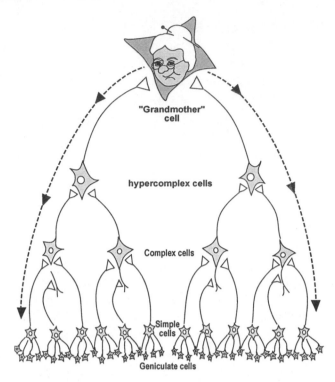

Figure 7-4.
Converging pathways from simple to complex cells, and then from complex to hypercomplex cells, create neurons with very specific and abstract response properties. If the process continued up the visual hierarchy, one could imagine the creation of the so-called grandmother cell that responds only to the face of one's grandmother.

is not and cannot be lost in awareness.[16] As Zeki observes, cells comprising *both* the early and the late stages of the visual processing stream must make a unique contribution to consciousness.[17] In this way the conscious mind is "spread out" across the activity of the many neurons that make up different regions of the brain.

The Cartesian Theater and the Binding Problem

If consciousness generally is distributed throughout the brain in this manner, then the question How is the self integrated? remains. Let us say, for the sake of argument, that all the cells that make a contribution to the conscious mind (including cells early and late in a sensory processing stream) *do* congregate in a central place in the brain. And let us further assume that our conscious mind is the product of the activity of these cells, and that this central place in the brain is the "pinnacle" of the mind and the self. The philosopher Daniel Dennett, in his book *Consciousness Explained*, dismissed the notion that all the neurons involved in consciousness somehow project their activity to a single brain region.[18] Dennett argued that this sort of reasoning required what he has called a "Cartesian Theater," an imaginary place in the brain where all conscious activity could be presented on an inner mental stage or screen for simultaneous viewing. Dennett named his "theater" after Descartes because it was Descartes who first suggested that the mind could be unified within a single place in the brain—namely, the pineal gland.

There are two major reasons why the idea of the Cartesian Theater doesn't work. As Dennett points out, and we have already discussed, the Cartesian Theater simply doesn't exist. There is no place in the brain in which all the brain's activity converges on "one pontifical cell." There is an additional problem with the idea of the Cartesian Theater. If we suppose that all brain activity contributing to consciousness is flashed on a mental "big screen TV" for simultaneous viewing, who is in the audience? This idea implies that there has to be an "inner homunculus"—a little person inside the head—who possesses the mind's eye and who is watching the show. But now we are left with another problem. To whom does this homunculus report? Yet another homunculus? With this line of reasoning we are inevitably led to an infinite series of homunculi and to a process that leads to nowhere (Figure 7–5).[19]

Scientists who study how the brain creates consciousness are particularly interested in the "binding problem."[20] Binding refers to the manner in which visual percepts are unified when cells located in different parts of the brain code for specific attributes. For example, color is processed in one part of the visual system and visual form in another. The brain needs a way to bind the correct shapes with the correct colors to form objects or images even though these two visual attributes are processed in different brain regions. What we have said about the visual system regarding its integration process becomes even more complex when the brain must coordinate features of a stimulus from multiple sensory domains, such as an object having both visual and auditory features. How are the color, shape, and honking horn of a red Corvette integrated into a unified perception? How does the brain bind the color red and the honking horn to the car, and the color brown and the barking to the dog it passes, and not the other way around? When we considered just a visual stimulus, the binding process involved only the visual centers of the brain. Now when considering the stimuli honking red Corvette or brown barking dog, binding must occur in both visual and auditory centers that are located in even more widely distributed areas of the brain.

Figure 7-5.
If the mind is created by a series of ever more complex grandmother cells, but the grandmother cells don't end up in one place, how is mental unity possible? It would appear that we need a Cartesian Theater where all the brain's parts can be simultaneously viewed by an inner homunculus. The difficulty with this type of reasoning is that it leads to an infinite regress of homunculi.

The brain must find ways to bind percepts together that are represented across separate brain regions. So how does the brain do this?

One way to explain binding in the visual system is that the brain uses synchronized oscillations to unify perception.[21] According to this account, the various neurons that are responsive to different visual attributes of a single object are bound together in awareness because they fire together in a synchronized fashion. The neurons coding for the shape, location, and color of the Corvette are all firing at one and the same frequency, and the attributes of the dog are firing at another frequency. A particular object then is represented coherently in the brain and can be distinguished from other objects. In his book *The Astonishing Hypothesis,* the Nobel Laureate molecular biologist-turned neuroscientist Francis Crick suggested that synchronized neuronal firing in the 35 to 75 Hertz range "might be the neural correlate of visual awareness."[22]

Another explanation for binding in the visual system, and mental unity in general, was offered by Nobel Laureate Gerald Edelman. Edelman also considered the problem of unification as the key to understanding consciousness. In his book *The Remembered Present: A Biological Theory of Consciousness* he posited that re-entrant cortical integration (RCI) represents the major integrative factor in the brain's construction of a unified consciousness.[23] According to Edelman, RCI is the back-and-forth signaling from multiple brain areas that allows segregated and distributed brain areas to "pull together" integrated representations. In this framework, Edelman contended that visual consciousness is unified, but that there is no need for all of the brain's inputs to end *physically* in the same place.

In fact, it is likely that the brain uses many mechanisms to perceptually bind objects in awareness, including convergence, synchronized oscillations, and re-entry. Nonetheless, whatever mechanisms the brain uses to bind objects in perception, some important questions remain. If consciousness is distributed across billions of individual neurons that are located in innumerable brain regions at different hierarchical levels of the nervous system, does it follow that each of these neurons individually "possesses" consciousness? And even if these neurons are networked together, is there something physically unified in the brain that has the same grain as the unified mind? It appears that there is still a "gap" between the objectively distributed and divisible brain and our subjective experience of a coherent and seamless "inner eye."

My reason for considering perceptual unity here has been to point out that the enigmas of visual and mental unity and the puzzle of the unification of the self that are addressed throughout this book are essentially the same: *If there is no area in the brain where all the regions that contribute to the self physically "come together," then how do we exist as whole, integrated, unified persons?*

The Ghost in the Machine

Before answering this question in the next chapter, I want to consider a similar and equally important problem for the unification of the mind and the self, and that is the unification of *action*. Just as the unification of the visual system contributes to our sense that we are unified beings, our ability to produce unified actions is essential to our feeling of wholeness as a person. When we act, we feel there is a unified self that is the source of what we do. But the *motor system*, like the visual system, is composed of millions of individual neurons. These neurons are organized to produce exquisitely integrated and unified actions, but there is no region or point in space at the top of the motor hierarchy at which we can locate the source of this unity.

Consider a simple action such as raising your arm. Suppose you say to yourself, "I will now move my arm" and you raise your arm. As you do this, you will experience an "inner I" as the source of that action; the "I" makes the conscious decision and exercises the "will" to move the arm. Suppose I, as your neurologist, search for the *source* of that "will" somewhere in your brain. I will find that there is no central, integrated, and unified physical locus that is the source of that action. There are no "commander-in-chief" neurons that I can identify in your brain as your "I" that ordered the action. There is no singular locus or top of the motor system, no "ghost in the machine" as the philosopher Gilbert Ryle famously put it, which can serve as the source of our unified "will."[24]

While looking for a way of pictorially representing the hierarchy of action, in a format similar to the depiction of the hierarchy of perception as shown in Figure 7–4, I came across a wonderful old book by the ethologist N. Tinbergen. In *The Study of Instinct,* which he wrote in 1951, Tinbergen analyzed a simple example of motor behavior, the instinctive behavior of the male three-spined stickleback fish.[25] I have fond memories of this fish, because it was a favorite subject of my psychology courses in college. Tinbergen described the levels of motoric behavior of this fish in a hierarchical fashion (Figure 7–6).

At the lowest level of this hierarchy is the single motor unit. A single motor unit consists of a single motor neuron and all the individual muscle fibers to which it is connected. It is the action of the muscle fibers that enables the fish to swim. At this level of the nervous system, the activity of a single motor unit is simple and undifferentiated. Any given

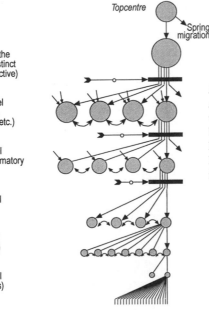

Topcentre

Spring migration

Level of the major instinct (reproductive)

2nd Level (fighting, nesting, etc.)

3rd Level (consummatory act)

4th Level (fins)

5th level (fin rays)

6th Level (muscles)

Figure 7-6.
An analysis by Tinbergen of the behavior of the stickleback fish. Tinbergen saw the behavior as hierarchical, with the highest level of the hierarchy the instinct and the lowest levels the individual muscles of the fish's fins.

motor unit will fire in the same fashion for each action that the fish takes, regardless of what that action is. When a neuron is activated as when the fish withdraws a fin in response to a jab by a piece of sharp coral or is engaged in a mating ritual, it does not matter a whit to that particular neuron what the rest of the fish is doing at the moment or why it is doing it. That neuron is just "following orders." The control for any action at the lower levels of the hierarchy comes from the higher levels of the nervous system. To find the source of the control, we must follow Tinbergen's hierarchy upward from single motor units, to the movement of entire muscles, and from there to the control of fin rays and further to fins, etc. Finally, at the top of the hierarchy, it is instinct that dictates control over the coordinated actions that make up the repetoire of the fish's motor behaviors.

Tinbergen's scheme appears pyramidal in shape, with many parts at the bottom of the pyramid converging on a single element at the top. But, just as in the perceptual hierarchy that appears to lead to the "grandmother cell" in the visual system (Figure 7-4), there is no single cell or brain region in reality that sits atop this motoric hierarchy. The instinct originates from the highest brain regions of the fish, and surely some particular areas of the fish brain are more necessary for instinctual behaviors than others. But *this instinct has no unified spatial locus in the brain.* Even though the instinct is unified in the behavior of the fish, it is not materially unified in the fish brain. The brain locus of an instinct, and hence the source of the unified action of the fish, is distributed across large regions of the fish brain.

We can also consider the hierarchical organization of human speech. If we trace the control of our speech, at the lowest level of control, there are the neurons connected to the individual muscles of the lips, tongue, face, and so on. The control of these neurons is located within the control of the joints, etc., whose control we can ultimately trace into the brain. What sits atop the hierarchy of this complicated behavior? If we look in the brain for the areas that control speech, we know first of all that the frontal portions of the left hemisphere are particularly important for the production of fluent speech, so that this area must be involved in the control of speech. We also know that the posterior portion of the left hemisphere is critical for the knowledge of the words we use in speech, and that this region of the left hemisphere is also necessary for the comprehension of speech and for self-monitoring as we listen to ourselves speak. We therefore must include this region in the act of speech production as well. We also know the right hemisphere is important for creating emotional inflection in speech production, so include this area too.

And if you gesture with your hands as you speak, we need to include the motor areas of both sides of the brain as a part of the overall act of expressing oneself. It is clear that vast areas of the brain are involved in the complicated act of speech production, yet somehow when we "will" to speak, the entire act is *unified* into a whole and coordinated behavior. But exactly how? Or by whom? Or what?

Once again, as when we considered the source of visual unity, when we search for the inner source of the center of the "will," we find ourselves at impasse. Just as there is no "pontifical neuron" sitting atop the perceptual hierarchy, there is no single brain region creating and controlling our actions and intentions. There does not appear to be any material "top" to either the perceptual or motor hierarchy. We cannot put a material "self" or "ego" at the top of any hierarchy. From the standpoint of the self, we surely experience ourselves as a unified person "in here" inside ourselves; we think that when we act, a unified self "wills" such actions. Yet our neurology and neuroscience can find no "ghost in the machine," no homunculus, no inner unified "biological soul" as it were. Where is the self then? What is it? What is its biological reality? Are we destined (doomed?) to a Cartesian Dualism, or is another explanation for the unity of the self possible? A new model, a new way of thinking about the self and the brain, is needed if we are to solve this 300-year-old problem.

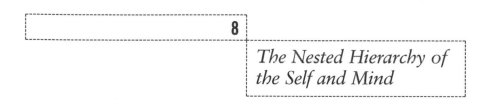

8

The Nested Hierarchy of the Self and Mind

In the preceding chapters we have described the many parts of the brain that contribute to the self. The diversity of the brain, however, stands in stark contrast to the subjective unity of the mind. In this chapter, I explore the belief that the essence of a mind, and a conscious and self-conscious self, extends beyond or is "more than the sum of the parts" of the material brain. This is the claim that the immaterial mind *emerges* from the many parts of the material brain.

Emergence and the Brain

In order to understand the claim that the self and the mind emerge from the brain, there are three key interrelated concepts to consider. The first concept is the idea of *emergence* itself. The doctrine of emergence, according to philosopher Jaegwon Kim, holds that

> although the fundamental entities of this world and their properties are material, when material processes reach a certain level of complexity, genuinely novel and unpredictable properties emerge, and that this process of emergence is cumulative, generating a hierarchy of increasingly more complex novel properties. Thus, emergentism presents the world not only as an evolutionary process but also as a layered structure—a hierarchically organized system of levels of properties, each level emergent from and dependent on the one below.[1]

One popular example of an emergent system is water, for which it is noted that the properties of liquidity, wetness, and transparency do not apply to a single water molecule, but to the aggregate "water." In biology, emergent properties are viewed as the result of *hierarchically* ordered living things. A hierarchy, in the general sense of the term, refers to an organized system composed of multiple parts arranged in a graded series of levels. In accord with Kim's definition, emergence in living things occurs as the product of a hierarchically organized system—the organism—in which each level of complexity of the organism produces *novel* emergent features from the levels below it. Emergent properties are also said to be *unpredictable* in that complete knowledge of the parts at a lower level of a hierarchy would not allow the prediction of the appearance of the emergent property at the higher level. In this way, the emergent feature is said to be "greater than the sum of its parts."

A second key concept of emergence theory is the notion of *constraint*. Although the term emergence connotes the way that the parts in a hierarchy combine to form wholes, constraint is the process by which higher levels in the hierarchy impose control over the lower levels. Campbell coined the term "downward causation" to refer to the control that a higher level of a hierarchy exerts on its contributing parts.[2] The biologist H. H. Pattee pointed out the importance of constraint in biological systems:

> If there is to be any theory of general biology, it must explain the origin and operation (including the reliability and persistence) of the hierarchical constraints which harness matter to perform coherent functions. This is not just the problem of why certain amino acids are strung together to catalyze a specific reaction. The problem is universal and characteristic of all living matter. It occurs at every level of biological organization, from the molecule to the brain. It is the central problem of the origin of life, when aggregations of matter obeying only elementary physical laws first began to constrain individual molecules to a functional, collective behavior. It is the central problem of development where collections of cells control the growth or genetic expression of individual cells. It is the central problem of biological evolution in which groups of cells form larger and larger organizations by generating hierarchical constraints on subgroups. It is the central problem of the brain where there appears to be an unlimited possibility for new hierarchical levels of description. These are all problems of hierarchical organization. Theoretical biology must face this problem as fundamental, since hierarchical control is the essential and distinguishing characteristic of life.[3]

It is through constraint that hierarchical systems operate. In biological systems such as a person, the individual cells of the human body constrain the microscopic organelles of the cell to perform cellular metabolism; the organs of the body constrain the cells so that they secrete enzymes; the entire body of the person constrains the organs to digest, breathe, and perform all the macroscopic functions necessary for the life of the body.[4]

There is often a reciprocal relationship between emergence and constraint in hierarchical systems. If you were to look at a single cell from the human lung, for example, under a high-powered microscope, you would see the thousands of miniscule organelles within the cell. Among these organelles would be found the mitochondria, the organelles responsible for generating energy from the oxygen we breathe via a process known as cellular respiration. These tiny organelles are a part of the cell that along with other cells make up the tissues that eventually give rise to the lung. The mitochondria contribute to the structure of the lung and therefore to the emergence of the lung at a higher level of the hierarchy of the body. The lung, at a higher level on the hierarchy, displays emergent features not possessed by mitochondria, such as the capacity to move air in and out of the body. If the lung did not breathe, the body would not have oxygen, and if we did not have oxygen, the mitochondria would not be able to carry on cellular respiration. In this manner the higher level property of breathing constrains the activity of the mitochondria. When the system is considered as a whole, the mitochondria contribute to the emergence of the lung, and the lung in turn constrains the mitochondria.

The third key concept of emergence theory that I wish to discuss is perhaps its most controversial. This concept is the notion of *nonreducibility*, the claim that the wholes created by an emergent system cannot be explained simply by or reduced to the properties of its constituent parts. According to Medawar and Medawar, in their book *The Life Science* the nonreducibility of a higher level to a lower level in a hierarchical system is a key characteristic of an emergent property.[5] They define emergence as the "philosophical doctrine opposed to *reducibility* which declares that in a *hierarchical* system each level may have properties and modes of behavior peculiar to itself and not fully explicable by analytic reduction."[6] According to the Medawars, if a property is emergent, it is *not* reducible to those parts. It follows that if a property in a hierarchy *is* reducible to the properties of things at lower levels of the hierarchy, it is not emergent.

According to philosopher John Searle, the basic idea underlying the principle of reduction was the notion that "certain things might be shown to be nothing but certain other sorts of things."[7] Searle also pointed out that a satisfactory scientific reduction involves a form of identity relation that he calls a "nothing-but" relation: a property A is said to be reducible to property B if it can be shown that A "is nothing but" B. In other words, we do not need to invoke a new or novel property to explain A over and above those principles by which we understand B. Searle identified several subtypes of reduction in his writings, but what Searle called *ontological reduction* is the form of reduction most relevant to emergence theory:

The most important form of reduction is ontological reduction. It is the form in which objects of certain types can be shown to consist in nothing but objects of other types. For example, chairs are shown to be nothing but collections of molecules. This form is clearly important in the history of science. For example, material objects in general can be shown to be nothing but collections of molecules, genes can be shown to consist in nothing but DNA molecules.[8]

Examples of successful ontological reductions in neuroscience include the identification of the manner in which motor action can be reduced to the physiology of the nerve and muscle, or the determination that paralysis can be reduced to a lesion of the motor system. These processes at one time considered mysterious and beyond the reach of natural science can now be explained in purely biological terms. Similarly, there currently is no "seizure-brain enigma" because we understand how the observable epileptic fit can be reduced to abnormal electrical discharges of cortical neurons in a particular brain region.

The three key aspects of emergence theory that I have enumerated are *emergence, constraint,* and *nonreducibility.* Keeping these general principles in mind, we now are ready to consider theories that view the mind as an emergent feature of the brain. The brain is generally thought of as a hierarchically organized system, and the concept of hierarchical organization is central to those theories that view the mind and the self as emergent phenomena. According to emergence theories of the mind, the self "emerges" from the complex interactions of the hierarchically organized parts of the brain. C. Lloyd Morgan was a leader of the school of emergentism. He viewed the emergence of mental phenomenon in terms of a hierarchical model of the brain. He wrote:

> In the foregoing lecture the notion of a pyramid with ascending levels was put forward. Near its base is a swarm of atoms with relational structure and the quality we may call atomicity. Above this level, atoms combine to form new units, the distinguishing quality of which is molecularity; higher up, on one line of advance, are, let us say, crystals wherein atoms and molecules are grouped in new relations of which the expression is crystalline form; on another line of advance are organisms with a different kind of natural relations which give the quality of vitality; yet higher, a new kind of natural relatedness supervenes and to its expression the word "mentality" may be applied.[9]

Morgan views the mind as emerging at the summit of the brain, just like the eye that sits atop the pyramid in Figure 1-2. According to emergentist theory, the "cyclopean eye" is an emergent phenomenon as well. As you will recall from the last chapter, the problem of the cyclopean eye refers to the question of how visual unity is possible with both eyes when either eye alone is capable of a complete and independent visual image. Why do we not see two of everything, one image coming from each eye? According to the principles of emergence theory, the images from each eye are components of the lower level of the visual hierarchy. These components are combined to create a single and unified cyclopean eye that "emerges" in consciousness as a single cyclopean image. It is this cyclopean eye that sits atop the visual hierarchy, just like the eye poised on top of the pyramid. The whole of the cyclopean eye *is* greater than the sum of the parts that are contributed by each eye alone. When we view with one eye open, we lack depth perception. When we view our environment with both eyes open, due to the differences between the images generated by each eye, the cyclopean eye possesses depth perception for the integrated image. Depth perception is an emergent property of vision not present when viewing with either eye alone.[10]

Roger Sperry Argues for the Emergence of an Immaterial Mind

The psychologist Roger Sperry, who received the Nobel Prize for his work on the split brain, argued that the mind constitutes an *emergent* phenomenon deriving from diverse parts of the material brain. Sperry claimed that the mind is "more than the sum of the parts" of the material brain and that the mind goes above and beyond the brain's physical limitations in important and sometimes mysterious ways. In Sperry's words: "conscious phenomena are different from, more than, and not reducible to, neural events. . . ."[11] All the features of emergence theory were present in his formulation of the relationship between the mind and the brain. Like most emergence theorists, Sperry viewed the mind-brain relationship in hierarchical terms and supposed that the neural elements of the brain combine in increasingly complex configurations until at the summit of organization, the mind emerges. Just as the unified cyclopean eye sits atop the visual hierarchy, Sperry argued the unified "I" sits atop the neural hierarchy of the entire brain. But Sperry took this idea further. He argued that since the mind was an emergent feature of the brain, the mind, therefore, could not be reduced to the brain. Since the mind could not be reduced to the physical brain, it was not a material substance like the brain. Lastly, another result of Sperry's formulation was the view that emergent mental forces or properties, while not material, can nonetheless influence the material body. Even though the mind is not material, it can *cause* material events to happen in the brain. In this way, Sperry suggested that the immaterial mind has *causal* properties over the material brain and constrains the brain. Sperry articulated his thoughts on the nature of consciousness as follows:

> consciousness was conceived to be a dynamic emergent of brain activity, neither identical with, nor reducible to, the neural events of which it is mainly composed. Further, consciousness was not conceived as an epiphenomenon, inner aspect, or other passive correlate of brain processing, but rather to be an active integral part of the cerebral process itself, exerting potent causal effects in the interplay of cerebral operations. In a position of top command at the highest levels in the hierarchy of brain organization, the subjective properties were seen to exert control over the biophysical and chemical activities at subordinate levels. It was described initially as a brain model that puts "conscious mind back into the brain of objective science in a position of top command . . . a brain model in which conscious, mental, psychic forces are recognized to be the crowning achievement . . . of evolution."[12]

> The causal power attributed to the subjective properties is nothing mystical. It is seen to reside in the hierarchical organization of the nervous system combined with the universal power of any whole over its parts. Any system that coheres as a whole, acting, reacting, and interacting as a unit, has systemic organizational properties of the system as a whole that determine its behavior as an entity, and control thereby at the same time the course and fate of its components. The whole has properties as a system that are not reducible to the properties of the parts, and the properties at higher levels exert causal control over those at lower levels. In the case of brain function, the conscious properties of high-order brain activity determine the course of the neural events at lower levels.[13]

More recently, mathematician Alwyn Scott in his book *Stairway to the Mind*[14] expresses a point of view similar to that of Sperry. Like Sperry, Scott suggests that consciousness "emerges" at the top of a hierarchically ordered nervous system. Scott compares the hierarchy of the nervous system to a flight of stairs or the rungs of a ladder. In this scheme, as in the model proposed by Sperry, consciousness emerges at the highest and most complex neural levels. According to Scott, "Just as life emerges from cycles of cycles of cycles of biochemical activity, consciousness seems to emerge from assemblies of assemblies of . . . of assemblies of neurons" and "as life emerges from several of the lower levels of the hierarchy, consciousness emerges from several of the upper levels." Scott calls this point of view *hierarchical* or *emergent dualism.*

There are problems with Sperry's account of the mind-brain relationship in my view. First, Sperry claimed that the mind emerges at the summit of a hierarchically ordered brain. But, as I described in chapter 7, there is no material summit of the brain or the self. There is no basis for the idea that the mind appears at the pinnacle of the brain because there is no place in the brain where all the brain's activity physically "comes together." Additionally, we are left with the Cartesian dilemma. If the brain is material, and the mind is immaterial, how does a nonmaterial mind control a material brain? There must be another way to reconcile the divisible brain with our internal sense of ourselves as unified and whole beings.

Non-Nested and Nested Hierarchies

The difficulty with Sperry's account lies in the way that he viewed the hierarchy of the brain. Sperry viewed the brain and the mind as parts of a particular type of hierarchy known as a *non-nested hierarchy.*[15] A non-nested hierarchy has a pyramidal structure with a clear-cut top and bottom in which higher levels control the operation of lower levels. A common example of a non-nested hierarchy is a military command. There is a general at the top who controls the lieutenants, who control their sergeants, and so on, down the chain of command until we finally reach the level of the individual troops. This would seem to be what Sperry had in mind when he spoke of a "top command" that subordinated lower levels of a hierarchy (Figure 8 1).

The non-nested hierarchy that Sperry envisioned is considered non-nested because, while the successive levels of the hierarchy interact, each level of the hierarchy is physically independent from all higher and lower levels. The various levels of a non-nested hierarchy are not *composed* of each other. Let me now reconsider our example of the military command that represents a non-nested hierarchy. The general commands and controls the lieutenants, but the general is not "made up of" the lieutenants.

An alternative framework for viewing the mind-brain relationship is another type of hierarchy known as a *compositional* or *nested hierarchy.* We refer to this type of hierarchy as nested because the elements com-

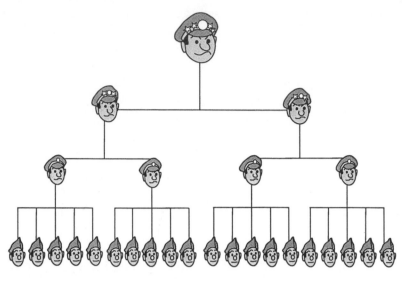

Figure 8-1.
An army is a good example of a non-nested hierarchy. The general, at the top of the pyramid, controls all lower levels down to the privates. Each level of a non-nested hierarchy is physically separate from all other levels.

posing the lower levels of the hierarchy are physically combined or *nested* within higher levels to create increasingly complex wholes. The important distinction between non-nested and nested hierarchies is the relationship between the lower and higher levels of the hierarchy. A non-nested hierarchy has a clear top and bottom, and the control of the hierarchy comes from the top. A nested hierarchy has no top or bottom, and the control or constraint of the hierarchy is embodied within the entire hierarchical system.[16]

All living things, including ourselves, are nested hierarchies (Figure 8–2). We are physically composed of minute organelles that are hierarchically organized to create a human being. In the hierarchy of a living person, it is the complete person who sits at the top of the hierarchy, and that person is not separate from the parts of which he or she is composed. Individual elements of the body that make up the person simultaneously contribute to the life of that person. The "parts" of the person in this way are nested within the totality of the human being.

I return to the example of the lung. The mitochondria make a contribution to the emergence of the lung, but this does not mean the lung is independent of the mitochondria. Indeed, the lung is totally dependent on the mitochondria for its life and, without the mitochondria, the lung, and the person along with it, would die. In this way, both the mito-

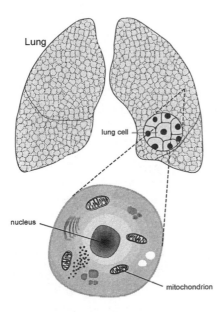

Lung

lung cell

nucleus

mitochondrion

Figure 8-2.
Organisms are nested hierarchies. Lower order elements, such as cellular organelles, combine to create higher order elements, such as organs. In this way, all higher level entities are physically composed of lower order elements. Even though the higher levels of the nested hierarchy display "emergent" features not present in lower levels, all entities at all levels continue to make a contribution to the life and operation of the entire organism.

chondria and the lung independently and interdependently make an essential contribution to the life of the person. Both are part of the nested hierarchy constituting the person.

The Nested Hierarchy of the Brain

With these considerations about hierarchies in mind, I present an alternative model to explain the relationship between the brain and the unified mind. I propose that the brain functions as a nested hierarchy, as do all biological systems, and that the proper model for the integration of the mind and the brain is that of a nested hierarchy. Consider again the face cells that were addressed in the last chapter. How is the mental representation of a face unified in awareness if so many areas of the brain are involved in its production? The convergence of neural pathways makes possible a cell so specific that it will only fire to face. This process might lead one to think that a *single* "grandmother" cell, at the top of the perceptual hierarchy, embodies the representation of an entire face in consciousness (Figure 7–4).

We have considered why this logic would be a mistake, and why, in reality, no single neuron embodies the experience of seeing a face. A "grandmother cell" might respond quite selectively to certain stimuli, such as faces. However, the awareness in consciousness of the face of one's actual grandmother requires the representation of an enormous variety of information about the lines of Granny's nose, the location of her mouth, the color and shape of her eyes, and so on. All this information is not contained in a single cell. Further, this information does not end up in the Cartesian Theater for simultaneous viewing because no such place exists. Rather, the entire nested system of the brain functions *interdependently* to create the visual image of the face. In the same way that mitochondria and the lung contribute to the life of the person, in the nested hierarchy of the mind, all the lower order elements—every line, shape, and patch of color that make up our awareness of the face—continue to make a contribution to consciousness.

We also can use the model of a nested hierarchy of consciousness to explain our conscious experience of the speeding red Corvette with its horn blasting that we considered in chapter 7. A complex stimulus of this nature is composed of so many elements that its neurological representation covers great areas of the brain and each part of the brain must make a contribution to its unified emergence into consciousness. In a brief review of the visual system (chapter 7) we saw how individual line segments are formed. A "line" of simple cells converges simultaneously onto the single complex cell that represents "a line." This process of convergence occurs for every line that appears in any image. In the scene with the speeding red Corvette, the roof and trunk of the car are composed of tens of thousands of individual line segments. These individual line segments of the car's outline then are combined into longer segments that produce the car's overall shape and form. The lower order features, for instance, the exact position of a small line sequence in space, emerge in awareness as "part of" something else, such as the outline of the car. A short line segment is "bound" to a longer segment to create the outline of the car, just as a small patch of red is "bound" to a larger red patch that is part of the door. The redness of the Corvette is "bound" to its shape that is bound to its movement that is bound to the honking horn, until all representations are "bound together" to create the entire image. The color, shape, and movement of the car are nested together within the image of the car and this image in turn is nested within the entire scene.

To say an element is *bound* to another is simply another way of saying that they are represented in awareness *dependently* and are *nested together*. It follows from this framework that the extent to which lower order features are bound into a higher order feature is the extent to which the lower order features lose their independence from each other. For example, the neurons responding to the redness of the Corvette are tightly bound to each other. These neurons make their contributions to awareness as a nested whole. Every single neuron in a red patch of the car makes a unique contribution to consciousness, but it *becomes* a "patch" of color because all the neurons that represent redness make their contribution to awareness in an *entirely* dependent, bound, and nested fashion. The binding concept also can be applied to the relationship between the redness and shape of the car. Color and shape are represented in awareness as a nested totality. We do not experience the color of the car independently from the experience of its shape. On the other hand, the experience of the dog that the car passes is bound to the car within the entire visual experience, but is not tightly bound to the color or shape of the car. The higher level or complex neurons that code for car and dog as entities make greater *independent* contributions to conscious awareness within the nested hierarchy of consciousness than do the simple neurons that code for the specific color or shape of the car.[17]

If there is no top or bottom to the nested hierarchy of the mind, what provides the topmost constraint that guides and controls our whole brain? What is the physical reality of the "inner I" that pulls together the mind and controls our actions? What keeps the millions of neurons in our brains from all going off in their own directions? How can we exist as single minds and unified selves?

Meaning and the "Inner I"

In the hierarchy of our conscious awareness, it is *meaning* that provides the constraint that "pulls" the mind together to form the "inner I" of the self. Think once again about our example of the nested hierarchy described by cyclopean perception and the mind's eye. In this example, the two visual images, one from each eye, do not, as Descartes had supposed, "physically" merge. There is no one place in the brain at which the images physically come together. Rather, the two images create a *mental condition* where their *meanings* are conjointly represented in awareness to produce a *higher level of meaning*. In the example of the cyclopean eye, the higher level of meaning is that of a single image now seen in depth. It is the higher meaning of the combined images that produces the "top-down" constraint on the individual elements. This constraint or control of the whole on the parts does *not suggest* the elimination of these individual parts from the mind because the image from each eye continues to make a contribution to the unified cyclopean eye. Instead, constraint leads to the elimination of the *independence* of each part from each other when operating within the framework of the nested hierarchy of consciousness. By saying that these parts are represented dependently I also am saying that they are represented *meaningfully* in consciousness. Thus, the *unified subjective experience* that we experience as the integrated self is the result of the *nested hierarchy of meaning* created by the brain.

Purpose Is the "Ghost in the Machine"

When the control of action or the nature of volition is considered as a nested hierarchy, it is *purpose* that provides the constraint and guiding force of the self. It is *purpose* that is the "ghost in the machine." Neurological theories usually do not make reference to purpose. There is little room for ideas like "free will" or "human purpose" in discussions of the neurological basis of behavior. Invoking purpose in an explanation of a neurological phenomenon is seen as a form of *teleological thinking*— an effort to invoke the end result of a process as its cause, which is a logical impossibility.[18] We cannot say, for example, that we possess the corneal reflex—the reflexive blink when something comes in contact with the cornea—*in order to* protect the eye. This form of teleological reasoning does not constitute a neurological explanation for the mechanism of the reflex. A neurological explanation of the corneal reflex entails a description of the nerves that provide sensation to the eye and the nerves that blink the eye, and the neurologist does not need to invoke the purpose of the reflex to explain its action. On the other hand, the corneal reflex does serve a *purpose* in that it protects the eye.

As pointed out at the beginning of this chapter, *all* living things are hierarchically organized such that its parts are *constrained* to perform certain goal-directed actions that serve a *purpose* for the organism. In a nested hierarchy, constraint is the means through which organisms achieve their goals. Another example of this relationship between constraint and purpose is demonstrated by the absorption of water by a plant via its roots. Parts of the plant (i.e., the roots) are constrained to perform the actions necessary for this vital function. This does not mean that the plant "knows" the purpose of this function or that the plant performs the actions of absorption "in order to" bring water to its leaves. It would be teleological thinking to explain the *mechanism* of water absorption on the basis of the plant having the *purpose* of absorbing water. Similarly, a human being's beating heart, which promotes the circulation of blood throughout the body, has a structure and biological design that enables it to perform the functions necessary to maintain the life of the organism. But the heart does not purposefully set out to perform the pumping of blood any more than the plant purposefully sets out to absorb water. Nonetheless, the roots of the plant and the beating heart have within their structures the biological organization to perform the actions that ensure the organism's survival.[19]

These examples demonstrate that it is difficult to describe biological functions that serve the purpose of ensuring the organism's survival in non-teleological terms. Theoretical biologist Ernst Mayr suggested that one approach might be to view biological systems as *teleonomic,* a word derived from the Greek word *telos,* meaning "goal" or "endpoint." According to Mayr, "a teleonomic process or behavior is one which owes its goal-directedness to the operation of a program."[20] Evolutionary processes produce living things that are teleonomic. Genetically programmed biological processes, such as the respiration of the mitochondria, are teleonomic. An organism can perform a process that is teleonomic in that the process serves an adaptive purpose for an organism, yet the organism does not have to anticipate or "know" the endpoint of that process.

It is fairly clear that plants and beating hearts do not anticipate the consequences of their actions. But what about a cat stalking its prey? This example is also an instance of a teleonomic process. The cat's stalking behavior is guided by a biological program (in this case we call it an instinct), and it has a clear endpoint, which is to catch and eat its prey. Let us consider if the beating heart has the same teleonomy as a cat chasing a mouse according to Mayr's conception of teleonomy. Does the beating heart have the same teleonomy as the early man who made the first stone tool?

Mayr wished to regard teleonomic processes as those that are end-directed, but not deliberately or intentionally so. Teleonomic phrases such as "the function of the heart's beating" or "the heart beats in order to" are acceptable as long as one realizes the metaphorical use of such language. But if teleonomic processes are not necessarily deliberate, purposive, intentional acts, then the question remains as to whether there is a biological and even philosophical distinction between the beating heart and the thinking and purposive brain of the toolmaker. And if there is a difference between the heart and the brain, how are we to describe the difference in scientific terms?

Although hierarchical constraint produces integrated teleonomic functions in all life, only certain teleonomic systems, events, acts, and so on are also *purposeful.* It is the degree of conscious purpose that distinguishes intentional from nonintentional teleonomic behaviors. Beating hearts do not have purpose in their actions; toolmakers do. Some neurological phenomena in humans also are teleonomic yet entirely nonpurposeful. The corneal reflex, which consists of the blink of the eye when it is touched, serves to protect the eye and is therefore a teleonomic behavior. However, this reflex can be invoked in someone in coma and the reflex is largely involuntary. While the corneal reflex is teleonomic in that it serves a purpose for the organism, it is not purposeful. The question is at what point do we consider a behavior purposeful? For example, Braithwaite had no problem attributing purposeful action to his cat:

> My cat's behaviour in pawing at the closed door, it may be said, is sufficiently similar to a man's behaviour in knocking at a locked door for it to be reasonable to infer that the cat, like the man, is acting as it does because of a conscious intention, or at least a conscious desire, to be let through the door.[21]

We can agree that the cat's behavior is to some extent intentional and goal directed. We may additionally agree that the man's behavior is a hierarchically more advanced, or at least more evolved, form of intentionality. For instance, animals including nonhuman primates have very limited voluntary control over their vocalizations. Primate researchers have no difficulty training a rhesus monkey to perform a bar press to obtain a reward, yet they have found it vastly more difficult to train these animals to produce a vocalization in the same way.[22] The monkey can control its limbs but not its vocalizations. While the brain regions controlling limb movement must have cortical representation, the brain structures that control vocalization and facial expression in the monkey are in the limbic system, a subcortical phylogenetically older area of the brain that is responsible for emotional, social, and self-preservative behaviors. A major difference, therefore, between the monkey and human vocalization is that humans can control their vocal apparatus. The human can *constrain* the many parts of the body that are required to produce speech.

My purpose in elaborating at some length on this topic is to point out that purposeful action can be distinguished from teleonomic (but nonpurposeful) behavior by its greater degree of constraint over a multitude of nested parts. Both birds and certain people fly south for the winter, yet only man has awareness that he is leaving to seek warmer weather in Boca Raton. The simple motor acts of both species are constrained by the highest levels of the nested action hierarchy; but, in the case of the bird, the highest level is a chain of instinctual behavior, with a minimal degree of either flexibility or foresight. On the other hand, for some human behavior, the extent of the constraint over space and time when traveling is extraordinary—buy clothes, tickets, bathing suits; tell friends and associates one will be out of town; go to the airport, and so on. The kind of "future directedness," the number and complexity of necesssary steps that human beings implement in order to purposively attain a goal, reflect an unparalleled degree of constraint when compared to that of any other form of life.[23]

The manner in which higher brain regions purposely control lower regions is one of the cornerstones of modern neurological thought. John Hughlings Jackson's hierarchical model of the nervous system is perhaps the single most influential model in the history of neurology. For Jackson, the nervous system evolved from simple reflexes that could be found at the lowest hierarchical levels of the nervous system to *voluntary* forms of action that are produced by the highest cortical levels of the brain.[24]

Jackson's hierarchical nervous system views higher cortical regions as controlling and suppressing lower levels. What appears at the top of a Jacksonian action hierarchy is not a pontifical cell. Jackson had no image of a "ghost in the machine" controlling lower levels of the nervous system. For Jackson, it was *purposeful action,* or what Jackson referred to as voluntary (as opposed to automatic) behavior that sits at the highest levels of the nervous system. Voluntary behaviors were the most complex, most specialized, least automatic, involved the greatest degree of consciousness, and had the greatest degree of independence from other movements. Voluntary action was also the most conscious form of action. It was voluntary or purposeful action that constrains the lower elements in the motor hierarchy, *not a single cell or brain region.*

The act of speaking further illustrates the constraint of purpose over a nested system of parts. When we speak, we do not *will* a particular muscle of the mouth to move in a specific and conscious way. We do not consciously send a command to the tongue to move left and then right and so on. Indeed, we couldn't do this even if we wanted to. First of all, the average speaker has no idea which particular muscles to move when speaking. We are not consciously aware which muscles of the mouth, tongue, pharynx, larynx, and so on must be called into action to produce a certain sound. Additionally, even if we did know which muscles to move, we lack the fine coordination required to voluntarily move a given muscle "just so" to produce a given speech sound. Finally, even if we were to possess the necessary knowledge and control to voluntarily move each muscle of speech into action, if we were required to do so when speaking, we would lose the overall integration of the speech act. We need to focus on the idea we wish to express, rather than on the way our lips and tongue are moving, or on the way a single fiber in the tongue is firing! The actions of the neurons at these lower levels of the hierarchy are *nested* within the higher levels of the hierarchy and the purpose of the act provides the *constraint* of higher levels on lower levels of the motor hierarchy, and in this case the purpose of speaking is the communication of an idea. When we speak, it is the idea we wish to express, the *purpose* of our speaking, that sits at the highest level of the action hierarchy. It is this purpose that brings unity to the speech act that constrains all the many muscles that are part of the act of speaking.

Jackson pointed out that proof of the hierarchical control of speech could be found when one considered patients with disease of the nervous system. Jackson studied the patient with aphasia.[25] Aphasia is the specific loss of language capacity due to brain dysfunction. Aphasia occurs in most right-handed patients as a result of damage to certain brain areas, which are usually in the left hemisphere in right-handed patients. Some patients with aphasia have problems with expression, so-called Broca's aphasia; while others who have their chief difficulty with comprehension are known as Wernicke's aphasics. Some aphasics may have various combinations of disturbances, sparing some functions, while involving others. Jackson found that the aphasic who could not say a word on command—for instance, in response to "say the word 'no' "—might be able to say it in response to a question. And a patient who could not utter "no" in response to a question might be able to say "no" when scolding his children or under states of emotional excitement.

In this instance, the lowest levels of speech, the more emotional and automatic, are the most resistant to—in Jackson's words—"dissolution of function," while the highest levels, the most voluntary, are more susceptible to disruption as a result of brain damage. An aphasic patient of mine nicely demonstrated this principle. He was a sixty-eight-year-old businessman who had a severe disturbance of speech due to a cortical stroke. As part of his language assessment he was given a series of objects to identify. The patient, who was prior to his stroke quite a raconteur, failed miserably on his ability to name even the simplest items such as a pen or watch. After a few minutes of this, he became noticeably upset and finally blurted out, "Damn it! I'm as smart as you are . . . as any man you'll ever meet!" While his ability to express specific thoughts was limited, he was always capable of producing a string of uninterrupted expletives.

Lesions in certain neocortical regions in the human reliably produce aphasia, a disorder of voluntary speech. But as we have already reviewed, as highlighted by Jackson, some aspects of emotional speech controlled by the limbic system may be preserved. Further, a dissociation between voluntary and nonvoluntary facial expression may occur with a stroke of either side of the brain. A patient with a cortical lesion often has a paralysis of the lower face on the side opposite the lesion. Thus, if a patient with a lower facial paralysis from a left cortical lesion is asked to "show me your teeth," the weakness of the opposite lower face becomes evident. However, when the patient is seen to spontaneously smile or laugh, a behavior controlled by the phylogenetically older and more primitive limbic system, the face moves symmetrically and normally. Conversely, neurologists recognize what is known as a "mimetic facial."[26] A patient with a lesion in the limbic system may have no difficulty exposing the teeth on command, but may appear to have a facial paralysis when laughing spontaneously.[27]

This dissociation of function was made clear to me as a resident when one night I admitted to the hospital a young man who was being evaluated for headaches. I found nothing wrong with him after taking a thorough history and performing a complete neurological examination. Later, as we spoke, we had the opportunity to laugh at something or other, and a noticeable droop on the right side of his face suddenly and somewhat ironically appeared and pointed to the presence of a tumor of the hypothalamus (brainstem). It fortunately was successfully removed.

Another fascinating but sometimes disabling condition called "pseudobulbar palsy" relates to these issues. A patient may develop lesions on both sides of the brain, such that the neocortical regions are disconnected from the lower centers of the brainstem that innervate the facial muscles. Under these conditions, the pathways of voluntary facial expression are severed, the patient losses volitional control over the face, and cannot, for instance, smile or move the mouth on command. If this weren't bad enough, the descending inhibitory pathways from higher brain regions are also damaged, so that the patient also cannot inhibit or suppress spontaneous emotional expression. In these circumstances, the patient is subject to extreme emotional outbursts of laughing or crying that may come over the patient seemingly out of the blue. One patient of mine, a young college-age woman, had a disease of the blood vessels that resulted in two strokes, one on each side of the brain. In my office, and in most social settings, she needed to constantly stifle a smile or laugh regardless of the topic or her mood. Sometimes the drive became too great, and she would burst into a loud prolonged laughing jag to the point of tears. The patient denied that significant emotion except frustration was attached to these occurrences.[28]

The condition of pseudobulbar palsy nicely demonstrates the principles of hierarchical control of the motor system. In the patient afflicted with this condition, the control of emotional expression at its highest levels is destroyed. This patient cannot smile to show approval or scowl to demonstrate anger. Yet there are circumstances when emotional expression bursts through without the constraint or control. The neurological underpinnings of emotion are intact, but are no longer under higher level control.

In summary, the self can be understood as a *nested hierarchy of meaning and purpose*. We do not experience multiple cognitive or conscious representations from each of the brain areas that contribute to the self because these regions serve as lower order elements in the nested hierarchy of the mind. Instead, many brain regions are coordinated into a single nested consciousness. The view that the brain functions as a nested hierarchy appears to have been largely overlooked in the neuroscientific literature. The nested nature of consciousness is not mentioned in the excellent and comprehensive special issue of *Consciousness and Cognition*[29] that is devoted to the topic of temporal binding and consciousness, and Scott[30] in his book, *Stairway to the Mind*, extensively discussed the issue of emergence in hierarchical systems, but the nested nature of the brain/mind in perception and action does not appear as part of his model.[31] In contrast, I suggest that the self, the "mind's eye" and our sense of will, is the product of the nested hierarchy of meaning and purpose created by the brain. In the next chapter we will consider how this viewpoint helps up to understand the ultimate nature of the united self.

9

Being and Brain

I cannot know as an object that which I
must presuppose in order to know any object.

Immanuel Kant, 1781

Descartes, Sherrington, and Sperry argued for the separation of body and mind. Their reasons for positing this separation were similar. These thinkers sought to explain how the unified mind, the "inner I" and the coherent self, was constructed from the diverse parts of the brain. In the final analysis, they concluded that the mind could not be reduced to the material brain. I have offered a solution to the problem of mental unification—namely, that the mind is a nested hierarchy of meaning and purpose created by the brain. The nested nature of the hierarchy of the "inner I" allows the self and the mind to be subjectively unified despite the diversity of the brain.

Does this proposal constitute *the* solution to the mind-body problem? Although I have tried to demonstrate why Descartes', Sherrington's, and Sperry's explanations for the separation of mind and brain were in error, there are *real* differences between the mind and brain, but not for the reasons proposed by these authors. In this chapter, I will argue that the reason the mind cannot be equated with the brain is the absolutely *personal* nature of meaning, purpose, and being. The mind is subjective and personal, and for this reason the mind and the self cannot be *reduced* to the brain.

The Subjective and Objective Points of View

Many scholars have made the argument that subjective and objective viewpoints on the brain are different in fundamental ways.[1] The philosopher Kant insisted that the perception of an object is presupposed by an experiencing self, and it therefore follows that the self can never be an object unto itself. The nineteenth-century philosopher Arthur Schopenhauer (1788–1860) was influenced by Kant's philosophy. Schopenhauer also insisted that no thing could be simultaneously subject and object. In Schopenhauer's words:

Our knowledge, like our eye, only sees outwards, and not inwards, so that when the knower tries to turn itself inwards, in order to know itself, it looks into a total darkness, falls into a complete void. That the subject should become object for itself is the most monstrous contradiction ever thought of: for subject and object can only be thought one in relation to the other. This relation is their only mark, and when it is taken away the concept of subject and object is empty: if the subject is to become the object, it presupposes as object another subject—where is this to come from?[2]

The distinction between subject and object was emphasized again by the evolutionary psychologists George Henry Lewes (1817–1878) and Herbert Spencer (1820–1903):

When I am told that a nervous excitation is transformed into a sensation on reaching the brain, I ask, who knows this? On what evidence is the fact asserted? On examination it will appear that there is no evidence at all of such a transformation; all the evidence points to the very different fact that the neural process and the feeling are one and the same process viewed under different aspects. Viewed from the physical or objective side, it is a neural process; viewed from the psychological or subjective side, it is a sentient process.[3]

When the two modes of Being which we distinguish as Subject and Object, have been severally reduced to their lowest terms, any further comprehension must be an assimilation of these lowest terms to one another; and, as we have already seen, this is negatived by the very distinction of Subject and Object, which is itself the consciousness of a difference transcending all other differences. So far from helping us to think of them as of one kind, analysis serves but to render more manifest the impossibility of finding for them a common concept—a thought under which they can be united.[4]

The relationship between the subjective or inner mind and the objective reality of the material brain remains a puzzle to this day. In fact, this old problem has found a new life in the current debates among philosophers and neuroscientists on the nature of consciousness. Philosopher Thomas Nagel argued that the subjective nature of the mind could not be eliminated from discussions of the brain in his classic paper "What Is It Like to Be a Bat?"[5] Nagel insisted on the subjective nature of mental phenomena and he argued against simple reductionism and physicalism because "every sub-jective phenomenon is essentially connected with a single point of view, and it seems inevitable that an objective, physical theory will abandon that point of view."[6] A central theme of Nagel's argument is that the subjective-objective dichotomy lies at the heart of the mind-body problem, and that "the subjectivity of consciousness is an irreducible feature of reality."[7]

Other contemporary philosophers, including John Searle, have argued that the mind is phenomenally irreducible to the brain. Searle pointed out that successful reductions in science aim to *remove* any subjective element in the analysis. A feature of the world that "appears" a certain way in nonreduced form is ultimately reduced to its scientific "reality." However, when we consider the mind, Searle argued that "we can't make that sort of appearance-reality distinction for consciousness because con-sciousness consists in the appearances themselves. *Where appearance is concerned we cannot make the appearance-reality distinction because the appearance is the reality.*"[8] This led Searle to suggest that "the ontology of the mental is an irreducibly first-person ontology."[9]

I agree with Searle that the mind cannot be reduced to the brain. In order to see why mind, and ultimately the self, cannot be reduced to the brain, and why the ontology of the mind and self is indeed an irreducibly first-person ontology, it is necessary to further explore the neurological origins and basis of meaning and purpose.

The Neurological Basis of Meaning

We first must understand what meaning and consciousness entail from the perspective of neurology. Lord Brain, one of the most influential neu-rologists of the twentieth-century, provided this beautiful example of how the brain creates meaning:

> When my hand has been exposed to cold air, I say, "My hand is cold," but when I grasp a stone I say, "This stone is cold." In each case what I am experiencing is a cold sense datum, but in the one case I feel it in my hand and in the other case as belonging to an object. How do I perceive the size, shape and solidity of the stone? The touch and pressure sense-data which contact with the object evokes in my fingers are localized and distinguished as relating to different parts of the skin. Furthermore, my fingers themselves will be bent or straightened and separated to a greater or less extent; and each successive movement and posture of any finger arouses sense-data from the tendons and joints. If you move your fingers

when your eyes are closed you are aware of these sense-data as originating in and referring to your fingers; but if you are holding an object in your hand these sense-data become fused with those just described and are felt as collectively conveying awareness of the size, shape and solidity of the object. Thus all the sense-data which are said to belong to an object when it is handled can in suitable conditions be experienced as belonging to the body.[10]

In neurology, we call the process of tactually identifying an object *stereognosis*. For a simple object such as a stone, recognition is almost immediate. But how does this happen? No single point of the body feels the entire stone; rather, the overall shape of the stone is extrapolated from the bending of the joints to accommodate it; its size by the distance between the fingers as they spread to cover as much surface of the stone as possible; its texture by the smoothness or roughness of the stone on the skin tips. If the task at hand is to identify the object, all these sensations that are actually occurring in the joints and skin are *perceived* as attributes of the object. The sensations within the hand are experienced within the "stone." When the sensations of the body are referred to the stone, these sensations have created a *meaning* for the subject.

How did brains that create meaning come into being? To understand how meaningful brains evolved, it is helpful to first point out what nervous systems can accomplish without meaning or consciousness. Neural complexity, in and of itself, does not create meanings or consciousness. Some very primitive reflexes, such as the blink of the eye to a puff of air (known as the corneal reflex), a reflex that is present in any animal with a cornea to protect, involve highly complex neural states. But this reflex will occur even if the animal is asleep. Thus, pure reflexes do not necessarily entail conscious neural states.

Consider, for example, frogs, cats, and dogs whose spinal cords have been surgically separated from the brain. The hind limbs in these animals still will withdraw reflexively in response to certain stimuli, even though the spinal cord connected to that limb is disconnected from the animal's brain. Chemical irritants, tickling, or noxious mechanical irritation would normally invoke pain, itch, or other sensations in the intact animal. But since the involved segments of the spinal cord that receive these stimuli are disconnected from the brain (specifically the part of the brain called the thalamus necessary for conscious pain perception), the animal "feels nothing." Sherrington pointed out that these reflexes occurred without mental accompaniment. Without the central connections to the brain, reflexes can occur and be accompanied by quite complex neural activity, but not by consciousness.[11]

Another circumstance that demonstrates neural complexity in the absence of mind is the unfortunate patient who has had the spinal cord severed. If the spinal cord is severed completely, there is a physical separation of the nervous system above and below the lesion. Neural pathways, which under normal circumstances convey pain impulses, can travel up the spinal cord only partway before being prevented by the cut through the spinal cord from reaching the parts of the brain where conscious sensation occurs. Under these circumstances, if one were to apply a painful stimulus to the foot, such as forcefully squeezing the toe, the foot might still withdraw—reflexively—yet the patient will report she "feels" nothing.

On the other hand, while some quite complex reflexes can occur *without* consciousness, some very simple organisms display behaviors that I would argue *do* involve meaning and consciousness. In the frog, a small, stationary stimulus situated directly in front of the animal evokes no response; it is for all intents and purposes invisible to the animal. But a small moving stimulus anywhere in the frog's visual field evokes an immediate dart of its tongue. Lettvin and coworkers recorded electrical activity from single fibers in the frog optic nerve during various stimulation procedures. They found one fiber population, called "net convexity detectors," that responded when a small dark stimulus entered the receptive field, stopped, and moved about in a jerky fashion—just the kind of activity a mosquito might make if it were flying about in range of the frog's tongue. In fact, they found these fibers so exquisitely suited to detect a flying insect that they suggested they were best described as "bug perceivers."[12]

For the bug perceivers of the frog brain to have "meaning" to the frog, the frog's brain has done something quite remarkable: it has created "an object" for the frog. Now you may say, "Dr. Feinberg, surely you're not suggesting that this frog is thinking to itself 'Oh what a lovely fly . . . I think I'll eat it!'" No, not at all. But let us look at what is happening. The neural activity that creates the meaning "bug" is certainly within the frog's brain. But the frog reacts to that neural activity as though it were not occurring within itself. The frog reacts to that neural activity *as if* it were in the world signifying fly as something that occurs outside the frog's brain and being. The creation of outside objects is the fundamental starting point of all minds and the manner in which meaning is created.

Sherrington called this projection of sensation on the body into the world *projicience,* and he had an explanation for its evolutionary origins. Sherrington reasoned that it was the development of the distance receptors (nose, ear, and eye), that enabled the registration of sensation from stimuli at a distance (smell, sound, and light). For an animal to register a stimulus that really is "out there in the world," the animal had to be wired to react to the stimulus as if it were external and not on the body where the sensory stimulation really is occurring.[13]

Meaning, Qualia, and the Mind-Body Problem

Now here is the crux of the mind-body problem. The very point at which certain neural firings take on *meaning* for the frog is also the point at which the frog's point of view of its own brain and the observer's point of view of the frog's brain diverge. The frog's brain has now taken on a dual aspect: from the "outside" or external point of view, the point of view of the neuroscientist who studies the frog, the frog's neurons are palpable, material, tangible objects; but from the frog's "inner" point of view, those same neurons mean "bug." It follows from this example of the frog's brain that meaningful neural states will always entail two *irreducible* perspectives: the "inside" subjective perspective and the "outside" objective perspective. The experience that the brain creates is meaningful only to one "I," its possessor. In this way, meaning and consciousness are *irreducibly personal.* When a neurological event carries meaning, the subjective aspects of the experience cannot be reduced to the objective neurological events.

Consider again the patient with the spinal cord injury. Suppose I, the neurologist, also acquired the same spinal injury, such that I, like my patient, had no sensation from the waist down. It would make little difference, from the standpoint of my consciousness, if I squeezed my patient's toe or my own. In either circumstance the withdrawal of the toe could occur but neither of us would "feel" anything. If there is no "first person" or "I" associated with the response, there is *no mind or subjective meaning* involved with the reflex. With the subjective aspect of the response entirely removed, the withdrawal of the foot occurred without a subject. If I as the neurologist wish to analyze in this circumstance the reflex, I have no problem reducing the entire reflex to the neurons that created it. I can reduce the entire neurological event, beginning to end, to the firing of the neurons involved in the spinal reflex without recourse to a "mind" or self or an inner "I." However, if either of us *feels* the toe as it is squeezed, if there is an "inner I" that has an experience that means "pain," we do have a problem reducing the neurological event to the brain. Once an event is meaningful, as was the case with the frog and the fly, the observer's point of view and the subject's point of view diverge.

We are now confronted with the difficult issue of qualia, or the "raw feels" of experience. Qualia are the feelings and sensations attached to experience. They are the sensations of "what it is like to be" in a certain brain state. Thus, tastes, smells, sounds, pains are qualia. Some philosophers, like Daniel Dennett, have denied that qualia exist;[14] others, like the philosopher Joseph Levine, claim that there is an unbridgeable gap between qualia and the brain.[15]

The problem of qualia, and the seemingly unbridgeable gap between *observing* a brain in a feeling state and *being* a brain that it is in a feeling state, is highlighted by the use of a fictional device that the philosopher Feigl called an "autocerebroscope."[16] Actually, no one to my knowledge has ever built an autocerebroscope, but nothing in theory would prevent the construction of a fully functional prototype. The autocerebroscope is a contraption that attaches to your head with a probe that goes through your skull. There is a viewer attached to the probe with a magnification device that allows you to observe the neurons of your own brain. Suppose one day, as you are merrily viewing your brain, you come upon your thalamus, the source of your feeling of pain. Suddenly you sneeze, and the scope's eyepiece pokes you in the eye! You now experience intense pain while you are looking through the scope at the very neurons in the thalamus that created that pain.

Now you ask yourself: Did you see anything through your autocerebroscope that was *equal* to the pain that you experienced? Was there anything that you observed that *explained* your pain? You surely saw the neurons responsible for your pain, and you could analyze the brain chemistry of these neurons, but does this allow you to *reduce* your pain to those neurons? It was your neurons themselves, not your image of the neurons through the viewer, that hurts! It occurs to you that there appears to be a *gap* between the neurons as they are observed by you and the neurons themselves as they are experienced by you within your brain. And you cannot find the source of this difference no matter how long and hard you observe your brain and think about the thalamus.

The problem of qualia and the uncertain ontological status of how things feel is also due to the irreducibility of the inside and outside perspectives of the nervous system. Consider again squeezing the toe of a patient who has spinal cord damage. When the spinal cord is intact, it should be obvious that the quale of having one's toe squeezed—the pain involved in the experience—differs fundamentally depending on whether one has the experience of the pain oneself or observes it as a brain having the experience of pain. What is the importance of these differences for the neurologist? If one actually feels pain, one experiences the quale "pain." When the neurologist observes the brain experiencing "pain" from the outside, she sees specific patterns of neural activity that can be accurately defined, but cannot see in the brain something neurological that is equivalent to the experience of "pain." When viewed from the outside therefore, the quale "pain" really does not exist materially. From the outside point of view, my patient's qualia are illusory. Qualia are personal and the relationship between a given *brain* and a given *mind* differs whether one *is* the person having that brain and that experience.

Therefore, the idea that "being something," like a bat, is necessary for an understanding of what it is like to be that thing, in my opinion, does not go far enough. *Being in a state is necessary for its existence.* It only exists relative to something being in that particular state. In order for there to be consciousness, there must be something *being* that consciousness.

This is why qualia, like meaning and purpose, have a fundamentally, irreducibly, first-person ontology. From the outside, we cannot ultimately reduce the experience of "pain" to the neural state that creates it because *there is nothing material from the outside perspective to reduce.* There is no materiality to the experience "pain" from the observer's point of view because the experience of pain from the inner point of view only exists as neural activity from the outside perspective.

This does not mean that qualia don't exist, or that the mind is "immaterial." I do not aim to support any form of Cartesian dualism. To deny that feeling or qualia or consciousness exists is not only wrong, it avoids the question of what qualia really are. I only wish to point out that qualia, like meaning and purpose, only exist from the subjective point of view of the self. Consciousness is a "personal mosaic." The neural states that carry meaning about objects in the world are uniquely "possessed" by the organism and are a *nested part of* that organism's totality. Qualia and being ultimately are not dissociable. Qualia and being are a unity. Teller puts this succinctly when he says "so-called qualia are not some separable feature of brain states which, logically, might or might not accompany them. Talk about qualia is just a confused way of talking about having an experience or of being in the state."[17] Qualia are meanings and meanings are personal. Our visions, our minds, our pains, are *personal* and have no *material* existence for anyone but ourselves. This is how neural states can mean something for the individual, can be that person's "mind," but for the observer, that mind does not materially exist.

The Brain Is Not About Itself

Now here comes the tricky part. What is it about the brain, what neuro-logical factor or property allows the brain to create subjective neural activities? There is a simple fact about the brain that is often neglected that provides the answer to this question. *The conscious brain has no sensation of itself.* It has been known since the time of Aristotle that the brain is insensate.[18] For instance, sticking a pin in the cortex itself evokes no pain that is referable to the brain itself. The brain has no sensory apparatus directed toward itself. As Globus puts it, the brain does not "represent in any way its own structure to the subject."[19] There is no way that the subject can become aware of his own neurons "from the inside." They can be known only objectively from the "outside." We have already seen that there is no "inner eye," no inner homunculus watching the brain itself, perceiving its own neurons, no "brain-skin" which feels the neurosurgeon's knife. When I test a patients' pinprick sensitivity by applying a pin to the hand, and I ask them to localize where on the body the sensation is, no one has ever pointed to their head. Conscious neural activity refers to things, not to the brain itself. Conscious neural states are *about* things, not about the neurons themselves (Figure 9–1).

Figure 9-1.
I have assessed many patients' ability to locate a painful stimulus on the surface of the body, yet never has a single one pointed to their head. From my perspective, however, the neurons responsible for the pain are located in the patient's brain. The brain is unique in the way it produces meanings that refer to things other than itself.

Just as meaning has a personal ontology, individual *purpose* also possesses a first-person ontology and exists only from the "inside" perspective of the self. From the observer's standpoint, we cannot locate in the brain an individual's purpose. The "will" is not something that can be touched or pointed to. One can identify the pattern of neural firing that creates volitional action within the brain, but there is nothing about the pattern of a particular neuron's firing that distinguishes its firing as part of a willful action per se. Just as meaning is embodied within the pattern of neural firing within the brain, individual purpose is *embodied* within the nested hierarchy of a person's actions. The ontology of purpose and action, like the ontology of meaning, is irreducibly personal.

Many philosophers have argued that one of the essential characteristics of the mind is the property of *intentionality*. The use of the word "intentionality" dates to medieval times. The term derives from the Latin verb *intendo,* which means to "point at" or "extend toward." Intentional phenomena are said to be *about* or *of* or *directed at* something. For example, beliefs are considered intentional because they are *about* a state of affairs. A fear is considered an intentional state because it is a fear *of* something. Perceptual states are considered intentional because if I experience an object in the world, whether I see, hear, touch, or smell it, then I have a perception *of* an object. In a similar way, action states are considered intentional when they are *directed at* something in the world.[20]

The seventeenth-century philosopher and psychologist Franz Brentano argued that intentionality is the defining feature of the mental, and only mental phenomena possess the characteristic of intentionality. Consider how Searle spoke about intentional states:

> The second intractable feature of the mind is what philosophers and psychologists call "intentionality," the feature by which our mental states are directed at, or about, or refer to, or are of objects and states of affairs in the world other than themselves."[21]

From the philosophical perspective, intentional mental states are directed at or *refer* to something other than themselves. On the basis of neurological considerations, I have argued that the origin of meaning and minds—from frog to human—are based on the fact that the conscious brain does not refer to itself. The similarity between the neurological perspective and the philosophical point of view is striking.

The Living Mind

The What, Where, and How of the Self

In the first chapter of this book, a number of questions were raised about the self. The first was "*What is the self?*" I believe the evidence supports the existence of a Kantian "I" at the center of each of us that is the subject of our conscious experience and the core of our being. The margins of the "I" are not entirely fixed, however, and they change throughout one's life. The patients in this book with altered egos demonstrate the dramatic, surprising, and sometimes frightening flexibility of the margins of the self.

Another question posed was "*Where is the self located in the brain?*" When we consider the brains of patients with perturbations of the self, one message comes through loud and clear: Many different areas of the brain contribute to the preservation of the self. From the asomatognosia cases we learn that the nondominant parietal lobe is essential to the feeling of ownership of a limb. Analysis of the neurology of patients with misidentification syndromes teaches us that many areas of the brain contribute to our personal relatedness to the world. The patients with personal confabulation demonstrate that both frontal lobes are necessary for a proper relationship between the self and the world, and the split-brain patients demonstrate the manner in which the corpus callosum contributes to mental unity. While the many parts of the brain create the self, however, there is no specific material locus of the self or the inner "I" within the brain.

The third question raised was "*How does the brain produce a unified self?*" The brain is extended and divisible, but the self is unified and integrated. The integration of the self cannot be explained by its emergence at the top of the hierarchy of a non-nested brain. The brain creates the unity of the self by producing a nested hierarchy of meaning and purpose, where the levels the self, and the many parts of the brain that contribute to the self, are nested within all other levels of the hierarchy. The brain has no pinnacle of consciousness, but we experience ourselves as unified because our meanings and our actions are unified within the nested self.

Beings and Brains

If Descartes' enigma is solved, and Descartes' dualistic solution to the mind-body problem was incorrect, then what is the answer to the final question *"What is the relationship between the brain and the mind?"* The answer leads to a most surprising and curious result. We know that the brain is a material object in the world. On the other hand, the neurological evidence confirms that the self has an entirely "first-person existence." The consciousness of each individual is uniquely related to the self. Our minds are a part of us, of our living being. The material existence of a mind depends solely on something *being* that mind.

If the existence of a mind presupposes a subjective personal point of view, and if a subjective point of view presupposes a being, the presence of consciousness presupposes life. The question then becomes What is it about life that allows the creation of a being, and what actually is a being?[1]

Evolution creates from nonlife living things—only some of which are beings. Being alive does not guarantee that a thing is a being. For instance, what about a plant? A plant is alive, it carries on respiration, metabolizes, moves, and so on. We humans have much in common with plants. We surely have a lot more in common with plants than with, for example, rocks. But is a plant a being? The majority of people don't think so. Despite the similarity between plants and ourselves, we do not consider plants beings because plants are simply not enough like "us" to be considered beings like us.

What about a frog? Is a frog a being? Although many people would claim that a frog is not a being, a case could be made that a frog is a primitive being. In the preceding chapters, it was argued that a frog has a primitive mind, and the presence of a mind is surely an important ingredient of a being. So, for me, a frog is a being. What about a chimpanzee? Is a chimp a being? Most people would agree that a chimp is a being. But again, what are the clear and objective criteria for this determination? It appears that all the features we do share with chimps—life, intelligence, some individual social identity—make chimps seem so much like us that we intuitively grant chimps "beinghood."

In the final analysis, there is no single criteria for determining whether or not something is a being, and the criteria that we do use do not seem terribly objective or clear-cut. On the other hand, there seems to be a cluster of features that we uniquely identify with being human, and it seems the more something possesses those features, the more likely we are to consider it a being. These features include, but are not restricted to, being alive, having subjectivity, and, finally, possessing a mind.

What about computers? Will the human race someday decide that an advanced computer is a being? Is it possible, at some point in the future, that someone could be charged with murder if they pulled the plug on a PC? Not a likely prospect. Even now, computers can be pretty smart at times, more so than frogs in many ways. In the years to come, computers will get even smarter. But a computer is not alive, and a computer is not a being. No matter how intelligent a computer may be, a frog on a lily pad soaking up some noonday sun is more a being than a computer. It follows that between frogs and computers, only the frog can have a mind. I doubt that computers will ever be considered conscious, because in order for a computer to be "conscious like us" and to have "feelings like us" it will need to be made like us and be alive like us. This is why I cannot take seriously the claim that a mind could be made out of silicon chips if only you could put them in the correct combination. It is more likely that the particular material substance of our brains is essential to the quality of our consciousness. To be enough like a human being to be considered conscious by us, a computer would have to be like us, of the same matter and process, and this includes being alive. In the nested hierarchy of an organism, all its parts—the cells, tissues, organs—are alive, and the life of the parts is what makes the entire thing alive. "Life" is simply not present in silicon chips.[2] Life itself is so indispensable to the mind that this probably rules out silicon-chip computers as candidates for consciousness or selves. In the final analysis, each mind is intimately connected to our lives and part of our lives as organisms. For this reason, our minds are just as much alive as our brains, and to have a mind is *to be* a living nested hierarchy of meaning and purpose. The mind is irreducibly personal. It begins and ends with the possessor of that mind and has an existence only for that person.

So here I am, inside my head, my inner mind, my pains, no more than illusion to you who read these words. There is a certain loneliness to all this, but this is the cost of the evolution of our brains. When self-aware minds developed their independence from the world, they separated from other selves, other beings, as well. As the life of every organism is surely unique, so is the mind. The ultimate personal uniqueness of each and every organism's mind and being is what we refer to as the "soul." The soul of each brain is indeed a unique, one-of-a-kind thing. We can donate an organ or provide blood for transfusions, but the meaning of oneself to oneself possesses a reality that can only be experienced by one person.

As our minds separate us from one another, however, so are they shared. The cases in this book demonstrate the dramatic ways in which the mind and the self can be altered. Transformations of the margins of the self, however, are not restricted to persons with brain damage. Each and every one of us, nearly every day, experiences change in the margins of the self. Whenever we identify with another person, put ourselves in another person's place, experience sadness when confronted with another's pain, or rejoice at another's good fortune, we partially merge with another's person's mind, thus sharing their subjective experience.

I am not suggesting that when we identify with others, anything materially, physically transfers between persons. However, I am proposing that under these circumstances a merging of minds does occur in more than a purely figurative sense. When we enter into states of mutual identification, when we love someone, for instance, or are bonded in friendship, or are part of a family, we enter into a new nested relationship of minds.

Notes

Chapter 1

1. I refer to these conditions elsewhere as *perturbations of the self* (Feinberg, 1997c). The clinical cases I describe in this book were collected over a fifteen-year period either during my training in neurology and psychiatry or later in my clinical practice. All the patients are real, but their identities have been concealed. Some of the clinical disorders I discuss here have been considered by neurologists in recent books. In his *Descartes' Error* (1994) and more recently in *The Feeling of What Happens* (1999), Antonio Damasio discusses some of the conditions I describe in this book. In the latter volume, Damasio offers his own theory of the neurobiology of the self and considers at length the role emotion plays in the neurobiology of the self. Damasio proposes that there are three levels of the self: the *proto-self*, that is an unconscious neural representation of the current state of the organism; the *core-self*, that is a conscious "second-order nonverbal account that occurs whenever an object modifies the proto-self"; and an *autobiographical self*, a conscious aspect of the self that is "is based on autobiographical memory which is constituted by implicit memories of multiple instances of individual experience of the past and of the anticipated future." The autobiographical self is "based on permanent but dispositional records of core-self experiences." The three levels of the self that are proposed by Damasio appear to be hierarchically arranged, with the proto-self the most basic and the autobiographical self the most advanced or complex aspect of the self. I do not explore in this book many of the brain regions, such as the brain stem, reticular formation, hypothalamus and thalamus that are necessary for the existence of basic consciousness, but Damasio provides an excellent and detailed discussion of these neuroanatomical structures, and the reader is referred to his work for a complete neuroanatomical discussion of these regions. In the present work, while I do not divide the self into discrete neuroanatomical levels, I do attempt to explain how different levels of the neuroaxis create the unified self, and therefore I view Damasio's and my approach as complimentary. For a helpful summary and commentary of Damasio's *The Feeling of What Happens*, see the recent review by Watt (2000). Richard Restak provides an insightful discussion of the neurology of the self and the problem of mental unity in *The Modular Brain* (1994). In *Phantoms in the Brain* (1998), Ramachandran and Blakeslee also analyze some of the neurological conditions that affect the self. In particular, see the chapters on anosognosia and Capgras syndrome for a consideration of some of the possible mechanisms of these disorders.

2. McGinn, 1999.
3. In order to understand how to read the scan, imagine that John is lying down, facing the ceiling, and you are standing at his feet, looking at his head. This vantage point puts the right side of his head on your left side. The pictures resulting from the scan can be thought of as horizontal slices through John's head. It is as if you cut an orange, slice by slice, and, after each slice, took a picture. In this book, the area of brain damage is cross-hatched. Throughout this book I refer to MRI and CAT scans. Although MRI scans and CAT scans are made using different technologies, both scans provide a picture of the brain's structure. For our purposes, the description of how to read John's MRI scan can apply to the reading of the CAT scans as well.
4. Schilder and Stengel (1928; 1931) provided the first clinical descriptions of pain asymbolia that they initially called "Schmerzasymbolie." In the most severe cases of pain asymbolia, the patient does not react to threats of physical harm of any sort. Persons with pain asymbolia understand on an "intellectual" level that something could hurt or injure them. The problem is that the patient does not show any emotional reaction to dangerous stimuli. For example, the patient understands that fire can cause burns, but will not flinch or withdraw if a match is held directly in front of the eyes. While the majority of cases with pain asymbolia have damage to the left hemisphere, some cases have been recorded that have damage to the right hemisphere (Berthier et al., 1988). Berthier and coworkers studied six cases with the condition, and all six patients had damage to an area of the brain called the insular cortex. They argued that the damage to this area of the brain interrupted the *connections* between the sensory cortex, an area of the brain responsible for the sense of touch, and the limbic system, a brain area that is responsible for emotions.
5. I am not a philosopher, but I address some philosophical issues in this book to determine how my neurological model fits with some philosophical positions. To my surprise and pleasure, some philosophical work fits quite nicely with the model of the brain and mind that I propose. This convergence of neurology and philosophy is encouraging because a correct theory of the self and the mind will need to satisfy both scientists and philosophers. I address those philosophical viewpoints that pertain most directly to brain functioning. For comprehensive and accessible reviews of philosophical and psychological ideas about the self, see Jerome Levin (1992) and Wilkes (1988). For in-depth philosophical discussions on the philosophy of self, see Cassam (1994; 1997). For recent discussions of the philosophy of mind and consciousness, see Searle (1984; 1992); Nagel (1979; 1986; 1995); P. S. Churchland (1986); Dennett (1991); Rosenthal (1991); Flanagan (1991; 1992); P. S. M. Churchland (1993; 1996); Chalmers (1996); McGinn (1997; 1999); Tye (1995); Block, Flanagan, and Güzeldere (1997).
6. William James, 1890; reprinted 1983, p. 345.
7. William James, 1892; reprinted 1985, p. 70.
8. Cited in Eccles, 1994, p. 1.
9. Horgan, 1999, p. 23.

Chapter 2

1. Classical descriptions of asomatognosic patients can be found in Macdonald Critchley's monumental work *The Parietal Lobes* (1953) and also in Gerstmann (1942). An analysis of the neuroanatomy of asomatognosia can be found in Feinberg et al., 1990.
2. For a review of the neglect syndrome and its clinical manifestations, see Heilman et al., 1993, and Heilman et al., 1997; Ramachandran and Blakeslee, 1998.
3. This case was cited in Nielsen, 1938.
4. Nielsen, 1938.
5. Spillane, 1942.
6. Ullman, 1960.
7. We examined a series of twelve patients with asomatognosia (Feinberg et al., 1990). All twelve had severe left hemispatial neglect. However, there were many patients in this study with neglect who did not demonstrate the syndrome of asomatognosia. Therefore we may conclude that neglect is a necessary but not sufficient condition for the occurrence of asomatognosia.
8. Gainotti et al., 1972; Albert, 1973.
9. Heilman and Van Den Abell, 1979.
10. Neurologist Marsel Mesulam (1985) suggests: "Patients with unilateral neglect ... behave not only as if nothing were actually happening in the left hemispace but also as if nothing of any importance could be expected to occur there" (p.149).
11. For other good examples of the drawings of patients with neglect, see Critchley, 1953; Mesulam, 1985.
12. Ullman, 1960.
13. Critchley, 1955.
14. Weinstein and Kahn, 1955; Weinstein and Cole, 1964; Weinstein et al., 1964.
15. Weinstein and Friedland, 1977; Weinstein, 1991.
16. Gilliatt and Pratt, 1952.
17. Critchley, 1974.
18. Halligan, Marshall, and Wade, 1993.
19. Halligan, Marshall, and Wade, 1995.
20. Critchley, 1974.
21. See the classic work *Denial of Illness* by Weinstein and Kahn (1955). Excellent works that contain general discussions of psychological denial are *Denial and Defense in the Therapeutic Situation* by Theodore Dorpat (1985) and *The Denial of Stress* (1983) edited by Breznitz. Lewis (1991) provides a very helpful review of psychological denial as it pertains to neurological illness.
22. On the topic of the relationship between confabulation and anosognosia for hemiplegia, see Feinberg et al. (1994); Feinberg (1997a); Feinberg and Roane (1997a). Critchley (1953) observed that when patients who were anosognosic for their hemiplegic arms were told to raise their paralyzed limbs, these patients would often insist that the arm really had moved or moved "less quickly" than the normal arm. V.S. Ramachandran (Ramachandran and Blakeslee, 1998) described a patient who claimed when Dr. Ramachandran

stood before her that she could touch his nose. The same patient claimed that she could clap with both her hands. We recently found a high degree of correlation between anosognosia, asomatognosia, and the tendency to confabulate limb movements (Feinberg, Roane, and Ali, 2000).

23. Babinski, 1914; 1918.
24. Anton, 1899. Anton's most famous case was a fifty-six-year-old seamstress named Ursula Mercz, who was blind yet denied her visual loss. For an excellent historical review and translation of some of Anton's work, see Förstl et al. (1993). See also McGlynn and Schacter (1989).

Chapter 3

1. The terms "ego-close" and "ego-distant" can be found in the writings of Paul Schilder, 1965, pp. 298–99.
2. Capgras and Reboul-Lachaux, 1923.
3. Gluckman, 1968; Christodoulou, 1986a; Luauté, 1986.
4. There are thousands of articles on the delusional misidentification syndromes, but two volumes that provide a comprehensive introduction to the subject are Ellis, Luauté, and Retterstol (eds.) 1994; and Christodoulou (ed.), 1986a.
5. Merrin and Silberfarb, 1976; Todd, Dewhurst, and Wallis, 1981; Christodoulou, 1986b; 1991; Kimura, 1986; Signer, 1987; Förstl, Almeida, and Owen et al., 1991; Signer, 1992; Spier, 1992; Mendez, Martin, Symth et al., 1992; Fleminger and Burns, 1993; Feinberg and Roane, 1997b.
6. Larrivé and Jasienski, 1931.
7. Davidson, 1941.
8. Anderson, 1988; Anderson and Williams, 1994.
9. Freud, 1909/1959.
10. Rank, 1952.
11. Freud, 1909/1959.
12. Dostoyevsky, 1971.
13. Ellis, Whitley, and Luauté, 1994. This article provides a valuable translation of the original article by Capgras and Reboul-Lachaux with enlightening commentary from the authors. (see note 14 below)
14. Courbon and Fail, 1927. Ellis, Whitley, and Luauté (1994) contains a translation of this article as well.
15. Burnham, 1956.
16. Feinberg et al., 1999.
17. Pick, 1903.
18. Patterson and Zangwill, 1944.
19. Levin, 1951
20. Levin, 1933.
21. Levin, 1953.
22. Levin, 1945.
23. Levin, 1968.
24. Feinberg, 1997c; Feinberg and Roane, 1997a; 1997b.

25. Benson et al., 1976.
26. Ruff and Volpe, 1981.
27. Feinberg and Shapiro, 1989. See also Burgess and Baxter et al., 1996.
28. Staton, Brumback, and Wilson, 1982.
29. Alexander et al., 1979. For a review of the limbic system, see LeDoux, 1996; also Ramachandran and Blakeslee, 1998.
30. Alexander et al., 1979.
31. Staton, Brumback, and Wilson, 1982.
32. Ellis and Young, 1990.
33. Landis et al., 1986.
34. Van Lancker and Klein, 1990; Van Lancker, 1991.

Chapter 4

1. Feinberg, 1997a; Feinberg and Roane, 1997b.
2. Berlyne, 1972.
3. Koppleman, 1980. For a review of the topic of confabulation, see also Moscovitch, 1995.
4. Stuss et al., 1978.
5. For an accesible yet comprehensive guide to memory research, see Schacter, 1996.
6. Van der Horst, 1932.
7. Victor, Adams, and Collins, 1989.
8. Bonhoeffer, 1901; 1904.
9. Eslinger, 1998. Damasio (1999) discusses at length the role that autobiographical memory plays in the creation of the self. See also Rubin (1986).
10. Cited by Schacter, 1996 from Tulving, 1983.
11. Eslinger, 1998.
12. Weinstein and Kahn, 1955.
13. Weinstein, Kahn, and Morris, 1956.
14. Weinstein and Lyerly, 1968.
15. Baddeley and Wilson, 1986.
16. Weinstein, Kahn, and Malitz, 1956.
17. In Weinstein and Kahn, 1955, p. 105, the authors describe their use of the "king story" as a vehicle for bringing out denial.
18. Weinstein, Kahn, and Morris, 1956.
19. Ibid.
20. Stuss et al., 1978.
21. Kapur and Coughlan, 1980.
22. Fischer et al., 1995.
23. DeLuca and Cicerone, 1991; for a review on the subject of the sequelae of frontal aneurysm rupture, see DeLuca and Diamond, 1995.
24. Stuss et al., 1978.
25. See also Stuss, 1991, for additional thoughts on this issue.
26. Gazzaniga, 1985.

Chapter 5

1. Feinberg and Shapiro, 1989.
2. Gluckman, 1968. Foley and Breslau (1982) briefly described seven cases with mirror misidentification. Like Gluckman's case, paranoid attitudes toward the mirror image were noted in patients of Foley and Breslau. Mirror misidentification has frequently reported to occur as part of the dementia of Alzheimer's disease. (See Rubin et al., 1988; Burns et al., 1990; and Mendez et al., 1992.) Spangenberg et al. (1998) reported a recent case of mirror misidentification that may have been due to vascular disease.
3. William James, 1892; Reprinted 1985, p. 43.
4. Gallup, 1970; 1977a; 1977b; 1982; Gallup et al., 1995. See also Povinelli et al., 1993; 1997. For a spirited debate on the issue of self-awareness in nonhuman primates, see Heyes, 1998.
5. For a review of some aspects of the double in religion, mythology, and folklore, see Todd and Dewhurst, 1955, 1962; and Christodoulou, 1986c.
6. Tymms (1949) provides a fascinating and extensive review of the theme of the double in world literature. In this work, Tymms reviews the double in Richter's work.
7. Cited by Tymms, 1949, p. 30.
8. Todd and Dewhurst, 1955.
9. Lhermitte, 1951; Damas Mora et al., 1980.
10. Todd and Dewhurst, 1955.
11. Ibid.
12. Devinsky et al., 1989.
13. Todd and Dewhurst, 1955.
14. Lippman, 1953.
15. Todd and Dewhurst, 1962.
16. Barth, 1890, cited by Todd and Dewhurst, 1962.
17. Rank, 1971, p. 83.
18. Ibid., p. 84.
19. Svendsen, 1934.
20. Sperling, 1954.
21. Nagera, 1969.
22. Murphy, 1962.
23. Frailberg, 1959.
24. Critchley, 1979.
25. The belief that a stranger is living in the house has been called the "phantom boarder syndrome." (See Rowan, 1984; Rubin et al., 1988; Burns et al., 1990; and Malloy et al., 1992.)

Chapter 6

1. Innocenti, 1986; Trevarthen, 1991.
2. Bogen (1993) provides an excellent review of the history of corpus callosotomy and the effects of corpus callosotomy on human behavior.

3. For a review of this work, see Gazzaniga (1985); Gazzaniga and Volpe (1981); Gazzaniga (1970); and Gazzaniga and LeDoux (1978).
4. Wigan, 1844a; 1844b. For a modern version of this hypothesis, see Puccetti, 1981.
5. Harrington (1987) does a remarkable job reviewing and analyzing the history of work on the nature of the two cerebral hemispheres. This is a must-read for anyone interested in the history of neurology and brain research.
6. Goldstein 1908, pp. 69–70; cited by Harrington, 1987.
7. Feinberg, et al., 1992; Feinberg, Roane, and Cohen, 1998.
8. Feinberg et al., 1992; Feinberg, 1997c. There have been several neuroanatomical studies of the alien hand syndrome, and controversy exists regarding the existence of clinical subtypes of the syndrome and its underlying anatomy. For additional review of these issues see Della Sala, 1991; Gasquoine, 1993; Tanaka et al., 1996; Chan and Liu, 1999.
9. Gazzaniga, 1970, p.107.
10. Geschwind, et al., 1995.
11. Ibid.
12. Goldberg and Bloom, 1990. This report also includes a discussion of possible mechanisms of alien hand syndrome.
13. Ibid.
14. Bogen, 1993.
15. Stuss and Benson, 1986, p. 88.
16. Sperry, Gazzaniga, and Bogen, 1969; Sperry, 1984.
17. Sperry, 1990; Trevarthen, 1991.
18. Bogen, 1993; Sperry, 1990; Trevarthen, 1991.
19. Examples and reviews of this fascinating research can be found in Levy, Trevarthen, and Sperry, 1972; Levy and Trevarthen, 1976; Levy, 1977, 1990; and Sperry, Zaidel, and Zaidel, 1979.
20. Trevarthen, 1974.
21. Levy, 1990, p. 235.
22. Ibid.
23. Trevarthen, 1991.
24. Feinberg, 1997a; Feinberg and Roane, 1997a.

Chapter 7

1. Kaas, 1989.
2. Van Essen, Anderson, and Felleman, 1992.
3. Kaas, 1993.
4. See, for example, Van Essen et al., 1992.
5. In philosophy, the problem of explaining the distributedness of the brain and the subjectively experienced seamlessness of consciousness is known as the "grain" problem, argument, or objection. The use of the term "grain" with reference to the philosophy of consciousness originates with Sellar (1963). The "grain argument" is a counterargument to Feigl's (1967) "identity argument." The identity argument asserts that mental states are identical with

neural states, for example, there is nothing about mental states that needs to be explained beyond the understanding of the neural states that create them. The "grain argument" points out that subjective experience is homogeneous, unified, and without grain (Teller, 1992), in contrast to the brain, which is a "'gappy,' heterogeneous, discontinuous conglomerate of spatially discrete events" (Meehl, 1966, p. 167). Based on these differences, neural events cannot be identical with mental states. See also Feinberg, 1997b, 2000.

6. Boring, in his monumental *A History of Experimental Psychology* (1959) opines that Descartes "marks the actual beginning of modern psychology."

7. Descartes (Les Passions de l'ame, Pt. I, article 30, 1649). Translation from Beakley and Ludlow, 1992, p. 111.

8. Descartes (Les Passions de l'ame, Pt. I, article 32, 1649). Translation from Clarke and O'Malley, 1996, p. 471.

9. Sherrington, 1947.

10. Ibid., p. xiv.

11. Sherrington, 1941, p. 277. The earliest use of the term "pontifical cell" that I have found is James, 1890/1983, p. 181.

12. For the reader who is interested in an introduction to the biology of the visual system, see Kandel, Schwartz and Jessell, 2000; A book that I have found particularly useful, especially on the issues that pertain to visual awareness, is Zeki's *A Vision of the Brain* (1993). I primarily used these two sources for this overview of the visual system.

13. Hubel and Wiesel, 1962; 1965; 1977; 1968; For summaries of Hubel and Wiesel's work, see Hubel and Wiesel, 1979; and Hubel, 1988.

14. Zeki, 1993, p. 298.

15. For a nice discussion of the idea of the "grandmother cell" and some of the history of the idea, see Barlow, 1995.

16. The cells of V_1, the primary visual area, have relatively small receptive fields that make the precise localization of a stimulus' position in space possible. On the other hand, V_5, an area further along the processing stream and specialized for movement perception, has cells with large receptive fields that respond to movement across large segments of visual space. The larger receptive fields of V_5 cells that are adequate or even necessary for the detection of motion are clearly inadequate for precise spatial localization. Therefore, processing information about a large moving object at a certain point in space would require the information of both V_1 and V_5 to be conscious. But this arrangement poses a real problem for visual unification. There is a wonderful experiment by Movshon, Adelson, Gizzi, and Newsome (1985) that illustrates this problem beautifully. They have demonstrated that when certain shapes are viewed behind a small circular aperture, conflicting movement information would be perceived at the level of the primary visual cortex (V_1). For instance, if the information went no further than V_1, adjacent sides of a horizontally moving diamond would appear to be traveling in different directions. Due to their small receptive fields, the cells of V_1 are able to encode the exact locus of a stimulus in space, but they are unable to discern the pattern of movement of a single object behind the aperture. The cells

of V5, unlike the cells of V1, are able to respond appropriately to the movement of the actual overall object. But if the "whole object" represented in V5 were the only conscious representation of the stimulus, the "local sign," for example, the exact topographical locus of a stimulus in space, would be lost. In order to know where the whole object moving in space is located, input from V1 and V5 is required. Therefore, the visual system must enable both V1 and V5 to make "explicit" contributions to visual perception.

17. Zeki, 1993, p. 301. In support of this position, Beckers and Zeki (1995) performed an experiment using a technique known as transcranial magnetic stimulation (TMS). In TMS, a magnetic pulse is applied to the scalp, creating a localized and reversible inactivation of the underlying brain. When the cells of area V1 of normal subjects are inactivated with a pulse applied to the back of the head, conscious motion perception that requires an active V5 is still possible, although the ability to judge the orientation of stationary objects, which requires exquisite point localization, is lost. Thus, the patient saw something "move" but didn't know exactly where it was. Based on this observation, Beckers and Zeki were able to conclude that V5 appears to make a conscious contribution to the perception of motion that is wholly independent of V1, the primary visual region.

18. Dennett, 1991.

19. Pinker addresses the issue of the homunculus from the standpoint of cognitive neuroscience in *How the Mind Works,* 1997, p. 79.

20. Recently, there has been a tremendous amount written about the "binding problem." For some reviews of this complicated topic, see Crick and Koch, 1990; Crick, 1994; von der Malsburg, 1995; König and Engel, 1995; Treisman, 1996; Hardcastle, 1997; Singer, 1998; 1999. There is a special issue of *Consciousness and Cognition* (volume 8, no. 2, June 1999) devoted to this topic that provides an excellent overview of the area. This issue contains an interesting article by Antti Revonsuo (1999) which specifically addresses the relationship between neuroscientific approaches to binding and the problem of mental unity from the standpoint of philosophy. Revonsuo distinguishes between perceptual binding, that he refers to as *stimulus-related binding* and the phenomenal unity of experience that he terms *consciousness-related binding*. He also refers to *cognitive binding*. He argues that some examples of stimulus-related binding, such as the demonstration of neural synchronization in an anesthetized (and therefore unconscious) animal, suggests that stimulus-related binding may be dissociated from consciousness-related binding. The degree that these forms of binding overlap requires further explication. In this book I deal with these various forms of binding as different aspects of the same fundamental neurophilosophical problem regarding the unity of the self. However, it is certainly possible, even likely, that different types of binding occur via different mechanisms.

21. In addition to the references in note 20, for some earlier papers on the role of oscillations in binding and awareness, see Gray and Singer, 1989; Gray et al., 1989; Engel et al., 1991; Crick and Koch, 1990; and Gray et al., 1992.

22. Crick, 1994, p. 245.

23. Edelman, 1989.
24. Ryle, 1949.
25. Tinbergen, 1951, p.125.

Chapter 8

1. Kim, 1992. Kim also addresses the issues of emergence and reduction in the philosophy of consciousness in Kim, 1995. In a recent book, Kim (1998) notes that emergentism is showing "strong signs of a comeback" not only in philosophy, but in "psychology, cognitive science, systems theory, and the like" (pp. 8–9). For an excellent overview of emergence theory in the philosophy of the mind, see Beckermann, Flohr, and Kim (1992).
2. Campbell, 1974.
3. Pattee, 1970, p.119.
4. Discussions of hierarchy theory and constraint in biological systems can be found in Whyte, Wilson, and Wilson (1969); Pattee (1973); Ayala and Dobzhansky (1974); Allen and Starr (1982); and Salthe (1985). Lively and engaging accounts of hierarchies in a host of settings can be found in the works of Arthur Koestler. Probably his best known work is *The Ghost in the Machine* (1967). For an excellent summary of his work see Koestler (1978). Koestler coined the term *"holon"* to describe the subwholes found in all hierarchies.
5. Medawar and Medawar, 1977.
6. Ibid., p. 177.
7. Searle, 1992, pp. 112–13.
8. Ibid., p.113.
9. Morgan, 1923, p. 35.
10. The brilliant scientist-philosopher Michael Polanyi (1965) provided an analysis of emergence as it pertains to stereoscopic vision. Polanyi's more general views on the emergence of consciousness can be found in Polanyi (1966) and (1968).
11. Sperry, 1977. Reprinted in Trevarthen, 1990, p. 383.
12. Ibid., p. 382. See also Sperry, 1965; 1966; and Sperry, 1984.
13. Sperry, 1977. Reprinted in Trevarthen, 1990, p. 384.
14. Scott, 1995, pp. 172, 5.
15. For a discussion of the differences between nested and non-nested hierarchies, see Allen and Starr, 1982, pp. 38–47; and Salthe, 1985, pp. 9–11.
16. Allen and Starr (1982) provided a definition of a nested hierarchy: "A nested hierarchy is one where the holon at the apex of the hierarchy contains and is composed of all lower holons. The apical holon consists of the sum of the substance and the interactions of all its daughter holons and is, in that sense, derivable from them. Individuals are nested within populations, organs within organisms, tissues within organs, and tissues are composed of cells" (p. 38). As noted in note 4, holons are subwholes or parts of hierarchies.
17. This model helps explain the aperture problem raised by the experiment of Movshon and coworkers previously discussed (chapter 7, note 16). We saw

how the cells of V1, the primary visual areas, have small receptive fields that make the precise localization of stimulus position in space possible. On the other hand, V5, an area specialized for movement perception, which receives input from, among areas, area V1, has cells with large receptive fields that respond to movement across large segments of visual space. The brain areas V1 and V5 appear as separate, hierarchically arranged brain regions, with V1 feeding V5 downstream, and V5 feeding upstream back to V1. When viewed in this fashion, V1 and V5 appear as part of a non-nested hierarchy with a larger number of neurons converging on a smaller number of neurons and the simultaneous emergence of more specific properties. Indeed, in this process, the emergence of higher order features *necessitates* that the cells beyond V1 be responsive to stimuli across a large portion of the visual field. But if this were the only conscious representation, the exact topographic locus of a stimulus in space would be lost. However, as we have seen, the mind does not lose the properties of the lower order neurons (i.e., the exact position of the stimulus is not lost despite the creation of new properties). The brain operates as a nested hierarchical system, wherein V1 neurons continue to make a contribution to awareness as well as contribute to the emergence of the higher order features present in the cells of V5.

18. At one time in the history of science, purpose was felt to be everywhere, especially when it came to human beings. The products of natural selection are so well suited to their tasks that it was assumed for centuries that someone or something had a purposeful hand in their design. Aristotle suggested that 'final causes' played a role in the creation of life, but this position is now seen, in the light of modern biology, as an example of "teleological thinking." We now know that fins were not "intentionally" designed so that fish could swim, or that human hands were intentionally "designed" so that we could grasp with opposable thumbs. In other words, natural selection does not set out with a predetermined goal in mind at its outset (see Mayr, 1974, p. 96; see also Searle, 1992, pp. 51–52).

19. Searle points out that some actions that may seem intentional actually are not. In order to make this point he compares the statements " I am thirsty" with the statement "My lawn is thirsty." In the first instance, there is a real conscious entity that possesses a true intentional desire to drink. Searle calls this *intrinsic* intentionality. In the second statement, we do not suppose the lawn actually "thinks" it is thirsty, or has a desire to drink, or intends to soak up some water. The lawn does not have an intentional desire to drink, and therefore the lawn does not have an intentional state. Rather, when we say the lawn is thirsty, we are speaking metaphorically. Searle refers to this condition as *as-if* intentionality (Searle, 1992, pp. 78–82). While agreeing with Searle, I would prefer to call the lawn's mechanism a teleonomic but non-purposeful action.

20. Mayr, 1974; 1982.

21. Braithwaite, 1953, p. 326.

22. Myers, 1976.

23. Our meanings and purposes did not just suddenly appear on the evolutionary landscape. Rather they have slowly evolved from the complexity of

organisms. With the highly evolved brain development of humans, the most advanced state of outside object projection, objectification, and differentiation from the self is made possible. Simple neural states such as those that result in reflexive behaviors ultimately evolved into complex neural states that carry ever more sophisticated meanings for the organism. There simply is no actual discontinuity between reflex and purposeful action, between the pupillary response to light and contemplating a Picasso painting. When compared with the simple reflexes of a snail, our human purposes seem prescient, our meanings sublime. I suspect, despite this, that if our intentions and awareness were compared with those of some hypothetical higher more evolved life form in some other place or time in the universe, they might appear to them as nothing more than reflexes.

24. It is a daunting task to acquaint oneself with the writings of J. H. Jackson. I refer the reader to one of Jackson's most famous works, his Croonian lectures of 1884 (reprinted in Taylor J., ed., *Selected Writings of John Hughlings Jackson*, vol. 2, 1958, pp. 45–75.) An excellent resource on Jackson's work is Harrington, 1987. Also see Levin, 1953.

25. Jackson, 1884 reprinted in Taylor, ed., vol. 2, 1958, p. 49.

26. Monrad-Krohn, 1924; Feiling, 1927.

27. See Damasio, 1994, pp. 139–143, for more on the dissociation between voluntary and spontaneous emotional expression.

28. See Ramachandran and Blakeslee, 1998, pp. 199–211, for an interesting take on pathological laughter.

29. *Consciousness and Cognition* (volume 8, no. 2, June 1999).

30. Scott, 1995.

31. Harth (1993) suggested a different solution to the "inner eye" problem. He proposed that the unification of the mind occurs not at the top, but rather at the bottom, of the sensory pyramid. According to Harth: "Unlike previous attempts that have placed the (Cartesian) theater at the highest level of cerebral activity, I believe that the unification is located at the only place where sensory patters are still whole and preserve the spatial relations of the original scene—at the bottom of the sensory pyramid, not at the top. It is there that all the sensory cues and cerebral fancies conspire to paint a scene. There is also an observer: it is the rest of the brain looking down, as it were, at what it has wrought. Consciousness, which arises in this self-referent process, not only unifies the immediate sensory messages but also becomes the joiner of everything around us, past, present, and future." The problem with Harth's approach is that while he claims that there is no "intelligent monitor at the top of the sensory pyramid," his model nonetheless posits a higher order "observer," an inner homunculus, observing the workings of the rest of the brain within a lower order "Cartesian Theater." The Cartesian Theater is simply moved from the higher centers of the brain to regions lower down on the sensory hierarchy. In contrast, I have tried to show how all levels of the neural hierarchy contribute to the unified mind and the self without positing an inner homunculus or a centralization of neural pathways.

Chapter 9

1. See Guzéldere, 1995, for a review of some contemporary viewpoints. Also see Velmans, 1991a; 1991b; 1995; Globus, 1973; 1976; Metzinger, 1995.
2. Schopenhauer, cited in Janaway, 1989, pp. 119–20.
3. George Henry Lewes, 1879, p. 459.
4. Herbert Spencer, 1883, p. 157.
5. Nagel, 1974.
6. Ibid., p. 437.
7. Nagel, 1986, p.7.
8. Searle, 1992, p. 122.
9. Ibid., p. 95.
10. Brain, 1951, p. 13.
11. Sherrington, 1947. Some surprisingly complicated behaviors turn out to be highly automatic. For instance, one can cut the spinal cord of a cat so that the portion of the spinal cord controlling the legs is disconnected from the brain. If the animal is then put on a treadmill, it is able to walk with a rhythmic pattern typical of the intact animal. No consciousness, no volition, only an isolated spinal cord and its local circuits control the stepping pattern.
12. Lettvin et al., 1959.
13. Sherrington, 1947, p. 324. The neural states that have meaning are no doubt within an organism's nervous system. But millions of years of evolution have established that the neural states caused by outside objects will *automatically* cause the animals to respond in a fashion appropriate to where the stimuli are in the world, not where the neural states *really* are which is in the brain. This is not some sort of mental magic. The brain has found a way to produce neural states that capture features of the world. But the brain of course does not literally "capture" the world. We should not be deceived into thinking that the brain actually "absorbs" these features of the environment. We can artificially stimulate the brain with an electrode, in the absence of such stimuli, and create the same sensory effects. Rather, it is more accurate to say that what the nervous system does is create *meanings*. Therefore, a sharp pinprick is a combination of touch, point localization, impulse to withdraw, etc. All these sensory and motor elements are integrated into a meaning for the organism. The consciousness of the pinprick for the organism is the meaning for the organism, a meaning that varies with different neural states. For a recent discussion of projection, see Velmans, 1996.
14. Dennett, 1992.
15. Levine, 1983.
16. Feigl, 1967.
17. Teller, 1992, p. 199.
18. Clarke and O'Malley, 1996, p. 9.
19. Globus, 1973, p. 1129. See also Globus, 1976.
20. See Dennett and Haugeland, 1987.
21. Searle, 1984, p. 14. See also Searle, 1983. In his book *Minds, Brains, and*

Science Searle enumerates four features of mental phenomena that do not seem to fit a "scientific" conception of the world. *Intentionality* is one of these features. The other three intractable features of mental phenomena are *consciousness* itself, the *subjectivity* of mental states, and *mental causation*. In this book, I have tried to show how these four features can fit within a fully scientific view of the brain and mind.

Chapter 10

1. If the life of the whole organism is built on the life of the parts, can we reduce the life of the cell to its parts as well? Some interesting questions are raised when we try to reduce entities within the nested hierarchy of a living thing. For example, is an organic molecule in my femur bone alive? Does such a molecule "die" if I take it out of my bone and place it on the table? Is a single carbon atom within my living femur alive as well? Where does one draw the line? Like consciousness, life has a personal ontology and some aspects of a life are irreducibly relative to the being that possesses it. Consider that lonely carbon molecule in my femur. To you, this molecule has the same ontology whether it is in my body or on the table next to me. In contrast, when that carbon molecule is part of my life, part of the nested hierarchy of my body, it possesses a personal ontology that is unique to me. That unique feature of being part of my living self is lost if that molecule is removed from my body.
2. For a refutation of the silicon chip argument, see Searle, 1997.

ALIEN HAND SYNDROME A clinical disorder in which the hand of the patient performs actions that are beyond the patient's control. The actions appear purposeful, but the patient claims the actions are involuntary. Alien hand syndrome is also known as the "Dr. Strangelove effect."

AMNESIA Loss of memory due to any cause.

ANEURYSM An abnormal dilatation of a blood vessel. When a brain aneurysm bursts it causes bleeding into the brain and the destruction of brain tissue.

ANOSOGNOSIA A term first used by Joseph Babinski in 1914, anosognosia literally means "lack of knowledge of the existence of disease." The patient with anosognosia is unaware of a neurological disability. A patient may be anosognosic for any neurological condition, but the most common form of anosognosia is unawareness of paralysis.

ANTEROGRADE AMNESIA A variety of amnesia (memory loss) in which the person cannot form new memories. Anterograde amnesia is a common occurrence in patients who demonstrate the syndrome of confabulation.

ANTON'S SYNDROME This syndrome was named after Gabriel Anton, one of the first investigators to describe the condition. Anton's syndrome is a form of anosognosia in which the patient is unaware of blindness. The blindness may be caused by disease anywhere in the visual system, but most commonly is due to bilateral strokes in the visual cortices of the brain.

APHASIA A disturbance of language that is caused by brain damage.

ASOMATOGNOSIA A term that literally means "lack of recognition of the body." A patient with asomatognosia denies that a part of the body belongs to him or her. The most common form of asomatognosia is denial of ownership of a paralyzed left arm.

AUTOBIOGRAPHICAL MEMORY A general term for memories about the self. Autobiographical memory may include the recall of facts about the self as well as the memories of specific events in one's life.

AUTOSCOPY A clinical condition also known as heutoscopy. Autoscopy refers to the visual hallucination of one's self. Autoscopy may be due to a variety of neurological and psychiatric conditions, and may also occur under conditions of psychological stress.

BEHAVIORAL NEUROLOGY A subspecialty of neurology that is primarily concerned with brain-behavior relationships. The behavioral neurologist specializes in the treatment of patients with neurological disorders that cause intellectual and emotional problems.

BILATERAL Pertaining to both sides of the brain or body

BINDING The mechanism by which the brain integrates multiple perceptual features into a single object. In the visual system, binding is the process the brain uses to integrate multiple visual features, such as color and shape, into a single object. The "binding problem" describes the question of how the brain can unify in consciousness multiple features of an object if different specialized brain regions code for different features of a stimulus.

BINOCULAR A term that refers to vision with both eyes.

BRAINSTEM A neurological term that refers to three structures—the medulla, pons, and midbrain—that connect the spinal cord with the higher brain structures.

BROCA'S APHASIA A variety of aphasia characterized by slow, hesitant, and effortful speech. The speech pattern of the Broca's aphasic is agrammatic and often characterized as "telegraphic" because it resembles the fragmented pattern of a telegram.

CAPGRAS SYNDROME A delusional misidentification syndrome in which the patient denies the identity of a person or persons. The patient with Capgras syndrome often claims that the misidentified person is an imposter or double of the "real" person and that there are two versions of the misidentified person. There may also be misidentification of places and objects. Capgras syndrome may be due to a variety of neurological and psychiatric conditions.

CARTESIANISM Another word for dualism, the belief that brain and mind are composed of different substances. See DUALISM.

CARTESIAN THEATER A term introduced by philosopher Daniel Dennett to describe an imaginary place in the brain where all the output of the brain that is destined for consciousness can "come together" for simultaneous viewing.

CAT SCAN The abbreviation for computerized axial tomography scan. A noninvasive imaging technique that is capable of producing pictures of the inside of the body or brain.

CENTRAL NERVOUS SYSTEM The nervous system is composed of the central nervous system that includes the brain and spinal cord as well as the peripheral nervous system that is composed of the nerves outside the spinal cord.

CEREBRAL CORTEX The most highly evolved portion of the brain, the cerebral cortex is the part of the brain responsible for our most advanced intellectual abilities. The cerebral cortex is the uppermost part of the nervous system. It is divided into two large and extensively folded hemispheres. Each hemisphere of the cerebral cortex is made up of millions of neural cells (grey matter) and nerve tracts (white matter).

CEREBRAL HEMISPHERE The brain is divided into two hemispheres, a left hemisphere and a right hemisphere. The single designation *hemisphere* applies to either one. Each cerebral hemisphere is composed of the cerebral cortex and three deep structures, the hippocampus, the amygdaloid nucleus, and the basal ganglia.

CEREBROSPINAL FLUID The fluid that circulates around the brain and within the brain's ventricles.

COMPLETION A filling-in of missing aspects of a stimulus, especially in vision.

COMPLEX CORTICAL CELLS A term that refers to a class of cells in the visual system. Complex cells receive converging input from multiple simple cortical cells. Complex cortical cells have more specific properties and larger receptive fields than simple cortical cells.

CONFABULATION An erroneous yet unintentional false statement. The patient who confabulates is not trying to deceive the examiner. Confabulations vary from long and dramatic narratives to short errors of simple facts. Confabulations are traditionally associated with disorders of memory, but many neurological conditions are associated with the tendency to confabulate.

CONFABULATORY COMPLETION A variety of completion in which the filled-in material is completely a product of the imagination, especially with reference to the completion that is present in split-brain patients.

CONSTRAINT The control a higher level of a hierarchy exerts over a lower level of a hierarchy.

CONTRALATERAL A term that refers to the opposite side of the body (e.g., the right hand is contralateral to the left hemisphere).

CONVERGENCE See TOPICAL CONVERGENCE.

CORPUS CALLOSOTOMY A term that refers to an operation on the brain in which part or all of the corpus callosum is cut. This operation creates what is known as the split brain. After a corpus callosotomy, the two halves of the brain are not in complete communication, and one hemisphere may possess information or perform actions out of the awareness of the other hemisphere.

CORPUS CALLOSUM The massive bundle of nerve fibers that connects the two hemispheres of the brain.

CORTEX See CEREBRAL CORTEX.

CORTICAL Pertaining to the cortex of the brain. See CEREBRAL CORTEX.

CYCLOPEAN EYE Named for the mythical monster "Cyclops," who had a single eye in the middle of his forehead, cyclopean vision is the normal result of vision that utilizes two eyes. The integration of the two images makes it seem as if we have a visual point of view that originates from a point somewhere between and behind the actual eyes.

DELIRIUM A mental disturbance characterized by confusion and agitation that is caused by a generalized disorder of brain function.

DELUSIONAL MISIDENTIFICATION SYNDROME A clinical condition in which a person mistakes the identity of a person, place, or thing. The misidentification cannot be attributed to a simple cognitive disorder. The misidentification is delusional because the patient persists in the misidentification even if the error is corrected.

DOMINANT A term that applies to a hemisphere of the brain when it plays a leading role in a certain function. In right-handed persons the left hemisphere is the language dominant hemisphere and the right hemisphere is dominant for directing attention.

DOWNWARD CAUSATION Another term for constraint. In a hierarchy, the control a higher level exerts over a lower level.

DUALISM The philosophical theory that holds that the brain is material and the mind is nonphysical, or at least not composed of the same substance as the brain.

EMERGENCE A property of a hierarchical system that is in a fundamental way "more than the sum of its parts." A property that is emergent cannot be *reduced* to its parts. Some writers claim that the mind is an emergent feature of the brain.

ENCEPHALOMALACIA A term that refers to an area of softened and dead brain tissue.

ENVIRONMENTAL REDUPLICATION Also known as reduplicative paramnesia, environmental reduplication refers to the mistaken belief that there are two nearly identical versions of a particular place.

EPISODIC MEMORY The form of memory that is tied to specific moments in one's life. Episodic memory refers to the memory of things personally experienced as opposed to the knowledge of facts one has learned.

FRÉGOLI SYNDROME A delusional misidentification syndrome in which the patient claims a person is in disguise or has taken on the appearance of someone else. The Frégoli delusion often takes the form of the belief that someone who is actually a stranger is "really" someone well known to the patient.

FRONTAL LOBES The most anterior lobes of the brain, the frontal lobes are highly developed in humans and make up a disproportionately large part of the human brain. The frontal lobes have extensive connections with other parts of the brain and they play a particular role in personality, self-regulation, and mental flexibility.

FRONTAL LOBOTOMY The operation in which the frontal lobes are surgically removed.

FRONTOCALLOSAL A region of the brain that involves both a portion of the frontal lobe as well as part of the corpus callosum.

GRANDMOTHER CELL A hypothetical cell so specialized that it responds only to the face of one's own grandmother. Although no one has ever found such specialized cells, in the visual system there are highly specific cells that respond preferentially to faces or hands. These cells are sometimes referred to as "grandmother cells" or "pontifical neurons."

HEMIFIELD One half, either left or right, of the visual field. Due to the crossing of the visual pathways in the brain, the left visual hemifield goes to the right hemisphere and the right visual hemifield goes to the left hemisphere.

HEMIRETINA A term that refers to one half of the retina of either eye. The information from the right hemiretinas of both eyes is sent to the right hemisphere and the information from the left hemiretinas of both eyes travels the left hemisphere.

HEMISPACE One half, either left or right, of the space around an organism.

HEMISPATIAL NEGLECT This term is also referred to as "neglect." A person with hemispatial neglect ignores stimuli on the side of the body or area of space opposite to a brain lesion. The most severe and longest lasting cases of neglect occur as a result of damage to the right hemisphere.

HEMISPHERE See CEREBRAL HEMISPHERE.

HEMORRHAGE A term that refers to any form of bleeding. In this book hemorrhage refers to bleeding into the brain that is often the result of ruptured cerebral aneurysms.

HIERARCHY An organized system composed of parts that are arranged in some sort of graded series of levels.

HIGHER ORDER A term that means more abstract, complex, or specific. In the visual neural hierarchy discussed in this book, a higher order cell is further along in the visual pathway and has more complex properties than a lower order neuron.

HOMUNCULUS This term literally means "manikin" or "little man." It describes an imaginary man who is inside the brain and available to view the output of the brain. At one time the homunculus was invoked as an explanation for the unity of consciousness.

HYDROCEPHALUS A ballooning of the fluid-filled ventricles of the brain due to the accumulation of cerebrospinal fluid.

HYPERCOMPLEX CORTICAL CELLS Cells located far along in the visual processing stream that receive their input from multiple complex cells. Hypercomplex cells have very specific properties and may respond preferentially to visual stimuli such as the side view of a face or the image of a hand.

INFARCTION An area of dead brain tissue that occurs as the result of the loss of blood supply to the affected region.

INFEROTEMPORAL CORTEX An area of the brain in the lower part of the temporal lobe that responds to very complex visual stimuli.

INTENTIONALITY Derived from the Latin verb *intendo,* which means to "point at" or "extend toward," intentional phenomena are about or directed at something. It is supposed by some philosophers to be the mark of mental phenomena.

IPSILATERAL A term that refers to the same side of the body as the side of the brain (e.g., the left arm is ipsilateral to the left hemisphere of the brain).

LIMBIC SYSTEM Also known as the emotional brain. A term that refers to a relatively ancient part of the brain that is responsible for emotion and motivation. The limbic system also plays a key role in memory function.

LOWER ORDER As opposed to higher order, a term that refers to cells with simple response properties.

MATERIALISM Refers to the philosophical theory that the mind has a physical basis like the brain.

MENINGIOMA A variety of brain tumor that is usually slow growing and benign.

MITOCHONDRIA The microscopic organelles contained within the cells of all aerobic (oxygen-requiring) organisms. The mitochondria are responsible for carrying on cellular respiration.

MODULE An area of the brain that is supposed to perform a particular discrete cognitive or emotional function. A modular approach to understanding of brain function claims autonomous brain regions perform relatively independent functions. The modularity approach is opposed to the holistic argument that posits the brain performs operations as a whole.

MOMENTARY CONFABULATION Also known as "provoked confabulation" or the "confabulation of embarrassment," momentary confabulations are short in duration and are often produced in response to questions that probe the patient's defective memory. Momentary confabulations often serve a "gap-filling" function.

MONOSYNAPTIC REFLEX A reflex that consists of two neurons, one sensory and one motor, connected by a single synapse. A synapse is the point at which two neurons make contact. The knee jerk is considered monosynaptic because the reflex involves one neuron carrying information from the knee to the spinal cord and a second neuron that runs from the spinal cord to the muscles that move the leg.

MOTOR NEURON The cell that runs from the spinal cord to the muscle fibers.

MOTOR UNIT A term that refers to a single motor neuron and all the muscle fibers to which it is connected.

MRI The abbreviation for magnetic resonance imaging scan. A method of obtaining pictures of the inside of the body. In neurology, an MRI scan of the brain produces a high-resolution picture of the brain's anatomical structure.

NEOCORTICAL The phylogenetically most recent areas of the brain. The neocortical regions are responsible for all higher thought processes.

NESTED HIERARCHY A term that describes a certain type of hierarchy. In a nested hierarchy, all higher levels of the hierarchy are physically composed of the elements at lower levels. An example of a nested hierarchy is a person who is composed of organs that are in turn composed of tissues that are composed of cells, and so on.

NEUROLOGY The medical specialty that focuses on disorders of the nervous system.

NEURON A single nerve cell.

NEUROPSYCHOLOGICAL TESTING A battery of tests that asseses a wide range of cognitive functions such as language, memory, attention, concentration, mental flexibility, and intelligence.

NON-NESTED HIERARCHY A hierarchy in which all levels of the hierarchy are physically independent.

ONTOLOGY A philosophical term that refers to what something really is when it is reduced to its essence. The ontology or ontological status of a thing is its true nature.

PAIN ASYMBOLIA An unusual clinical condition that is caused by damage to the brain. The patient with pain asymbolia is able to discriminate various painful stimuli, but these stimuli do not create the appropriate emotional response. Persons with this condition do not realize that painful stimuli, such as a sharp pin or a match flame, are hurtful and might be harmful.

PARIETAL LOBE One of the four lobes of the brain, the left parietal lobe plays a significant role in a variety of functions including language abilities, and the ability to calculate, read, and perform skilled movements. The right parietal lobe plays a prominent role in attentional, spatial, and emotional behaviors.

PERSONAL CONFABULATION A term that describes a variety of confabulation in which the patient tells a specifically autobiographical fictional narrative. The personal confabulation is often a metaphorical representation of the patient's problems.

PINEAL GLAND A small unpaired gland that is located deep in the middle of the brain. The fact that the pineal is unpaired was a chief reason Descartes chose it as the liaison between the brain, which is composed of two hemispheres, and the unified mind.

PROJECTION Also known as projicience. The process whereby stimuli on the body surface are experienced as in the world. Since all stimuli that come from the world are received on the body, these stimuli are all projected when they are experienced in the world. An example of projection is light stimuli that when received on the retina are experienced by the receiver as originating from a point away from the eye.

PROSOPOGNOSIA A clinical condition caused by brain damage in which the patient cannot visually recognize faces. The patient with prosopognosia can recognize persons by nonfacial visual cues such as clothes or by nonvisual cues such as the sound of a person's voice.

PSEUDOBULBAR PALSY A condition that is often caused by bilateral cortical strokes that disconnect the higher cortical motor regions from lower centers that control the musculature of the face, tongue, and throat. The patient with pseudobulbar palsy may experience pathological laughing or crying.

PSYCHIATRY The medical specialty that focuses on mental disorders. There is increasing overlap between psychiatry and neurology.

QUALIA A philosophical term to denote the way things feel. The subjective feeling of pain and the smell of a rose are examples of qualia.

RECEPTIVE FIELD The area of space around an organism or on the surface of the body that influences a cell's firing. It is the area of space that a particular cell monitors.

REDUCTIONISM The scientific program that attempts to explain all higher order structures or events by the analysis of lower order parts and processes.

REFLEX An involuntary nervous reaction. The operation of a reflex does not require consciousness. An example of a reflex is the knee jerk, where a tap in the knee produces an involuntary jerk of the leg. This reflex will occur even if the person is asleep or in coma.

RETROGRADE AMNESIA This term refers to a variety of amnesia (memory loss) in which the patient loses memories of experiences that occurred prior to the onset of the amnesia.

SIMPLE CORTICAL CELLS The cells that are located in area V1 of the brain that respond to simple lines in specific orientations.

SPLIT BRAIN A patient or animal that has undergone a corpus callosotomy. See CORPUS CALLOSOTOMY.

SPONTANEOUS CONFABULATION A variety of confabulation that occurs without provocation from the examiner. Spontaneous confabulations are often long in duration and may contain bizarre or fantastical content.

STEREOGNOSIS The capacity to identify objects by touch alone.

STROKE A term that refers to an injury to the brain caused by lack of blood supply to that region.

SYNAPSE The site of the connection between two neurons.

SYNCHRONIZED OSCILLATIONS A possible solution to the binding problem, the theory of synchronized oscillations posits that neurons from different brain regions are "bound" together in consciousness by the temporal correlation to their firing. In this way separate brain regions responsible for different features of a single object can be unified in consciousness.

TELEOLOGY A doctrine that attempts to explain the end result of a process as its cause. In biological theory, it is the school of thought that invokes purpose and predetermined goals to explain the mechanism of natural processes.

TELEONOMY According to Mayr, a teleonomic process is one that owes its goal directedness to the operation of a program. A teleonomic system does not necessarily foresee the endpoint of its operation. Rather, the achievement of an end result is built into the operation of a teleonomic process. Evolutionary processes produce biological systems that are teleonomic. Teleonomic processes are prominent in development, physiology, and behavior.

TEMPORAL LOBE One of the four lobes of the cerebral cortex. In addition to visual and auditory functions, the temporal lobes play a particular role in memory and emotional functions.

THALAMUS A deep brain structure, the thalamus plays a major role in sensory processing. The thalamus receives most of the sensory information that comes into the nervous system and relays this information to the cortex for further processing.

TOPICAL CONVERGENCE The neural pattern in which several presynaptic neurons simultaneously make connections with a common single postsynaptic neuron. The convergence of multiple lower order neurons onto a single higher order neuron plays a role in the creation of complex perceptual features. The convergence of complex cells that respond to simple lines onto hypercomplex cells that code for a complex stimulus such as a face is an example of topical convergence.

UNILATERAL Pertaining to one side of the brain or body.

VENTRICLE A term that refers to any one of the brain cavities within which the cerebrospinal fluid flows.

V1 This designation refers to cortical area V1. V1 is the primary visual area of the brain and it is the first cortical area to receive visual information. V1 contains simple cortical cells that code for elementary shapes such as single lines.

V5 This designation refers to cortical area V5. V5 is a visual area of the brain that contains cells that are selectively responsive to visual information about an object's movement.

VISUAL AGNOSIA A clinical condition caused by brain disease in which the patient cannot recognize objects by visual means but may be able to do so by other means such as by feeling the object. The patient is not blind, however, and elementary visual functions are preserved.

WERNICKE'S APHASIA A variety of aphasia. The patient with Wernicke's aphasia has difficulty with the comprehension of language. The speech output in this condition is fluent but may be meaningless or have frequent word substitutions.

Bibliography

Albert, M. D. "A simple test of visual neglect." *Neurology*. 23: 658–64, 1973.

Alexander, M. P., D. T. Stuss, and D. F. Benson. "Capgras syndrome: A reduplicative phenomenon." *Neurology*. 29: 334–39, 1979.

Allen, T. F. H., and T. B. Starr. *Hierarchy. Perspectives for Ecological Complexity*. Chicago: University of Chicago Press, 1982.

Anderson, D. N. "The delusions of inanimate doubles: Implications for understanding the Capgras phenomenon." *Br J Psychiat*. 153: 694–99, 1988.

Anderson, D. N., and E. Williams. "The delusions of inanimate doubles." *Psychopathology*. 27: 220–25, 1994.

Anton, G. "Über die Selbstwahrnehmung der Herderkrankungen des Gehirns durch den Kranken bein Rindenblindheit und Rindentaubheit." *Arch Psychiatrie*. 32: 86–127, 1899.

Ayala, F. J., and T. Dobzhansky, eds. *Studies in the Philosophy of Biology. Reduction and Related Problems*. London: Macmillan, 1974.

Babinski, J. "Contribution à l'étude des troubles mantaux dans l'hémiplégie organique cérébrale (anosognosie)." *Rev Neurol (Paris)*. 27: 845–48, 1914.

——. "Anosognosie." *Rev Neurol (Paris)*. 31: 365–67, 1918.

Baddeley, A. D., and B. Wilson. Amnesia autobiographical memory and confabulation. In Rubin, D. C., ed. *Autobiographical Memory*. Cambridge: Cambridge University Press, 1986.

Barlow, H. The neuron doctrine in perception. In: Gazzaniga, M. S., ed. *The Cognitive Neurosciences*. Cambridge: MIT Press, 1995.

Barth, A. *Folk-Lore*. I:227, 1890.

Beakley, B., and P. Ludlow, eds. *The Philosophy of Mind: Classical Problems/Contemporary Issues*. Cambridge: MIT Press, 1992.

Beckermann, A., H. Flohr, and J. Kim, eds. *Emergence or Reduction? Essays on the Prospects of Nonreductive Physicalism*. New York: Walter de Gruyter, 1992.

Beckers, G., and S. Zeki. "The consequences of inactivating areas V1 and V5 on visual motion perception." *Brain*. 118: 49–60, 1995.

Benson, D. F., H. Gardner, and J. C. Meadows. "Reduplicative paramnesia." *Neurology*. 26: 147–51, 1976.

Berlyne, N. "Confabulation." *Brit J Psychiat*. 120: 31–39, 1972.

Bertheir, M., S. Starkenstein, and R. Leiguarda. "Asymbolia or pain: A sensory-limbic disconnection syndrome." *Ann Neurol*. 24(1): 41–49, July 1988.

Block, N. Flanagan, O, Güzeldere G. eds. *The Nature of Consciousness*. Cambridge: MIT Press, 1997.

Bogen, J. E. The callosal syndromes. In Heilman K. M., and E. Valenstein, eds. *Clinical Neuropsychology.* 3rd ed. New York: Oxford University Press, 1993, p. 360.

Bonhoeffer, K. Die akuten Geisteskrankheiten der Gewohnheitstrinker. Jena: Gustav Fisch, 1901. "Der Korsakowsche Symptomenkomplex in seinen Beziehungen zu den verschiedenen Krankheitsformen." *Allg Z Psychiat.* 61: 744–52, 1904.

Boring, E. G. *A History of Experimental Psychology.* 2nd ed. New York: Meredith Corporation, 1959.

Brain, W. R. *Mind, Perception and Science.* Oxford: Blackwell Scientific Publications, 1951.

Braithwaite, R. B. *Scientific Explanation: A Study of the Function of Theory, Probability and Law in Science.* London: Cambridge University Press, 1953.

Breznitz, S., ed. *The Denial of Stress.* New York: International Universities Press, Inc., 1983.

Burgess, P. W., D. Baxter, M. Rose, and N. Alderman. Delusional paramnesic misidentification. In: Halligan, P. W., and J. C. Marshall, eds. *Method in Madness: Case Studies in Cognitive Neuropsychiatry.* UK: Psychology Press. 1996.

Burnham, D. L. "Misperception of other persons in schizophrenia." *Psychiatry.* 19: 283–303, 1956.

Burns, A., R. Jacoby, and R. Levy. "Psychiatric phenomena of Alzheimer's disease. II: Disorders of perception." *Br Psychiat.* 157: 76–81, 1990.

Campbell, D. T. Downward causation in hierarchically organized biological systems. In: Ayala, F. J., and T. Dobzhansky, eds. *Studies in the Philosophy of Biology.* Berkeley and Los Angeles: University of California Press, 1974, pp. 179–86.

Capgras, J., and J. Reboul-Lachaux. "L'illusion des sosies dans un délire systématisé chronique." *Bull Soc Clin Méd Ment.* 11: 6–16, 1923.

Cassam, Q. *Self-Knowledge.* New York: Oxford, 1994.

——. *Self and World.* New York: Oxford, 1997.

Chalmers, D. J. *The Conscious Mind.* New York: Oxford, 1996.

Chan, J. L., and A. B. Liu. "Anatomical correlates of alien hand syndromes." *Neuropsychiatry Neuropsychol Behav Neurol.* 12(3): 149–55, 1999.

Christodoulou, G. N., ed. *The Delusional Misidentification Syndromes.* Basel: Karger, 1986a.

——. "Role of depersonalization-derealization phenomena in the delusional misidentification syndromes." *Bibliotheca Psychiatrica.* 164: 99–104, 1986b.

——. "The origin of the concept of 'Doubles'." *Bibliotheca Psychiatrica.* 164: 1–8, 1986c.

——. "The delusional misidentification syndromes." *Br. Psychiatry.* 14: 65–69, 1991.

Churchland, P. S. *Neurophilosophy.* Cambridge: MIT Press, 1986.

——. *Matter and Consciousness.* Cambridge: MIT Press, 1993.

——. *The Engine of Reason, the Seat of the Soul.* Cambridge: MIT Press, 1996.

Clarke, E., and C. D. O'Malley. *The Human Brain and Spinal Cord.* 2nd ed. San Francisco: Norman Publishing, 1996.

Courbon, P., and G. Fail. "Syndrome d'illusion de Frégoli et schizophrénie." *Bull Soc Clin Méd Ment.* 15: 121–24, 1927.

Crick, F. H. C. *The Astonishing Hypothesis.* New York: Basic Books, 1994.

Crick, F., and C. Koch. "Towards a neurobiological theory of consciousness." *Semin Neurosci.* 2: 263–75, 1990.

Critchley, M. *The Parietal Lobes.* New York: Hafner Press, 1953.

——. "Personification of paralyzed limbs in hemiplegics." *Br Med J.* 30: 284, 1955.

——. "Misoplegia or hatred of hemiplegia." *Mt Sinai J Med.* 41: 82–87, 1974.

——. *The Divine Banquet of the Brain and Other Essays.* New York: Raven Press, 1–12, 1979.

Damas Mora, J. M. R., F. A. Jenner, and S. E. Eacott. "On heautoscopy or the phenomenon of the double; Case presentation and review of the literature." *Br J Med Psychol.* 53: 75–83, 1980.

Damasio, A. R. *Descartes' Error.* New York: G. P. Putnam's Sons, 1994.

——. *The Feeling of What Happens. Body and Emotion in the Making of Consciousness.* New York: Harcourt Brace & Company, 1999.

Davidson, G. M. "The syndrome of Capgras." *Psychiat Q.* 15: 513–21, 1941.

Della Sala, S., C. Marchetti, and H. Spinnler. "Right-sided anarchic (alien) hand: a longitudinal study." *Neuropsychologia.* 29: 1113–27, 1991.

DeLuca, J., and K. D. Cicerone. "Confabulation following aneurysm of the anterior communicating artery." *Cortex.* 27: 417–23, 1991.

DeLuca, J., and B. J. Diamond. "Aneurysm of the anterior communicating artery: A review of neuroanatomical and neuropsychological sequelae." *J of Clin and Exp Neuropsychol.* 17(1): 100–21, 1995.

Dennett, D. C. Consciousness. In: Gregory, R. L., ed. *The Oxford Companion to the Mind.* New York: Oxford University Press, 1987, pp. 160–64.

——. *Consciousness Explained.* Boston: Little Brown, 1991.

——. Quining qualia. In: Marcel, A. J., and E. Bisiach, eds. *Consciousness in Contemporary Science.* Oxford: Clarendon Press, 1992, pp. 42–77.

Dennett, D. C., and J. C. Haugeland. Intentionality. In: Gregory, R. L., ed. *The Oxford Companion to the Mind.* New York: Oxford University Press, 1987, pp. 383–86.

Descartes, R. *Les passions de l'âme.* 1649. Translated in Beakley and Ludlow, 1992; Clarke and O'Malley, 1996.

Devinsky, O. E. Feldmann, K. Burrowes, and E. Bromfield. "Autoscopic phenomena with seizures." *Arch Neurol.* 46: 1080–88, 1989.

Dorpat, T. L. *Denial and Defense in the Therapeutic Situation.* New York: Jason Aronson, Inc., 1985.

Dostoyevsky, F. *The Possessed.* London: Heinemann, 1971.

——. *The Double.* Letchworth: Prideaux Press, 1976.

Eccles, J. C. *How the Self Controls Its Brain.* Berlin and Heidelberg: Springer-Verlag, 1994.

Edelman, G. M. *The Remembered Present. A Biological Theory of Consciousness.* New York: Basic Books, Inc., 1989.

Ellis, H. D., J. Luauté, and N. Retterstøl, eds. *The Delusional Misidentification Syndromes.* Basel: Karger, 1993.

Ellis, H. D., J. Whitley, and J. Luauté. "Delusional misidentification. The three original papers on the Capgras, Fregoli and intermetamorphosis delusions." *History of Psychiatry.* 117–46, 1994.

Ellis, H. D., and A. W. Young. "Accounting for delusional misidentifications." *Br J of Psychiatry.* 157: 239–48, 1990.

Engel, A. K., P. König, A. K. Kreiter, and W. Singer. "Interhemispheric synchronization of oscillatory neuronal responses in cat visual cortex." *Science.* 252: 1177–79, 1991.

Eslinger, J. "Autobiographical memory after temporal lobe lesions." *Neurocase.* 4: 481–95, 1998.

Feigl, H. *The "Mental" and the "Physical."* Minneapolis: University of Minnesota Press, 1967.

Feiling, A. "A case of mimic facial paralysis." *Neurol Psychopath.* 8: 141–45, 1927.

Feinberg, T. E.. Anosognosia and confabulation. In: Feinberg T. E, and M. J. Farah, eds. *Behav Neurol and Neuropsychol.* New York: McGraw-Hill, 1997a.

——. "The irreducible perspectives of consciousness." *Sem in Neurol.* 17: 85–93, 1997b.

——. "Some interesting perturbations of the self in neurology." *Sem in Neurol.* 17: 129–35, 1997c.

——. "The nested hierarchy of consciousness: A neurobiological solution to the problem of mental unity." *Neurocase.* 6: 75-81, 2000.

Feinberg, T. E., L. A. Eaton, D. M. Roane, and J. T. Giacino. "Multiple Frégoli delusions after traumatic brain injury." *Cortex.* 35: 373–87, 1999.

Feinberg, T.E., L. D. Haber, and N. E. Leeds. "Verbal asomatognosia." *Neurology.* 40: 1391–94, 1990.

Feinberg, T. E., and D. M. Roane. "Anosognosia, completion and confabulation: The neutral-personal dichotomy." *Neurocase.* 3: 73–85, 1997a.

——. Misidentification syndromes. In Feinberg T. E., and M. J. Farah, eds. *Behav Neurol and Neuropsychol.* New York: McGraw-Hill, 1997b, pp. 391–97.

Feinberg, T. E., D. M. Roane, and J. Ali. "Confabulatory Limb Movements in Anosognosia for Hemiplegia." *J of Neurol, Neurosurg, and Psychiat.* : 511-13, 2000.

Feinberg, T. E., D. M. Roane, and J. Cohen. "Partial status epiliepticus associated with asomatognosia and alien hand-like behaviors." *Arch Neurol.* 55: 1574–76, 1998.

Feinberg, T. E., D. M. Roane, P. C. Kwan, et al. "Anosognosia and visuoverbal confabulation." *Arch Neurol.* 51: 468–73, 1994.

Feinberg, T. E., R. J. Schindler, N. Gilson Flanagan, and J. D. Haber. "Two alien hand syndromes." *Neurology.* 42: 19–24, 1992.

Feinberg, T. E., and R. M. Shapiro. "Misidentification-reduplication and the right hemisphere." *Neuropsychiat Neuropsychol Behav Neurol.* 2: 39–48, 1989.

Fischer, R. S., M. P. Alexander, M. D'Esposito, and R. Otto. "neuropsychological and Neuroanatomical correlates of confabulation." *J of Clin and Exp Neuropsychol.* 17(1): 20–28, 1995.

Flanagan, O. *The Science of Mind.* 2nd ed. Cambridge: MIT Press, 1991.

——. *Consciousness Reconsidered.* Cambridge: MIT Press, 1992.

Fleminger, S., and A. Burns. "The delusional misidentification syndromes in patients with and without evidence of organic cerebral disorder: a structured review of case reports." *Biological Psychiatry.* 33: 22–32, 1993.

Foley, J. M., and L. Breslau. "A new syndrome of delusional misidentification." *Ann Neurol.* 12: 26, 1982.

Förstl, H., O. P. Almeida, and A. Owen et al. "Psychiatric, neurological and medical aspects of misidentification syndromes: A review of 260 cases." *Psychological Medicine.* 21: 905–50, 1991.

Förstl, H., A. M. Owen, and A. S. David. "Gabriel Anton and 'Anton's symptom': On focal diseases of the brain which are not perceived by the patient (1898)." *Neuropsychiat Neuropsychol Behav Neurol.* 1: 1–8, 1993.

Frailberg, S. *The Magic Years.* New York: Scribners, 1959.

Freud, S. Family romances. Originally appearing in Rank O. *Desmythus von der Geburt des Helden.* Leipzig and Vienna: Deuticke, 1909, pp. 64–68. Translated in Strachey, J., ed. *The Standard Edition.* London: The Hogarth Press, 1959, pp. 237–41.

Gainotti, G., P. Messerli, and R. Tissot. "Qualitative analysis of unilateral and spatial neglect in relation to laterality of cerebral lesions." *J Neurol Neurosurg Psychiat.* 35: 545–50, 1972.

Gallup, G. G., Jr. "Chimpanzees: Self-recognition." *Science.* 167: 86–87, 1970.

——. "Absence of self-recognition in a monkey (Macaca fascicularis) following prolonged exposure to a mirror." *Development Psychobiol.* 10: 281–84, 1977a.

——. "Self-recognition in primates: A comparative approach to the bidirectional properties of consciousness." *Am Psychologist.* 32: 329–38, 1977b.

——. "Self-awareness and the emergence of mind in primates." *Amer J Primatol.* 2: 237–48, 1982.

Gallup, G. G., D. J. Povinelli, S. D. Suarez, J. R. Anderson, J. Lethmate, and E. W. Menzel. "Further reflections on self-recognition in primates." *Animal Behaviour.* 50: 1525–32, 1995.

Gasquoine, P. G. "Alien hand sign." *J Clin Exper Neuropsychol.* 15: 653–67, 1993.

Gazzaniga, M. S. *The Bisected Brain.* New York: Appleton-Century-Crofts, 1970.

——. *The Social Brain. Discovering the Networks of the Mind.* New York: Basic Books, Inc., 1985.

Gazzaniga, M. S., and J. E. LeDoux. *The Integrated Mind.* New York: Plenum, 1978.

Gazzaniga, M. S. and B. T. Volpe. Split-brain studies: implications for psychiatry. In: Arieti, S., H. Keith, and H. Brodie, eds. *American Handbook of Psychiatry.*, 2nd ed. New York: Basic Books, 1981.

Gerstmann, J. "Problem of imperception of disease and of impaired body territories with organic lesions." *Arch Neurol Psychiat.* 48: 890–913, 1942.

Geschwind, D. H., M. Iacoboni, M. S. Mega, D. W. Zaidel, T. Cloughesy, and E. Zaidel. "Alien hand syndrome: interhemispheric motor disconnection due to a lesion in the midbody of the corpus callosum." *Neurology.* 45: 802–8, 1995.

Gilliatt, R. W., and R. T. C. Pratt. "Disorders of perception and performance in a case of right-sided cerebral thrombosis." *J. Neurol Neurosurg Psychiat.* 15: 264–71, 1952.

Globus, G. G. "Unexpected symmetries in the 'World Knot'." *Sci.* 180: 1129–36, 1973.

——. Mind, structure, and contradiction. In: Globus G. G., G. Maxwell, and I. Savodnik, eds. *Consciousness and the Brain – A Scientific and Philosophical Inquiry.* New York: Plenum Press, 1976, pp. 271–93.

Gluckman, L. K. "A case of Capgras syndrome." *Aust NZ J Psychiat.* 2: 39–43, 1968.

Goldberg, G. and K. K. Bloom. "The alien hand sign. Localization, lateralization, and recovery." *Amer J of Phys Med Rehab.* 69: 228–38, 1990.

Gray, C. M., A. K. Engel, P. König, and W. Singer. "Synchronization of oscillatory neuronal responses in cat striate cortex: temporal properties." *Visual Neurosc.* 8: 337–47, 1992.

Gray, C. M., P. König, A. K. Engel, and W. Singer. "Oscillatory responses in cat visual cortex exhibit inter-columnar synchronization which reflects global stimulus properties." *Nature.* 338: 334–37, 1989.

Gray, C. M., and W. Singer. "Stimulus-specific neuronal oscillations in orientation columns of cat visual cortex." *Proc Natl Acad Sci USA.* 86: 1698–1702, 1989.

Güzeldere, G. "Problems of consciousness: A perspective on contemporary issues, current debates." *J Consc Stud.* 2: 112–43, 1995.

Halligan, P. W., J. C. Marshall, and D. T. Wade. "Three arms: A case study of supernumerary phantom limb after right hemisphere stroke." *J of Neurol, Neurosurg, and Psychiat.* 56: 159–66, 1993.

——. "Unilateral somatoparaphrenia after right hemisphere stroke: A case description." *Cortex.* 31: 173–82, 1995.

Hardcastle, V. G. "Consciousness and the neurobiology of perceptual binding." *Sem in Neurol.* 17(2): 1997.

Harrington, A. *Medicine, Mind, and the Double Brain: A Study in Nineteenth-Century Thought.* Princeton: Princeton University Press, 1987.

Harth, E. *The Creative Loop. How the Brain Makes a Mind.* Reading, MA: Addison-Wesley, 1993.

Heilman, K. M., and T. Van Den Abell. "Right hemispheric dominance for mediating cerebral activation." *Neuropsychologia.* 17: 315–21, 1979.

Heilman, K. M., R. T. Watson, and E. Valenstein. Neglect and related disorders. In: Heilman K. M., and E. Valenstein, eds. *Clinical Neuropsychology.* New York: Oxford University Press, 1993, pp. 279–336.

——. Neglect: Clinical and anatomic aspects. In Feinberg, T. E., and M. J. Farah, eds. *Behavioral Neurology and Neuropsychology.* New York: McGraw-Hill, 1997, pp. 309–317.

Heyes, C. M. "Theory of mind in non human primates." *Behav and Brain Sciences.* 21: 101–48, 1998.

Horgan, J. *The Undiscovered Mind.* New York: The Free Press, 1999.

Hubel, D. H. *Eye, Brain, and Vision.* New York: Scientific American Library, 1988.

Hubel, D. H., and T. N. Wiesel. "Receptive fields, binocular interaction and functional architecture in the cat's visual cortex." *J. Physiol (Lond.).* 160: 106–54, 1962.

——. "Receptive fields and functional architecture in two non striate visual areas (18 and 19) of the cat." *J Neurophysiol.* 28: 299–89, 1965.

——. "Receptive fields and functional architecture of monkey striate cortex." *J Physiol (Lond.).* 195: 215–43, 1968.

——. "The Ferrier Lecture: Functional architecture of macaque monkey visual cortex." *Proc R Soc Lond B.* 198: 1–59, 1977.

——. "Brain mechanisms of vision." *Sci Am.* 241(3): 150–62, 1979.

Innocenti, G. M. General organizations of callosal connections in the cerebral cortex. In Jones, E. G., and A. Peters, eds. *Cerebral Cortex,* vol. 5. New York: Plenum, 1986, pp. 291–353.

Jackson, J. H. Evolution and dissolution of the nervous system. Croonian lectures delivered at the Royal College of Physicians, March 1884. Reprinted in Taylor J, ed. *Selected Writings of John Hughlings Jackson.* New York: Basic Books, Inc., 1958, vol. 2, pp. 45–75.

James, W. *The Principles of Psychology.* Cambridge: Harvard University Press, 1983.

——. *Psychology. The Briefer Course.* Notre Dame, Ind.: University of Notre Dame Press, 1985.

Janaway, C. *Self and World in Schopenhauer's Philosophy.* Oxford: Clarendon Press, 1989.

Kaas, J. H. "Why does the brain have so many visual areas?" *J Cogn Neurosci.* 1: 121, 1989.

——. "Evolution of multiple areas and modules within neocortex." *Persp Devel Neurobio.* 1: 101–7, 1993.

Kandel, E. R., J. H. Schwartz, and T. M. Jessell, eds. *Principles of Neural Science.* Norwalk: Appleton & Lange, 2000.

Kant, I. *Critique of Pure Reason,* 1781. Translated in: Meikiejohn, J.M.D. ed. London: J. M. Dent and Sons, 1934.

Kapur, N., and A. K. Coughlan. "Confabulation and frontal lobe dysfunction." *J. Neurol Neurosurg Psychiat.* 43: 461–63, 1980.

Kim, J. "Downward Causation" in Emergentism and Nonreductive Physicalism. In: Beckermann, A., H. Flohr, and J. Kim, eds. *Emergence or Reduction? Essays on the Prospects of Nonreductive Physicalism.* New York: Walter de Gruyter, 1992, pp. 119–38.

——. "The Non-Reductivist's Troubles with Mental Causation" In: Heil, J., and A. Mele. *Mental Causation.* Oxford: Clarendon Press, 1995, pp.189–210.

——. *Mind in a Physical World. An Essay on the Mind-Body Problem and Mental Causation.* Cambridge: MIT Press, 1998.

Kimura, S. "Review of 106 cases with the syndrome of Capgras." *Bibl Psychiatry.* 164: 121–30, 1986.

Koestler, A. *The Ghost in the Machine*. Harmondsworth: Hutchinson Publishing Corp. Ltd., 1967.

——. *Janus: A Summing Up*. New York: Random House, 1978.

König, P., and A. K. Engel. "Correlated firing in sensory-motor systems." *Curr Opin in Neurobiol*. 5: 511–519, 1995.

Koppleman, M. D. "Two types of confabulation." *J. Neurol Neurosurg Psychiat*. 43: 461–63, 1980.

Landis, T., J. L. Cummings, D. F. Benson, and P. Palmer. "Loss of topographic familiarity: An environmental agnosia." *Arch Neurol*. 43:132–36, 1986.

Larrivé, E. and H. J. Jasienski. "L'illusion des sosies: une nouvelle observation du syndrome de Capgras." *Annls Méd Psychol*. 89: 501–7, 1931.

LeDoux, J. *The Emotional Brain. The Mysterious Underpinnings of Emotional Life*. New York: Simon & Schuster Inc., 1996.

Lettvin, J. Y., H. R. Maturana, W. S. McCulloch, and W. H. Pitts. "What the frog's eye tell the frog's brain." Proceeding Institute of Radio Engineers. 47: 1940–51, 1959. Reprinted in: McCulloch, W. S., ed. *The Embodiment of Mind*. Cambridge: Harvard University Press, 1965.

Levin, J. D. *Theories of the Self*. Washington, D.C.: Taylor and Francis, 1992.

Levin, M. "Bromide delirium and other bromide psychosis." *Amer J Psychiat*. 89:1125–58, 1933.

——. "Delirious disorientation: The law of the unfamiliar mistaken for the familiar." *Ment Sci*. 91: 447–53, 1945.

——. "Delirum: A gap in psychiatric teaching." *Am J Psychiat*. 107: 684–94, 1951.

——. "Reflex action in the highest cerebral centers." *J Nerv Mental Dis*. 6: Vol. 118, 1953.

——. "Delirium: An experience and some reflections." *Am J Psychiat*. 124: 8, 1968.

Levine, J. "Materialism and qualia: The explanatory gap." *Pacific Philosoph Quart*. 64: 354–61, 1983.

Levy, J. Manifestations and implications of shifting hemi-inattention in commissurotomy patients. In Weinstein, E.A., R. P. Friedland, eds. *Advances in Neurology*. New York: Raven Press, 1977.

——. Regulation and generation of perception in the asymmetric brain. In: Trevarthen C, ed. *Brain Circuits and Functions of the Mind*. New York: Cambridge University Press, 1990, pp. 231–48.

Levy, J., and C. Trevarthen. "Metacontrol of hemispheric function in human split-brain patients." *Exp Psychol Hum Percept Perform*. 2: 299–312, 1976.

Levy. J., C. Trevarthen, and R. W. Sperry. "Perception of bilateral chimeric figures following hemispheric disconnection." *Brain*. 95: 60–78, 1972.

Lewes, G. H. *Problems of Life and Mind*, vol. II, p. 459; cited by Jackson, J. H. *Selected Writings of John Hughlings Jackson*. Taylor, J. ed. Vol. I. New York: Basic Books, 1958, pp. 41–42.

Lewis, L. Role of psychological factors in disordered awareness. In: Prigatano, G. P., and D. L. Schacter, eds. *Awareness of Deficits after Brain Injury: Clinical and Theoretical Issues*. New York: Oxford University Press, 1991. pp. 223–39.

Lhermitte, J. "Visual hallucination of the self." *Brit Med J*. 1: 431–34, 1951.

Lippman, C. W. "Hallucinations of physical duality in migraine." *Nerv Ment Dis.* 117: 345–50, 1953.

Locke, J. *An Essay Concerning Human Understanding.* New York: Dover, 1959 (originally published 1690).

Luauté, J. P. "Joseph Capgras and his syndrome." *Bibl psychiat.* 164: 9–21, 1986.

Malloy, P., C. Cimino, and R. Westlake. "Differential diagnosis of primary and secondary Capgras delusions." *Neuropsychiat, Neuropsychol, and Behav Neurol.* 5(2): 83–96, 1992.

Mayr, E. "Teleological and teleonomic: A new analysis." *Boston Stud Philos Sci.* 14: 91–117, 1974.

——. *The Growth of Biological Thought.* Cambridge: Harvard University Press, 1982.

McGinn, C. *The Character of Mind.* New York: Oxford University Press, 1997.

——. *The Mysterious Flame.* New York: Basic Books, 1999.

McGlynn, S. M., and D. L. Schacter. "Unawareness of deficits in neuropsychological syndromes." *J. Clin Exp Neuropsychol.* 11: 143–205, 1989.

Medawar, P. B., and J. S. Medawar. *The Life Science: Current Ideas of Biology.* New York: Harper & Row, 1977.

Meehl, P. The compleat autocerebroscopist: A thought experiment on Professor Feigl's mind/body identify thesis. In Feyerabend P. K., and G. Maxwell, eds. *Mind, Matter and Method.* Minneapolis: University of Minnesota Press, 1966, pp. 103–80.

Mendez, M. F., R. J. Martin, K. A. Symth, and P. J. Whitehouse. "Disturbances of person identification Alzheimer's Disease: A retrospective study." *J Nerv Ment Dis.* 180: 94, 1992.

Merrin, E. L., and P. M. Silberfarb. "The Capgras phenomenon." *Arch Gen Psychiat.* Vol. 33 August 1976.

Mesulam, M. M. *Principles of Behavioral Neurology.* Philadelphia: F. A. Davis Company, 1985.

Metzinger, T. The problem of consciousness. In: Metzinger, T., ed. *Conscious Experience.* Paderborn, Germany: Imprint Academic, 1995, pp. 3–37.

Monrad-Krohn, G. H. "On the dissociation of voluntary and emotional innervation in facial paresis of central origin." *Brain.* 47: 22–35, 1924.

Morgan, C. L. *Emergent Evolution.* London: Williams & Norgate, 1923.

Moscovitch, M. Confabulation. In Schacter D. L., ed. *How Minds, Brains, and Societies Reconstruct the Past.* Cambridge: Harvard University Press, 1995, pp. 226–51.

Movshon, J. A., E. H. Adelson, M. S. Gizzi, and W. T. Newsome. The analysis of moving visual pattern. In: Chagas C., Gattass R., and Gross V, eds. *Pattern Recognition Mechanisms.* New York: Springer, 1985, pp. 117–51.

Murphy, L. B., et al. *The Widening World of Children.* New York: Basic Books, 1962.

Myers, R. E. Comparative neurology of vocalization and speech: Proof of a dichotomy. In: Harnad, S. R., H. D. Steklis, and J. Lancaster, eds. *Origins and Evolution of Language and Speech.* Ann New York Acad of Sci, Vol. 280. 745–60, 1976.

Nabokov, V. *Despair*. New York: Vintage Books, 1989.

Nagel, T. "What is it like to be a bat?" *Philosophical Review*. 83: 435–50, 1974.

——. *Mortal Questions*. New York: Cambridge University Press, 1979.

——. *The View from Nowhere*. New York: Oxford University Press, 1986.

——. *Other Minds*. New York: Oxford University Press, 1995.

Nagera, H. The imaginary companion: Its significance for ego development and conflict solution. In: *The Psychoanalytic Study of the Child*. Vol XXIV. New York: International Universities Press, Inc., 1969, pp. 165–96.

Newman, J., ed. Special Issue: Temporal binding and consciousness. In: Baars, B. J., W. P. Banks, and A. Revonsuo. *Consciousness and Cognition*. Vol. 8(2). Orlando: Academic Press, 1999.

Nielsen, J. M. Gerstmann syndrome; finger agnosia, agraphia, confusion of right and left acalculia; comparison of this syndrome with disturbances of body scheme resulting from lesions of right side of brain. *Arch Neurol Psychiat*. 39: 536–60, 1938.

Pattee, H. H. The problem of biological hierarchy. In Waddington, C. H., ed. *Towards a Theoretical Biology 3*. Chicago: Aldine, 1970.

Pattee, H. H., ed. *Hierarchy Theory. The Challenge of Complex Systems*. New York: George Braziller, Inc., 1973.

Patterson, A., and O. L. Zangwill. "Recovery of spatial orientation in the post-traumatic confusional state." *Brain*. 6754–68, 1944.

Pick, A. "On reduplicative paramnesia." *Brain*. 26: 260–67, 1903.

Pinker, S. *How the Mind Works*. New York: W.W. Norton & Company, 1997.

Polanyi, M. "The structure of consciousness." *Brain*. 88: 799–810, 1965.

——. *The Tacit Dimension*. New York: Anchor Books, 1966.

——. "Life's irreducible structure." Science. 160: 1308–12, 1968.

Povinelli, D. J., G. G. Gallup, Jr., T. J. Eddy, D. T. Bierschwale, M. C. Engstrom, H. K. Perilloux, and I. B. Taxopeus. "Chimpanzees recognize themselves in mirrors." *Animal Behaviour*. 53: 1083–88, 1997.

Povinelli, D. J., A. B. Rulf, K. R. Landau, and D. T. Bierschwale. "Self-recognition in chimpanzees: Distribution, ontogeny, and patterns of emergence." *J of Compar Psychol*. 107: 347–72, 1993.

Puccetti, R. "The case for mental duality: Evidence from split-brain data and other considerations." *Behav Brain Sci*. 4: 93–123, 1981.

Ramachandran, V. S. "Consciousness and body image: Lessons from phantom limbs, Capgras syndrome and pain asymbolia." *Philos Trans R Soc Lond B Biol Sci*. 353(1377): 1851–59, November 29, 1998.

Ramachandran, V. S., and S. Blakeslee. *Phantoms in the Brain. Probing the Mysteries of the Mind*. New York: William Morrow, 1998.

Rank, O. *Der Mythus Vonder Geburt des Heldem*. Leipzig and Vienna: Deuticke; Reprinted in Rank O. *The Myth of the Birth of the Hero: A Psychological Interpretation of Mythology*. New York: Robert Brunner, 1952.

Revonsuo, A. "Binding and the phenomenal unity of consciousness." *Consciousness and Cognition*. 8: 173–185, 1999.

Restak, R. M. *The Modular Brain*. New York: Scribner's, 1994.

Rosenthal, D. M. ed. *The Nature of Mind*. New York: Oxford University Press, 1991.

Rowan, E. "Phantom boarders as a symptom of late paraphrenia." *Am J Psychiat*. 141: 580–81, 1984.

Rubin, D. C. ed. *Autobiographical Memory*. Cambridge: Cambridge University Press, 1986.

Rubin, E. H., W. C. Drevets, and W. J. Burke. "The nature of psychotic symptoms in senile dementia of Alzheimer's type." *J of Geriatric Psychiat and Neurol*. 1: 16, 1988.

Ruff, R.L., and B. T. Volpe. "Environmental reduplicaton associated with right frontal and parietal lobe injury," *Neurol Neurosurg Psychiat*. 44: 382–86, 1981.

Ryle, G. *The Concept of Mind*. London: Hutchinson and Company, Ltd., 1949.

Salthe, S. N. *Evolving Hierarchical Systems: Their Structure and Representation*. New York: Columbia University Press, 1985.

Schacter, D. L. *Searching for Memory. The Brain, the Mind, and the Past*. New York: Basic Books, 1996.

Schilder, P. *Medical Psychology*. New York: John Wiley & Sons, Inc., 1965, pp. 298–99.

Schilder, P., and E. Stengel. "Schmerzasymbolie." *Z ges Neuro Psychiat*. 113: 143–58, 1928.

——. "Asymbolia for pain." *Arch Neurol Psychiat*. 25: 598–600, 1931.

Scott, A. *Stairway to the Mind: The Controversial New Science of Consciousness*. New York: Springer-Verlag, 1995.

Searle, J. R. *Intentionality*. New York: Cambridge University Press, 1983.

——. *Minds, Brains and Science*. Cambridge: Harvard University Press, 1984.

——. *The Rediscovery of the Mind*. Cambridge: MIT Press, Bradford Books, 1992.

——. Breaking the hold: silicon brain, conscious robots, and other minds. In: Block, N., F. Owen, and G. Güzeldere, eds. *The Nature of Consciousness: Philosophical Debates*. Cambridge: MIT Press, 1997, pp. 493–502.

Sellars, W. *Science, Perception, and Reality*. London: Routledge and Kegan Paul, 1963.

Sherrington, C. *The Integrative Action of the Nervous System*. New Haven: Yale University Press, 1947.

——. *Man on His Nature*. New York: Macmillan, 1941.

Signer, S. F. "Capgras' syndrome: The delusion of substitution." *Clin Psychiat*. 48: 147–50, 1987.

——. "Psychosis in neurologic disease: Capgras symptom and delusions of reduplication in neurologic disorders." *Neuropsychiatr Neuropsychol Behav Neurol*. 5: 138–43, 1992.

Singer, W. "Consciousness and the structure of neuronal representations." *Philos Trans R Soc Lond B Biol Sci*. 353(1377): 1829–40, 1998.

——. "Time as coding space?" *Curr Opin Neurobiol*. 9(2): 189–94, 1999.

Spangenberg, K. B., M. T. Wagner, and D. L. Bachman. Neuropsychological analysis of a case of abrupt onset mirror sign following a hypotensive crisis in a patient with vascular dementia. *Neurocase*. 4: 149–54, 1998.

Spencer, H. *The Principles of Psychology*. Vol 1. New York: D. Appleton and Co., 1883, p. 157.

Sperling, O. E. An imaginary companion representing a prestage of the super-ego. In: *The Psychoanalytic Study of the Child,* Vol. IX, pp. 252–58, 1954.

Sperry, R. W. Brain bisection and mechanisms of consciousness. In: Eccles, J. C., ed. *Brain and Conscious Experience*. New York: Springer-Verlag, 1966, pp. 298–313.

——. Mind, brain, and humanist values. In: Platt, J. R. *New Views on the Nature of Man*. Chicago: University of Chicago Press. Reprinted in *Bull Atom Scientists*. 22: 2–6, 1966.

——. "Forebrain commissurotomy and conscious awareness." *J Med Phil*. 2(2): 101–26, 1977.

——. "Consciousness, personal identity and the divided brain." *Neuropsychol*. 22(6): 661–73, 1984.

——. Forebrain commissurotomy and conscious awareness. In: Trevarthe C., ed. *Brain Circuits and Functions of the Mind*. New York: Cambridge University Press, 371–88, 1990.

Sperry, R. W., M. S. Gazzaniga, and J. E. Bogen. Interhemispheric relationships: The neocortical commissures; syndromes of hemispheric disconnection. In: Vinken, P. J., and G. W. Bruyn, eds. *Handbook of Clinical Neurology*. Amsterdam: North-Holland, 1969, pp.273–90.

Sperry, R. W., E. Zaidel, and D. Zaidel. "Self-recognition and social awareness in the disconnected minor hemisphere." *Neuropsychologia*. 17: 153–66, 1979.

Spier, S. A. "Capgras' syndrome and the delusions of misidentification." *Psychiatr Annals*. 22: 279–85, 1992.

Spillane, J. D. "Disturbances of the body scheme, anosognosia, and finger agnosia." *Lancet*. I: 42–44, 1942.

Staton, R. D., R. A. Brumback, and H. Wilson. "Reduplicative paramnesia: A disconnection syndrome of memory." *Cortex*. 18: 23–36, 1982.

Stuss, D. T. Disturbance of self-awareness after frontal system damage. In: Prigatano, G. P., and D. L. Schacter. *Awareness of Deficit After Brain Injury. Clinical and Theoretical Issues*. New York: Oxford University Press, 1991, pp. 63–83.

Stuss, D. T., M. P. Alexander, A. Lieberman, H. Levine. "An extraordinary form of confabulation." *Neurology*. 28: 116–72, 1978.

Stuss, D. T., and D. F. Benson. *The Frontal Lobes*. New York: Raven Press, 1986, p. 88.

Svendsen, M. "Children's imaginary companions." *Arch Neurol Psychiat*. 32: 985–99, 1934.

Tanaka, Y., A. Yoshida, N. Kawahata, R. Hashimoto, and T. Obayashi. "Diagnostic dyspraxia. Clinical characteristics, responsible lesion and possible underlying mechanism." *Brain*. 119: 859–73, 1996.

Teller, P. Subjectivity and knowing what it's like. In: Berckermann A, Flohr H, and Jaegwon K, eds. *Emergence or Reduction? Essays on the Prospects of Nonreductive Physicalism*. Berlin/New York: Walter de Gruyter, 1992, pp. 180–200.

Tinbergen, N. *The Study of Instinct.* Oxford: Clarendon Press, 1951.

Todd, J., and K. Dewhurst. "The double: its psychopathology and psychophysiology." *J Nerv Ment Dis.* 122: 47–55, 1955.

——. "The significance of the doppelganger (Hallucinatory double) in folk-lore and neuro-psychiatry." *Practitioner.* 188: 377–82, 1962.

Todd, J., K. Dewhurst, and G. Wallis. "The syndrome of Capgras." *Br J Psychiat.* 139: 319–27, 1981.

Treisman, A. "The binding problem." *Curr Opin Neurobiol.* 6(2): 171–78, 1996.

Trevarthen, C. Functional relations of disconnected hemispheres with the brain stem and with each other: Monkey and man. In: Kinsbourne, M, and W. L. Smith, eds. *Hemispheric Disconnection and Cerebral Function.* Springfield: Charles C. Thomas, 1974, pp. 187–207.

——. Integrative functions of the cerebral commissures. In: Nebes, R. D., and S. Corkin, eds. *Handbook of Neuropsychology.* New York: Elsevier, 1991, pp. 49–83.

Trevarthen, C., ed. *Brain Circuits and Functions of the Mind.* New York: Cambridge University Press, 1990.

Trojano, I., C. Crisci, B. Lanzillo, R. Elefante, and G. Caruso. "How many alien hand syndromes? Follow-up of a case." *Neurology.* 43: 2710–12, 1993.

Tulving, E. *Elements of episodic memory.* Oxford: Claredon Press, 1983.

Tye, M. *Ten Problems of Consciousness: A Representational Theory of the Phenomenal Mind.* Cambridge: MIT Press, 1995.

Tymms, R. *Doubles in Literary Psychology.* Cambridge: Bowes & Bowes, 1949.

Ullman, M. Motivational and structural factors in denial of hemiplegia. *Arch Neurol.* 3: 306–18, 1960.

Van der Horst, L. "Ueber die psychologie des Korsakowsyndroms." *Msschr. Psychiat Neurol.* 83: 64–84, 1932.

Van Essen, D. C., C. H. Anderson, and D. J. Felleman. "Information processing in the primate visual system: An integrated system perspective." *Am Assoc Adv Sci.* 1992. Reprint *Science* 255: 419–23, 1992.

Van Lancker, D. "Personal relevance and the human right hemisphere." *Brain and Cognition.* 17: 64–92, 1991.

Van Lancker, D., and K. Klein. "Preserved recognition of familiar personal names in global aphasia." *Brain and Lang.* 39: 511–29, 1990.

Velmans, M. "Is human information processing conscious?" *Behav Brain Sci.* 14 (4): 651–69, 1991a.

——. "Consciousness from a first-person perspective." *Behav Brain Sci.* 14 (4): 702–26, 1991b.

——. "The relation of consciousness to the material world." *J Consc Stud.* 2: 255–65, 1995.

——. What and where are conscious experience? In: Velmans, M. ed. *The Science of Consciousness.* New York: Routledge, 1996, pp. 181–96.

Victor, M., R. D. Adams, and G. H. Collins. *The Wernicke-Korsakoff Syndrome and Related Neurologic Disorders Due to Alcoholism and Malnutrition.* 2nd ed. Philadelphia: F. A. Davis Company, 1989.

von der Malsburg, C. "Binding in models of perception and brain function." *Curr Opin Neurobiol.* 5: 520–26, 1995.

von Hagen, K., and E. R. Ives. "Anosognosie (Babinski), imperfection of hemiplegia. Report of 6 cases, one with autopsy." *Bull Los Angeles Neurol Soc.* 2: 95–103, 1937.

Watt, D. F. "Emotion and Consciousness: Part II. A review of Antonio Damasio's The feeling of what happens: Body and emotion in the making of consciousness." *J Consc Stud.* 7: 72-84, 2000.

Weinstein, E. A. Anosognosia and denial of illness. In: Prigatano, G. P., and D. L. Schacter, eds. *Awareness of Deficit After Brain Injury. Clinical and Theoretical Issues.* New York: Oxford University Press, 1991, pp. 240–57.

Weinstein, E. A., and M. Cole. Concepts of anosognosia. In: Halpern, L. E., ed. *Dynamic Neurology.* Jerusalem: Jerusalem Post Press, 1964.

Weinstein, E. A., M. Cole, M. Mitchell, and O. G. Lyerly. "Anosognosia and aphasia." *Arch Neurol.* 10: 376–86, 1964.

Weinstein, E. A., and R. P. Friedland. Behavioral disorders associated with hemiinattention. In Weinstein, E. A., and R. P. Friedland, eds. *Advances in Neurology.* Vol. 18. New York: Raven Press, 1977, pp. 51–62.

Weinstein, E. A., and R. L. Kahn. *Denial of Illness.* Springield: Charles C Thomas, 1955.

Weinstein, E. A., R. L. Kahn, and S. Malitz. "Confabulation as a social process." *Psychiatry* 19: 383–96, 1956.

Weinstein, E. A., R. L. Kahn, and G. O. Morris. "Delusions about children following brain injury." *J Hillside Hosp.* 5: 290–98, 1956.

Weinstein, E. A., and O. G. Lyerly. "Confabulation following brain injury." *Arch Gen Psychiat.* 18: 348–54, 1968.

Whyte, L. L., A. G. Wilson, and D. Wilson. *Hierarchical Structures.* New York: American Elsevier, 1969.

Wigan, A. L. *A New View of Insanity: The Duality of the Mind.* London: Longman, Brown, Green and Longmans, 1844a.

——. "Duality of the mind, proved by the structure, functions, and diseases of the brain." *Lancet.* 1: 39–41, 1844b.

Wilkes, K.V. *Real People.* New York: Oxford, 1988.

Zeki, S. *A Vision of the Brain.* Oxford: Blackwell Scientific Publications, 1993.

Index